THE FICTION OF RUTH PRAWER JHABVALA

The Fiction of Ruth Prawer Jhabvala

The Politics of Passion

Laurie Sucher

MACMILLAN

First published 1989

Published by
THE MACMILLAN PRESS LTD
Houndmills, Basingstoke, Hampshire RG21 2XS
and London
Companies and representatives
throughout the world

Typeset by Wessex Typesetters
(Division of The Eastern Press Ltd)
Frome, Somerset

Printed in the People's Republic of China

British Library Cataloguing in Publication Data
Sucher, Laurie, 1942–
The fiction of Ruth Prawer Jhabvala: the
politics of passion.
1. Fiction in English. Indian writers.
Jhabvala, Ruth Prawer – Critical studies
I. Title
823
ISBN 0–333–42196–5

To the memory of my parents
Augusta and Irving Sucher

Contents

Acknowledgements   x

PART ONE   QUEST

1 **Introduction: Ruth Prawer Jhabvala and her Fiction**   3
   Overview   13
   The Later Novels and Short Stories   18

2 **Dangerous Quest**   22
   Being Known   22
   Unsuitable Attachments   27

PART TWO   TO THE ASHRAM

3 **Gurus: Short Stories**   39
   'An Experience of India'   40
   'A Spiritual Call'   44

4 **Gurus: *A New Dominion* or *Travelers***   48
   Dominion: the Political Context   48
   Britons in the New Dominion: Raymond and Lee   50
   Names   54
   Ashrams   56
   'Gothic' Aspects   61

PART THREE   THE DEMON-LOVER

5 **'The Housewife'**   69

6 'Desecration'   77

   Knowing and Being Known   81

   The 'Unknown Woman'   92

7 **Demon-Lovers and Holy Mothers: *Heat and Dust***   98

   'Going Too Far'   103

   Parallel Structures   107

   Olivia and the Anglo-Indians   109

   Motifs: Graveyards, Husbands, Pianos, Hijra   115

   Nature Imagery   121

   The 'New' Story: Holy Mothers   124

   Wives and Widows in Satipur   127

   Disregarding Pollution Taboos   131

   Anti-Romantic Lovers   133

   Literary Allusion: *A Passage to India*   134

   'Harry' and E. M. Forster   136

PART FOUR   BACK IN THE WEST

8 **Difficult Adjustments: Three Stories**   143

   Homosexual Men, Heterosexual Women   143

   'A Birthday in London'   149

   'Commensurate Happiness'   157

   'Grandmother' and Other Old Women   161

9 *In Search of Love and Beauty*   168

   The Gothic Way and the Greek Way: Three
     Generations of Searchers   168

   New York as a Setting   169

   Critical Response   176

Contents

The Pantheon of *In Search of Love and Beauty*   177

'The Point'   184

Two Houses   187

Natasha's Answer   192

10 The International 'Trick': *Three Continents*   **200**

Some Preparatory Stories   201

Three Continents   205

Victims of Global Disinheritance   216

'Expiation': Other Victims   221

Notes   228

Selected Bibliography   238

Index   247

Acknowledgements

My thanks go to Professor Susan Squiers, English Department, SUNY at Stony Brook, where this study was first conceived as a doctoral thesis; to Arun Aurora of the Foreign Languages Department, Chicago Public Library; to 'Andrea', who like Ruth Jhabvala is a refugee from state terror, this time in Guatemala, and who took good care of my children while I worked; and finally, to my husband, Michael Gaster.

Part One
Quest

1
Introduction: Ruth Prawer Jhabvala and her Fiction

Sly and compassionate, sad and funny, the fiction of Ruth Prawer Jhabvala has, by 1988, enchanted British readers for more than three decades; her North American audience, while somewhat newer, is no less enthusiastic. 'An immense literary achievement,'[1] 'subtle, concise, and magnificent'[2] her work has been called, and she herself 'a genius if the word means anything', while India is 'a marvellous whetstone for her sharp humanity and retractable claws'.[3]

Her reputation among American audiences, who first got to know her through her regular contributions to the *New Yorker* magazine, was heightened with the 1983 award to her of the MacArthur Foundation's prestigious 'genius' grant. Though it is as a writer of fiction that she has earned the highest praise, her simultaneous career as screenwriter, in successful and steady collaboration with director James Ivory and producer Ismail Merchant, has probably brought about the widest recognition. One sign of her growing importance as novelist is the recent reissuing of most of her earlier work.[4]

By now many readers are familiar with the outlines of her unusual biography, which is yet so quintessentially of our time. She was born in Cologne on 7 May 1927, into what was, on her mother's side, a well-established German-Jewish family: Eleonora Cohn married the lawyer Marcus Prawer, a Polish Jew recently arrived in Germany; like many others, he fled enforced conscription in the First World War. In the Second World War, the immediate family – Ruth Prawer Jhabvala's parents and one brother – only narrowly escaped the catastrophic fate of most European Jews, sailing to England as late as April 1939.[5] But most of the others were lost: 'My father's entire family, part of my mother's family, the children I first went to school with, and most of my parents' family friends – in fact, our entire social and family circle.'[6]

The four Prawers came to England as 'displaced persons', among those lucky enough to be allowed to live anywhere. The children survived and prospered – Ruth Prawer Jhabvala's brother, Siegbart Prawer, is Professor of German Literature at Oxford and an established author in his own right[7] – but Marcus Prawer committed suicide in London in the fifties.

Such were the disastrous losses and upheavals of this writer's early life. A study could be, and no doubt will be, made of Ruth Prawer Jhabvala's Jewish themes, foremost among which is the use of the refugee/wanderer protagonist. That she – that anyone – finds the resources to produce creative work after having lived through such events is, one might say, wonderful in itself; but what is most remarkable is the quality of her art, and its lasting contribution to literature.

Already writing fiction in German as a child, Ruth Prawer negotiated the switch to English, and has spoken in later life of bureau drawers stuffed with unfinished plays, stories and novels, evidence that writing came to her 'as naturally as breathing'.[8] She studied English Literature at London University, earning the MA degree. Her thesis was 'The Short Story in England, 1700–1750', a nice hint at her future career as master of the short story.[9]

Ruth Prawer met and then married C. S. H. Jhabvala, an Indian student of architecture. With him she moved to India in 1951, and there she remained for some two and a half decades. Their three daughters grew up in Delhi. In India, R. Prawer Jhabvala, as she somewhat cryptically signed herself, became a writer: most of her nine novels and five collections of stories were written and set there, though published in England and the United States, and intended, she asserts, for a Western audience.[10]

Her Indian fiction is spun by an 'initiated outsider' – the phrase is John Updike's – working from within a domestic world.[11] If nothing else, the remarkable point of view elicits comment: a Bombay literary headline hit upon a similar phrase, naming her 'Outsider with Unusual Insight'.[12] This perspective was not available to any of the great Anglo-European novelists who have addressed themselves to cross-cultural issues: one thinks of the very different worlds of James, Forster and Conrad. For all their exotic settings, her novels of middle-class Indian life present an incongruous but inescapable similarity to those of Jane Austen, since in many ways – the large family, the strict codes of behaviour, the constant presence of relations – that setting has more in common with eighteenth-century England than it has with the modern West, as the writer herself has pointed out.[13] In an early interview, she allowed, too, that 'perhaps my way of looking at things may have been somewhat similar to hers – a sort of ironic detachment? May be.'[14] A close reading of Jhabvala's earliest novels reveals conscious allusion to *Pride and Prejudice*.[15]

It should be said that the family into which Ruth Prawer married is Parsi, and that the Parsis – Persians – are themselves something of an outsider group in India. Very much like Jews in their diaspora, they value education, actively pursue professional status and retain a somewhat separate identity. Ruth Jhabvala has spoken of the fortuitous accident that her husband's business partner was one of a large Hindu extended family, and that she was able through him to enter into its life.[16] It is thus that the particularities of modern Hindu domestic life are woven into her novels and stories in Indian settings, which thereby take on something of the function of sociological texts, painlessly educating us in the mores and manners of a foreign culture. But, as I hope to show, the appeal of this fiction is far deeper than that.

Many of Ruth Jhabvala's Indian critics have been offended by her ambivalent view of India. Merchant–Ivory's *Shakespeare Wallah*, with the screenplay by Jhabvala, was a case in point: the Indian characters in the film were not exemplary – 'a maharaja, a movie actress and a playboy were not felt to be the best representatives of the New India' and for this reason the film was actually booed at the Berlin Film Festival.[17] One of Jhabvala's best known Indian critics, Vasant Shahane, speaks of her 'constant sneering at the expense of India, as depicted in the attitudes, postures and gestures of the characters in *Heat and Dust*'.[18] Shahane is puzzled by the crucial relationship of Harry and the Nawab in that novel, and much of Jhabvala's humour either eludes or irritates him. For example, when a travelling English girl jokes that she came to India 'to find peace . . . but all I found was dysentery' (*Heat and Dust*, p. 21), Shahane comments, 'it seems curious that this girl should think of 'peace' and 'dysentery' as two links of a connected or contrasted experience; in fact, they cannot be related at all'.[19]

Ruth Jhabvala's candid admissions of her personal struggles as a European in India (in 'Myself in India'), together with her penchant for irony, even her satiric distances from her self-satisfied, middle-class targets of whatever nationality, have occasionally led her into political trouble. Ironies that might be appreciated coming from one of our own are perhaps resented when they come from an outsider's pen.

Ruth Jhabvala's biography literalises outsiderhood, the outsiderhood of the exile. In 1975 she moved once again, this time to New York City, and her latest fiction at the time of this writing is set there, or in an international context. But the outsiderhood of the artist is different, and the work itself shows the other side of *that*, evincing an almost magical ability to enter deeply into diverse individual consciousnesses, with an understanding that transcends difference.

This book is a close study of the four most recent of Ruth Jhabvala's novels, together with several of her related short stories, culled from the several dozen now in print. I have chosen to write about these works alone, rather than attempt to scan the whole of her published fiction, which by the time of this writing represents a sizeable output indeed. It is not for lack of interest that I have bypassed the other six novels: it simply seems more fruitful to talk about the aspects of Ruth Jhabvala's work that most interest me by approaching a smaller piece of it. As it happens, while I was engaged in this study, another critic more ambitious than I was writing that broad and general appreciation – I am speaking of Yasmine Gooneratne's admirable and sensitive critique *Silence, Exile and Cunning: The Fiction of Ruth Prawer Jhabvala* (New Delhi: Orient-Longman, 1983). Though I did not have the benefit of her work while writing this study, I refer readers to it and to her thorough bibliography.

A New Dominion, Heat and Dust, In Search of Love and Beauty and *Three Continents* are the maturest statements of Jhabvala's preferred themes: the tragi-comedies of self-deception, and the loss and shedding of illusions. As might be expected, she marks the plight of the outsider-refugee, his/her strategies for survival, and the heightened consciousness that outsiderhood confers. Her fiction usually centres on the lives of women, which leads her to observe the issues that feminism grapples with: how women get, use and maintain power in a society that renders them effectively powerless. She also plays with the great literary theme of love and death, or the paradoxes of eroticism – what might be called a neo-Gothic motif. Thus, her focus on the tragi-comic relations between charismatic men and their willing victims (mostly, but not solely, female).

As a reader whose home ground, so to speak, is the feminist literary criticism of the sixties and seventies, I am particularly interested in this neo-Gothic motif, in the various unexpected guises and settings in which it is encountered here. For underlying these Austenian comedies of manners, these sensitive explorations of cultural differences, these subtly precise psychological portraits, runs a 'dark' river of emotion and intensity. As with Jane Austen, ctitics tend to speak of Ruth Jhabvala's 'cool', even 'cold', ironic distancing. Yet – and I would argue that the same is true of Austen – the irony masks, even heightens, a deep core of feeling. If the cynic is a disappointed idealist, the ironist is a disappointed – that is, experienced – romantic.

In this quasi-Lawrencian vision, love is dark, paradoxical, even terrible. The story 'Desecration' tells the tale. Willing victims fall prey to demon-lovers; love and death are linked, forming two sides of the same coin. This romantic paradox, while it is subject to comic undercutting, stubbornly resists analysis, persisting even into her characters' experienced old age. We meet it, for example, in the story 'The Man with the Dog', which unveils an 'unsuitable' relationship between an elderly, cross-cultural, pair.

Throughout Ruth Jhabvala's work, authorial legerdemain enables us to see double, as it were: at once to validate and acknowledge the 'dark' side, and to hold it up to the light of reason and the ironic amusement that reason brings. This doubleness of vision is for me the triumph of her fiction. We are led to mark her characters' vulnerability to love at once with compassion and with irony. The irony is not malicious but grounded in a tragic view of life in which victims feel and suffer, and the callous are rewarded. The naïve – such as Daphne of 'A Spiritual Call' – are exploited by the canny – her lecherous guru. Even the more experienced – such as Mark of *In Search of Love and Beauty* – are prey to their own obsessional sexuality, their fatal taste for strong silent lovers – such as Kent, stony-faced, powerfully built and essentially mediocre.

I will discuss those of Ruth Jhabvala's novels that most closely examine this Gothic sexual theme, in which sexual love verges on hysteria, terrible in its intensity, transcendent and compelling. Those (men) who call it forth from women and other (homosexual) men are super-phallic, demonic, almost anti-human. Remote or alien, they are often socially or intellectually inferior. What is wonderful about these novels and related stories is the almost

magical transmutation of this hothouse atmosphere of super-
charged and repressed sexuality into its comic opposite, and back
again. As the dynamics of Gothic sexuality are regarded with
detachment and compassion, they tend to lose their exhilarating
terrors and deflate to comedy. This is most evident in *Heat and
Dust*, in which the double vision is expressed in two parallel story
lines set two generations apart. But the other works also evidence
the mutually exclusive truths – that is, the paradox – that love is
tragic and love is also comic. That the work conveys both sides of
the paradox is attributable to the narrative skill and sense of balance
of its author, who effortlessly negotiates a tightrope stretched
between the two points of view.

Although the artistic vision oscillates between romance and
irony, there is none the less a movement toward the relinquishment
of naïveté, the shedding of illusion. Ruth Jhabvala's fiction urges
us to seek with her a maturer vision of the tragic/romantic. Through
its characterisations and story lines, it compels dis-illusionment –
which is seen to be a good thing, a spiritual imperative, indeed
virtually a quest. I argue that in her hands the imperative to shed
illusion becomes particularly a *feminine* quest. For those who attend
to the *feeling* level of existence – here primarily women and
homosexual men – are, logically, most vulnerable to the illusions
of desire. We who desire, desire what seems most unlike ourselves:
that which has the invulnerability of remoteness. This remoteness
more often than not hides something disarmingly simple. The
strong, mysteriously silent male, unlike those whom he holds in
thrall, is revealed to be motivated by expediency, acquisitiveness,
class revenge, or simply the narcissistic pleasure of collecting
admirers. Often he himself is a naïve. Ruth Jhabvala's comedy often
rests on dialogue at cross-purposes, cross-cultural misunderstand-
ing. Romantic love may be seen as a special subcategory thereof.

I think it is fair to say that my perspective is probably more
politically feminist than my subject's. Even her decision to use her
husband's family name, despite its difficulty for Western readers,
suggests a certain traditionalism (and one imagines that had she
chosen differently she might have more quickly gained a large
audience: 'Prawer' is, for us, much more easily spelled and
remembered!). Judging by her screenplay adaptation of Henry
James's *The Bostonians* we can guess that she would not define
herself as a feminist. As are all the films of Merchant–Ivory
Productions, it is rendered with great intelligence, taste and beauty;

in my view, however, the film endorses and even expands on
James's anti-feminism.[20] The character of Olive Chancellor, the
New England suffragist, is held up to ridicule; her love for another
woman is presented in the most pathetic light; the chivalrous
Southerner who is her successful rival is given every advantage of
casting and dialogue. The encoded appeal to male homosexuality
makes the film particularly dishonest, I think. The anti-feminist
theme shades imperceptibly into the kind of subtle, or not-so-
subtle, misogyny occasionally encountered among male homosexuals.

In a similar vein, Merchant–Ivory's next production, an adaptation of *A Room with a View*, again validates E. M. Forster's romantic
and homosexual phallo-centrism – which would be fine, except for
the unbelievable heterosexual plot conventionally overlaid upon
it. Both films are tellingly cast: slightly chubby, rather silly, heroines
play opposite lean and twinkling heroes.

Merchant–Ivory Productions is perhaps only peripherally related
to the fiction of Ruth Prawer Jhabvala; and yet their films and her
fiction have been evolving in parallel paths for some years. *The
Guru*, *The Autobiography of a Princess* and *Roseland* – each relates to
themes treated contemporaneously in Ruth Jhabvala's fiction: to
take these examples, respectively, *A New Dominion*, *Heat and Dust*
and *In Search of Love and Beauty*. The latest Merchant–Ivory films
seem to be grappling with an unstated but underlying theme of
homosexuality and, of course, *Maurice* brings the theme out into
the open. Ruth Jhabvala's later fiction examines relationships
between heterosexual women and homosexual men; they are
rich with insights into women's psychology and women's lives,
although they do betray some uneasiness in their portrayal of
homosexuality, which the novels seem to suggest is all right for
men, but not for women.

Taken as a whole, Ruth Jhabvala's work at this point constitutes
an exploration, told from a woman's point of view, of the sexual
politics of passion. It confirms and illustrates the premise of
feminism, the societal derogation of women. It even confirms
feminism's imperative: that women resist that social and psychological derogation. In other words, as has been said, she paints a
faithful portrait of the reality that her readership knows, as well
as the reality (India) that they do not know. C. P. Snow comments:
'Someone once said that the definition of the highest art is that
one should feel that life is thus and not otherwise. I do not know

of a writer living who gives that feeling with more unqualified certainty than Mrs Jhabvala.'[21] In this fiction, women resist alone – and perhaps that too is realistic. They do not, by and large, have the support, love or friendship of other women – which is viewed as highly suspect. The female protagonist is emotionally isolated, unable or unwilling to draw strength from others like herself.

Ruth Jhabvala returns often to the idea of *quest*; her characters search tirelessly for something. Her women characters, particularly, desire something transcendent: a level of being, perhaps, that might be deeper, more connected and less alienated, more joyful, *better*. Her protagonists attempt this connection in a number of ways: spiritual practice (with or without ironic quotation marks), love and travel. Those ways often converge in the India of her fiction, where their limits are revealed. Always, the woman protagonist is thwarted: by her own romantic idealism, by the realities of economics, politics and power, or by a social system that devalues her.

For making these attempts the protagonists elicit our laughter, evoke our sympathy and earn our respect. They fail to discover the nameless, infinitely attractive, diabolically elusive source of their yearnings. The guru is a charlatan, the beloved a heel. The lover is disillusioned; she renounces; she falls in love again. The failure of the quest for transcendence through eros is met, by author and characters alike, by a dialectic of religious/ascetic renunciation and its opposite: ironic, ever more experienced, reaffirmation of the quest in the world of the senses.

This dialectic may be seen in cultural terms: Asian mysticism versus European pragmatism. Ruth Jhabvala herself has spoken of the opposition:

Once somebody said to me: 'Just see, how sweet is the Indian soul that can see God in a cow!' But when I try to assume this sweetness, it turns sour: for, however much I may try and fool myself . . . it is soon enough clear to me that the cow *is* a cow, and a very scrawny, underfed, diseased one at that. And then I feel that I want to keep this knowledge, however painful it is, and not exchange it for some other that may be true for an Indian but can never quite become that for me. . . . Sometimes it seems to me how pleasant it would be to say yes and give in and wear a sari and be meek and accepting and see God in a cow. Other times it seems worth while to be defiant and

European and – all right, be crushed by one's environment, but all the same have made some attempt to remain standing.[22]

With a characteristic and deceptive unassuming tone and sly humour in its rendering of intonation and dialect, the passage opposes renunciation to activism. Yet it refers by implication, I think, to another set of opposites and another ambivalence, in the sphere of sexuality. To 'say yes and give in and wear a sari and be meek and accepting' is not only to see God in a cow: it is to see God in a man.

Traditional Indian life places women in a position of real dependence and inferiority to men: purdah continues. Ruth Jhabvala's British or American women travellers, by contrast, are blithely and unconventionally independent, even in their own countries: they reject the norms of patriarchal society simply by the act of setting out alone. Of all people, they in particular confront the traditional and male-supremacist society of India with a great uneasiness. They do not and cannot ignore its romantic and erotic reverberations.

In a way, Ruth Jhabvala's work explores Freud's infamous question 'What do women want?' She shows, however, that it is not only women who stand implicitly accused of 'masochism', but any romantic idealist. Men and women alike, her idealistic protagonists fall for an assortment of unscrupulous, narcissistic, dominating men. Female or male, they find themselves wanting to be 'bullied' by their male lovers. This troubling phenomenon they regard with bewilderment, but do not deny. They yearn to be *known*, but they have a horror of that yearning.

The men they 'fall for' can be counted on to know how, and not to scruple, to use people for their own advantage: a police chief; a deposed prince; a conniving guru; a master musician, arrogant in his mastery; the famous founder of a modern school of psychotherapy; a street hustler turned 'world leader'. The women – or men – who fall in love with these icons of power hope to be known and loved: they are not, for they have gravitated to men who *know* them only in the sense of knowing how to use them. The protagonist remains, then, more or less isolated, still searching. Sensitive, altruistic, even self-denying, idealistic and deeply responsive to nature, Jhabvala's female protagonists have another trait in common: they are almost completely alienated from other women.

The female friendships depicted – and there are many – are parodies of friendship, abusive relationships, really, between an excessively tolerant underling and a narcissistic bitch. As I mentioned, the women protagonists often have friendships with male homosexuals – whose homosexuality is viewed without phobia or hysteria: as 'normal', that is, no more pathological than heterosexuality, and sometimes less so. But any suggestion of support or mutual nurturance between women (not to mention love) is parodied or treated with revulsion. From the work as a whole emerges a picture of women's flight and alienation from other women. The relationships, or non-relationships, of mothers and daughters throughout the work are particularly significant. So conspicuous is the failure of friendship, love or support between women that a simultaneous undercurrent is suggested, of longing for connection with other women and with the maternal aspects of the transcendent. One of my aims in this critique is to offer an interpretation of images, metaphors and ideas that seem to suggest, throughout these stories and novels, women's quest for the maternal.

Read from this feminist perspective, the work offers a fascinating study of women's isolation and alienation in a male-centred society; indeed, Ruth Jhabvala's chosen settings are often aggressively dominated by a charismatic male: the ashram, or the psycho-spiritual centre. But it is one that her protagonists, isolated though they be, know enough to resist. The particular nature of the relationship that develops between the 'charismatic man' and his disciples is only one of the thorny issues to which Jhabvala brings her original and witty intelligence.

Another of her innovations is the focus on the single British or American woman traveller: I know of no other author who has so seriously addressed the issues that surround and confront *her*. The connection here is between travelling or wandering, on the one hand, and the Gothic sense of sexuality as dark, intense, even hysterical. In her study *Literary Women*, Ellen Moers has written of this connection. Her chapter title 'Travelling Heroinism' casts the heroine as traveller and adventuress, testing her mettle and daring all.

Both predilections – for travelling and for romantic love – imply a certain disaffection; both suggest dissatisfaction with the circumstances of one's life, so profound a dissatisfaction that escape appears the only solution. Escape into foreign places, escape into sexual fantasies, even, for that matter, escape into novels – all are related half-solutions, perhaps necessary steps along the various pathways of self-development. Charlotte Brontë, the mother of travelling heroines (although it is difficult to think of her as a mother, when in her passionate rebellion she embodies modern daughterhood) saw this clearly. Moers cites a passage from *Shirley*, in which a little girl named Rose Yorke interrupts her reading of Mrs Radcliffe's Gothic novel, *The Italian*, to expatiate on that novel, on travel and on life:

> In reading it, you feel as if you were far away from England – really in Italy – under another sort of sky, – the blue sky of the south, which travellers describe. . . . I must see the outside of our round planet at least. . . . I am resolved that my life shall be a life; not a black trance like a toad's, buried in marble.[23]

Wandering women, *femmes errantes* in both senses, the many Jhabvala women who have rejected the paths laid out for them by convention, pay a price. Striking out for distant shores, they may become chronic outsiders, ironically more vulnerable than their conventional sisters to the charms of charismatic and mysterious men who offer them a false sense of belonging. These passionate and independent-minded protagonists descend in a straight line from Jane Eyre or Lucy Snowe. For all her Austenian style, irony and detachment, Ruth Jhabvala by her choice of these protagonists manages to align herself with Charlotte Brontë as well.

OVERVIEW

Ruth Jhabvala's novels to date may be conveniently divided into three phases, each bearing on the issues of romantic idealism, the shedding of illusions and the search for wholeness. In a telling passage from the essay 'Myself in India', she outlines a sort of wheel of predictable responses to India: first, everything marvellous, next, everything not so marvellous, next, everything abominable, and then back again to phase one, second cycle.[24] Clearly, this very formulation is a paraphrase of the ongoing process of idealism and disillusionment that forms the essence of Ruth Jhabvala's literary and psychological vision.

Her first two novels, *To Whom She Will* (1955) and *The Nature of Passion* (1956), treat the theme of disillusionment in its gentlest, most benign form: the comic mismatching of pairs of lovers, who, as the novels progress, discover the differences between illusion and reality. Accordingly, they change partners, end the liaison or modify their expectations, and comedic harmony is re-established. The fictional world is comfortable, domestic and sensuously appealing; part of the point of these novels is to reveal to the Western reader an India which the author loves, and in which she resides at the time of their writing.

To Whom She Will was reissued in the United States as *Amrita* – in my view a lamentable simplification which forfeits a key idea. The British title is explicated by an epigraph taken from the Vedic epic the *Panchatantra* in a translation by H. Ryder:

For if she bides a maiden still
She gives herself to whom she will
Then marry her in tender age
So warns the heaven-begotten sage.[25]

The *Panchatantra* prescribes an entire code of manners, in this detail specifying that a girl must be married before the onset of puberty, to 'forestall any mishap to her virginity and to permit her mother-in-law to train her in household ways before she develops strong tendencies of her own'.[26] The warning of the 'heaven-begotten sage' rests unheeded in the case of Amrita, who valiantly, if naïvely, attempts to give herself to whom she will: thereby hangs the plot of the novel.

The second novel, a rich and delightful domestic comedy, is given another evocative title – the same in the British and American editions – which suggests the direction of Ruth Jhabvala's future work, one which concerns me in this study: *The Nature of Passion*.

In addition to the incisive and appreciative detailing of a culture with which her readership is largely unfamiliar, Ruth Jhabvala is interested in this first phase in a number of social issues: the clash of generations in a society in transition; the influence of the West on modern-day middle-class India; and the lingering effects of colonialism.

The milieu is that of the moneyed and privileged in a society in which millions are hungry. The point is made in Ruth Jhabvala's much-quoted essay 'Myself in India', first published in 1965: 'Not

for one moment should we lose sight of the fact that a very great
number of Indians never get enough to eat. . . . From birth to
death they never for one day cease to suffer from hunger. *Can* one
lose sight of that fact? God knows, I've tried.'[27] These early novels
illustrate that choice and that attempt. The outrage, the concern
with social injustice that will appear later, is for now put aside, as
if to acquaint the Western audience with the urban middle class
and aspects of Indian life that come less readily to mind.

The next novel to be set in Delhi, *Esmond in India* (1958),
introduces a set of darker themes that will be worked out in
succeeding novels. The tragi-comedy of manners is a seemingly
effortless rendition of a complicated series of relationships representing a cross-section of Indian life. At its centre is Esmond, a
villainous – manipulative and embittered – Briton, in some respects
the first of a line of destructive males who will come to be in Ruth
Jhabvala's later novels, indifferent objects of the fevered affections
of an over-idealistic woman. In contrast to those who will follow
him, though, and despite his cynical relationship with Betty, the
bitchy Englishwoman, Esmond seems a 'closet' homosexual. Consequently, the misunderstandings between him and the Indians
are even more abundant.

This novel contains one of Ruth Jhabvala's most positive depiction of a mother–daughter relationship. Esmond's mismatched
wife Gulab, their toddler Ravi, and Gulab's mother Uma, enjoy an
intimate domesticity that lends a charm and a tenderness to this
novel (even though Gulab is a naïve, and Uma as intelligent as her
daughter is stupid). In the context of Jhabvala's oeuvre, this
relationship of grandmother, daughter and grandson is a touchstone of warmth that will never reappear. The significant configuration with which the novel ends will reappear, however, and
often: the female protagonist, Shakuntala, is poised on the brink
of disaster – about to elope with Esmond – and there the novel
leaves her. This open-ended but pessimistic conclusion is met with
again and again, in *A New Dominion*, 'An Experience of India' or *In
Search of Love and Beauty*, to some extent in *Heat and Dust* as well,
and most notably in the latest novel at the time of writing, *Three
Continents*.

The last work of this first phase, *The Householder* (1960), represents
a return to the harmonious vision of the first two novels, in a more
melancholy, almost elegiac, mode. The novella is a moving portrait
of a struggling schoolteacher, Prem (whose name means 'servant'),

and his delightful bride Indu. Western characters are treated satirically, as seen through Prem's eyes, while the colours and textures of his own world are casually and effortlessly revealed. Rich in comedy, and full of tenderness, the novel is one of Ruth Jhabvala's triumphs.

The next phase of Jhabvala's fiction, which might be called 'Delhi and the West' – I see the emphasis in that order – is characterised by a mounting discomfort with the traditional values that were to some extent endorsed and upheld in the first romantic comedies. The next two novels, *Get Ready for Battle* (1962) and *A Backward Place* (1965) fall into this category. The pair signal a more lively interest in the clash of Western and Indian values as they are embodied in European and Indian characters and their relationships, friendly, erotic, inimical or distant as they may be.

In *Get Ready for Battle*, Sarla Devi (whose name derives from the Sanskrit for 'Simplicity') fights stubbornly with her traditional, but proudly up-to-date, family over issues of social justice, activism and reform – concepts alien to the traditional Hindu ethos, and deriving, of course, from modern democratic idealism. Sarla Devi is herself something of an eccentric. Her family views her as odd, unfeminine, even ridiculous. Though there are elements of satire in her characterisation, she represents conscience and struggle in a world of greed and expediency, a world in which the wretched become more wretched still while the rich prosper. Hayden Williams, one of Jhabvala's early critics, saw her as a 'yogi'.[28]

Sarla Devi's simplicity and anti-materialism, which, of course, backfire in the real world, prefigure the same qualities in a much later character, Natasha of *In Search of Love and Beauty*, also something of an authorial stand-in, and also a person of conscience in a world without conscience. Both Sarla Devi and Natasha are satirised when their naïve do-gooding fails. Our last glimpse of Sarla Devi sees her embarking on what we know will be a futile attempt to help a teenaged prostitute. Similarly, in the later novel we learn that Natasha was forced to give up her job as an assistant in a home for retarded children when one of her charges beat her to the ground. When these sympathetic and compassionate characters are held up to ridicule the result is a certain discomfort, as though the author's wit has been turned against the wrong targets. Certainly, it cannot be said that she is unwilling to laugh at herself.

Get Ready for Battle marks a shift in emphasis, a turning away from the relatively benign comedic discord of the earlier novels. Ruth Jhabvala has taken up the challenge that she earlier eschewed, that of addressing herself to the heartless corruption and implacable strength of the social and economic machine. Sarla Devi's struggle is inevitably and tragically met with defeat. Had she struck to fiction, like her author, she might have had greater success!

The second novel in this phase, *A Backward Place*, using varying degrees of detachment that range from gentle irony to acid satire, introduces Western characters who represent different kinds or degrees of 'adjustment' to India. It presents three more or less unsatisfactory solutions to the problem of being a Western woman in India. First there is Judy, one of the few sympathetic characters in the novel, who actually does 'wear a sari'. Her love for her husband Bal (whose name means 'Lord') is drawn with a tenderness that derives in part from the naïveté of both characters. He is an endearingly muddled lord, an unsuccessful actor, a charming but irresponsible dreamer. With three small children, no family other than an aged aunt, and very little money, Judy must decide whether to accede to Bal's dubious schemes to move from Delhi to Bombay, where he believes he will find success in films. Although the novel partially endorses the move, as a kind of liberating response to the rationalistic self-imprisonment of bourgeois materialism, it also gives ample proof of Bal's folly and irresponsibility. We leave the little family, again, on the brink of an adventure that may well end in disaster.

Next comes Clarissa, whose name evokes not one but two famous literary predecessors, and who is, like one of them, an upper-middle-class Englishwoman with 'lesbian tendencies'. There the similarity to Virginia Woolf's character ends. She is not loved by her creator. At once ridiculous, arrogant, snobbish and pathetic, she is the first of a number of lesbians glimpsed from afar. The pathological light in which she is viewed contrasts strangely and significantly, as I have mentioned, with the open, matter-of-fact and sympathetic treatment of male homosexuals. The disparity will emerge more sharply in the later fiction, particularly *In Search of Love and Beauty*.

At any rate, Clarissa deserves her 'friendship' with the even more egotistical and even more pathetic Etta, the third in the trio of Western women. Etta is an ageing Hungarian courtesan, still attempting, now rather unsuccessfully, to trade on her erstwhile glamour as a Westerner. Each of these three Western women –

wife, lesbian, and 'kept' woman – faces the sad discovery that India presents no solution for her. As comic foils to them are the Hochstadts, a visiting German professor and his wife, whose superficial and enthusiastic love for India is revealed, layer by layer, as a combination of stupidity, posturing and conceit.

THE LATER NOVELS AND SHORT STORIES

These six novels lead up to the four which will be closely read in this study: *A New Dominion* (1972); *Heat and Dust* (1975); *In Search of Love and Beauty* (1983); and *Three Continents* (1987). In these last novels the comedy is deepened by a dimension of seriousness, which marks a new phase. Jhabvala moves on to further explore and unravel the tangled web of emotions that is called love. She shows us the effects of the malady, for such it appears to be, in the personae of women and homosexual men. She investigates the combination of spiritual longing and erotic obsession that her characters know as love, and where these emotions overlap she discovers to us the figure of the guru.

She is as interested in the false guru as she is in the false lover. The first of these novels explores the ashram of a magnetic and sinister guru. A number of stories investigate the same theme and will be discussed in this context: 'A Spiritual Call', 'How I Became a Holy Mother', 'An Experience of India' and 'The Housewife'.

The second of the novels focuses on an Englishwoman's infatuation with the guru's nineteenth-century predecessor in India, a magnetic and (perhaps) sinister nawab. Here is found Ruth Jhabvala's most pointed deconstruction of the Gothic-romantic, especially as it applies to Western women in India. Two related stories continue the exploration of the links between romance and pornography: they are 'Passion' and 'Desecration', the latter especially.

In the third novel, the author continues her investigation of the appeal of the charismatic male guru, now in the persona of Leo Kellermann, a German refugee psychiatrist who collects around himself a devoted coterie of earnest disciples eager to scrutinise their own and each other's psyches. His quasi-therapeutic, quasi-cultish and marvellously named 'Academy for Potential Development' is the latter-day Western equivalent of the swami's ashram.

Central both to the ashram and to such communities as 'The Academy', which purport to offer special opportunities for development, Ruth Jhabvala's fiction places a charismatic male. Swami or psychiatrist, he is a master of the techniques of exploitation – if such mastery were needed. It is not: his disciples bring him such fevered vulnerability that his skill is all but superfluous.

Jhabvala's last novel at the time of writing, *Three Continents*, represents an interesting progression. It takes the theme to its logical conclusion: its heroine–narrator is at once sharply observant and hopelessly deluded – which makes for some narrative problems. By the end of the novel the protagonist has entered into an entrapment so complete that the tale slips into the realms of the fantastic. Curiously, its Gothic conclusion is offset by a subliminal comedic aura.

A new theme emerges in the most recent novels, and reveals another arena in which women are liable to illusion. This is the relationship of heterosexual women and homosexual men (whom the women often believe to be heterosexual). The stories 'Commensurate Happiness', 'Grandmother' and 'A Summer by the Sea' further explore this theme, which represents another reworking of illusion in the service of limiting or false expectations for women.

This fiction satirises 'esoteric' phenomena (ashrams, cults and the like): the disciples' fervour, and that of the leaders, is merely sexual at its core. Yet Jhabvala's seeking protagonists also may discover a real, vital and true spiritual essence. At times it appears in the personae of *women* seers. *A New Dominion* and *Heat and Dust* both contain women seers not viewed satirically, who possess wisdom and the power to help those who come to them. More often, however, this healing and transcendent power comes through contemplation, withdrawal and communion with beauty in nature.

Ruth Jhabvala's fiction suggests, without of course explictly positing, a spirituality that I would characterise as female-centred, a transcendent joy available primarily through the beauty of nature, which demands receptivity, a skill at which women are perhaps more adept. Quietness and receptivity are celebrated. Despite the bleak light in which her fiction presents intimate, nurturing or loving relatonships between women, of which, as I have said, there is a conspicuous absence, it offers to them a female-centred and redemptive spirituality.[29] Sarla Devi, Natasha or Maji in *Heat and Dust* are able to tap into a transcendent joy that seems to come from the sky.

In *A Backward Place*, it is from the sky that Judy draws the courage to follow Bal to Bombay, to leave the deadening and artificial props of bourgeois life; from the sky so 'large and beautiful' (p. 179) at which 'one had only to look up and it was peaceful'. She compares her life in England, where she never remembers having seen the sky: 'Nothing had spoken. . . . Who spoke from the sky here? Why did it seem to her that someone spoke?' (p. 179).

A meditative receptivity may bring about resolution of the nagging contradictions of experience. In the same novel Sudhir – who in combination with Judy serves as authorial spokesperson – muses on India, and thinks, during a nighttime train journey which becomes symbolic of the human condition, that

> Everyone always talked about [India] incessantly, compulsively, and yet never said anything that was the least conclusive or that seemed to him now, *shut in with an assortment of strangers and travelling through a landscape which was too dark to be seen and could therefore only be guessed at*, [my emphasis] that perhaps the paradox was not a paradox after all or, if it was, was one that pleasurably resolved itself for the sake of him who accepted it and rejoiced in it and gave himself over to it, the way a lover might.   (pp. 184–5)

Jhabvala is a moralist, and like all moralists is angry at what she sees. As her work shifts in its setting from East to West and leaves the realm of the disenfranchised (from a global perspective), it situates itself in a darker, more pessimistic, mode. It is as if for all that India failed to live up to the glory of its promise for her characters, and perhaps for her, it is still her first love. The Indian characters at least redeem themselves by a warmth and directness that is lacking in, say, the German refugees in Manhattan who form the cast of characters of *In Search of Love and Beauty*.

An equation suggests itself here: the more active, successful, powerful and worldly the character, the more there is a chill about him or her. In the New York-based novel, our sympathy is most engaged by the most passive of characters, the adopted refugee, 'poor Natasha' (p. 12). She can only look on in helpless sympathy as the others are driven in circles by their own needs and interests. Like her author, Natasha is small and dark, a Holocaust survivor, a moralist, a writer. Paradoxically, despite her intense receptivity, she represents the only character in the novel *not* vulnerable to the charms of the charismatic Leo Kellermann – though he is the cause of her (probable) death.

In Jhabvala's fiction, action arises out of self-interest, which, naturally, is likely to conflict with the interests of others. The cleanest life, therefore, is logically the most withdrawn one. In this respect Jhabvala perhaps draws on an Asian religious world view, although the idea of renunciation has, of course, many Western religious and literary incarnations. Henry James, Jean Rhys, E. M. Forster, all of whom Ruth Jhabvala has adapted for the screen, may be characterised as adherents of the ideals of receptivity and quietism. All distrust power and worldly success, which probably accrue at someone else's expense.

Despite the easy assurances of the 'Human Potential Movement' and its representatives – people like Leo Kellermann, or worse, the Rawul, there is not enough to go round. So thinks Natasha in *In Search of Love and Beauty*. Clearly, not enough love, with 'everyone needing such an awful lot of it' (p. 225). We compound the problem by our indifference to each other; worse, we exploit; worse yet, exploitativeness is not evenly distributed: there are those who have power to hurt, and those who do not, winners and losers. Yet all suffer, even the ostensible winners, for the ability to exploit others does not guarantee happiness either.

Despite all this, however, Ruth Jhabvala's vision, I would argue, is fundamentally affirmative. Disillusionment is a good thing because it brings us closer to truth; and truth is a good thing: this world of suffering lovers and struggling householders is overarched by a transcendent joyousness, available to whoever is willing to stop and listen for it. Nor are we enjoined to renounce desire completely: luckily for us, the process of disillusionment never ends; there is always further to go. The world of the senses is far too droll to give up. The characters are correct to hold on to their idealistic desires, though, clearly, they had better give up the idea of attaining them all. The shedding of illusions may be a painful process, but we are invited to dare it. The landscape may be too dark to be seen and we may be shut in with an assortment of strangers, but each has a tale to tell, and in the listening, and the telling, light and recognition may enter in.

2
Dangerous Quest

BEING KNOWN

'Sofia, Sofia, what are you thinking?' asks the husband of his unfaithful wife in Jhabvala's short story 'Desecration' (first concluding the collection *How I Became a Holy Mother*, later concluding the collection of reprinted stories, *Out of India*). Of course, she cannot answer; to do so would risk 'changing his look' of 'tender respect' – the respect that requires her to live apart from the vulgar society of others, to remain in elegant, splendid isolation with him. However, the strain of never revealing herself, of managing to 'bear it by herself' proves finally impossible. Her suicide is a response to the isolation ordained to the romantic heroine, and all who would imitate her.

The romantic heroine's isolation is a result of the self-fragmenting bind she is caught in, that is, the irremediable opposition between the lady and the woman who lives inside her. The lady, 'above reproach', is only a fiction: everyone knows that she is a woman too, a guilty daughter of Eve. The tension between these mutually contradictory images – beautiful, highborn goddess, and living, breathing female – sets up and even compels the lady's lapse into shameful self-revelation, of just the sort that Sofia gives way to. For the human impulse toward self-revelation is persistent and inescapable, despite every effort to quell it.

Sofia's 'nervous prostrations', so poignantly reminiscent of those of other literary wives (one cannot help thinking of Virginia and Leonard Woolf), bring out the 'inexhaustible' patience of her husband, who 'stayed awake all night and held her hand (she clutched his)' (p. 192). Yet in a sense, he is her jailer, and no matter how saintly his patience, it is beside the point. To live up to her name Sofia must become wise; but before wisdom comes knowledge. As a woman, knowing is denied her, though 'being known' presumably is not. Yet to her horror she never is known as she wishes to be, in the sense of being understood by another

22

human being – only 'known' in the sexual and pornographic sense.

All of Ruth Jhabvala's lovers wish *to be known*: to transcend the ordinary competitive, isolating and fragmenting conditions of daily interaction, in which one hides from others, and even from oneself, a primal level of feeling and the socially subversive impulses that it includes. Whether treated seriously or parodically, that wish to be known recurs throughout Jhabvala's fiction: sometimes, as in 'Desecration', its tragedy is plumbed; more often, it is presented with a wry irony. For example, the women of 'The Academy for Potential Development' wish 'to be known, to be found out and probed to the core of their being' (*In Search of Love and Beauty*, p. 13). And at Swamiji's 'Universal Society for Spiritual Regeneration in the Modern World' (*A New Dominion*, p. 139), a disciple will thrill to the 'speaking without words that went right through her and reached it seemed to her into regions which no one had hitherto penetrated' (p. 83). There too Lee rhapsodises about her guru: 'How he *knew* her, knew how to deal with her, handle her, make her his: and that not in private just between the two of them but before a whole roomful of people' (p. 102).

The grammar of this transaction is clearly passive. Jhabvala's lovers, heterosexual women and homosexual men, search for self-knowledge in the form of mythic, phallic, masculinity: a mysterious stranger – perhaps masked, at any rate, remote, awesome and frightening – who knows without being known. The divine male, the most elevated judge, the most powerful knower alone would be sufficiently 'penetrating' to see through our disguises and *love us anyway*: such love alone would be worth having. Perhaps this explains the fascination and seductiveness of the manipulators that Ruth Jhabvala's characters are continually falling in love with. If the nawab, the swami, the psychiatrist or the dashing young man is transparently manipulative, that both is and is not a point against him – for the lover secretly *wishes* to be objectified: to be 'handled' as Lee is handled by Swamiji. S/he is constantly warring with impulses toward being 'handled' – toward being objectified and hence annihilated.

Ruth Jhabvala's heterosexual and homosexual lovers alike find themselves on the thin edge of painful self-awareness. They themselves cannot fail to see the self-destructiveness of their desires. Why it should be that to be *known* is to be annihilated is a subject open to question, and her portrayals of suffering lovers and the callous objects of their love direct us to ponder the question. Perhaps because culture and civilisation condemn or devalue the humane and universal impulses of need and emotional express-iveness, naming each 'feminine', to be known as oneself is somehow to be shamed and abased. Whatever the causes of the desire to abase oneself, the desire remains. What to do with it, Jhabvala's fervent lovers ask themselves and us, in moments of puzzled lucidity.

In the short story 'Passion' (*A Stronger Climate*), Betsy realises that Har Gopal, her lover, thinks of her as a 'fallen woman' (p. 76), but 'this very humiliation actually increased, exacerbated her passion for him' (p. 77). Shakuntala in *Esmond in India* loves the odious Esmond's 'angry solitude': she finds in it 'great dignity' (p. 137), and wants him also 'to look deep, deep into my heart and my soul' (p. 147). In *In Search of Love and Beauty* Mark knows that Kent's 'impassive manner' and 'faraway look' hide no more than a rather vulgar desire to be seen in the right places and with the right people: yet Mark helplessly watches himself and others fall prey to Kent's devastatingly attractive remoteness. In the same novel, Louise and Natasha actually debate the issue: what *should be* our response to the powerful attractiveness of the successfully manipulative (Leo Kellermann, the psychiatrist-guru, for example)?

In Sofia's case, the pristine image her husband holds of her – for his own reasons – is just what must be shattered if she is to know the joy of self-revelation. The Police Chief who 'desecrates' her is only half the 'wrong man': his abasement of her is a sought-after corrective to her husband's falsely elevated image of her. The only problem, to return to my formulation, is that he does not *love her anyway*. This difficulty, which leads to her suicide, is not, it should be clear, an idiosyncrasy peculiar to the two of them. The divine knower does not exist, at least in our world. *Everyone* wishes to be known – everyone, that is, of 'finer feeling'. If the knower is also to be known, he would be found also to be weak and fallible, for all are human. The vulnerable – tragically or ludicrously – are those of us who persist in the search for recognition from this imaginary being, those of us who have not yet succeeded in the life-long task of integrating the sacred and the profane, if the beloved is sacred and we are profane. Jhabvala's novels and stories thus document the tragi-comedy of the compelling quest for a non-existent knower.

Feminist activism by definition rejects the passive as a mode of being – as indeed it should. However, one encounters occasionally the tendency in feminist thought to adhere to the values of exteriority and action, and to view as suspect the celebration of passivity in women's lives. Jhabvala stands in opposition to this reductive tendency. In a way, her work is a celebration of an 'active' passivity, that is, a chosen and willed stance of receptivity. Her most sympathetic protagonists are those who float on a sea of experience, never attempting to *husband* its riches – that is, to use or to exploit it – but only to appreciate, to understand, to pity – and not to forgive.

If Ruth Jhabvala's fiction endorses a religion, it is a quietistic religion of private and contemplative withdrawal, passive 'waiting' for grace through meditation. Natasha, for example (*In Search of Love and Beauty*), practises this religion without a name or a god, even describing her meditation, that active waiting: 'waiting, and yet at the same time having received what she was waiting for' (p. 169). Some of the wisest Indian characters practise a deeply revivifying meditation (Maji in *Heat and Dust*; 'The Old Lady' in the story by that name (*Like Birds, Like Fishes*); Banubai in *A New Dominion*; or the laughing Swami of *The Householder*, and his follower, Sohan Lal – perhaps the same Sohan Lal who appears again, twenty years older, in *In Search of Love and Beauty*, as the disciple of Sujata.

'Active passivity' also characterises Ruth Jhabvala's scrupulously observant narrators: Lee or Raymond in *A New Dominion*, or the unnamed narrator of *Heat and Dust*. Indeed, her Western wanderers in India are given to aimless travel, to journeys that unfold randomly and without clear motive or plan.

Receptivity also implies non-instrumentality. Ruth Jhabvala's sympathetic characters absolutely refuse to take advantage of others, or even, sometimes, to act out of ordinary self-interest. Miss Tuhy, the title character of 'Miss Sahib' (*An Experience of India*), is an elderly version of this character, and with the additional vulnerabilities of age, she suffers the miserable fate of one who has always refused to exploit others. Alone among her poor Indian neighbours she does not keep a still more wretched servant boy, and she is despised by them for it.

In the earlier novel *Get Ready for Battle*, the comparison is explicitly made: the contemplative Sarla Devi tries, ineffectually, to better the condition of a community of impoverished shanty-dwellers, and is contrasted with her entrepreneurial, successful son, who is instrumental in their further degradation. In this world of getting and spending, merely not to exploit tends to bring abut one's own exploitation. The quietism of Miss Tuhy elicits her neighbours' contempt; and everyone laughs at Sarla Devi – even we, the readers, who love her.

In the more individual realm of personal relations, such passivity – the desire to be known – must fail as ignominiously, as ultimately it becomes narcissistic and delusional. The breathless lover is always in a state of hysterical delusion: s/he has taken a man for a god. Since God is thought of as male, this delusion is socially sanctioned, even encouraged in theory. But women engage in its practice at their extreme peril. For more than men, who may permit themselves the luxury of passionate *grands amours*, women are traditionally liable to social ostracism, shame and 'ruin' if they give in to the impulse – as Charlotte Brontë pointed out long ago.[1]

Yet Ruth Jhabvala's protagonists do exactly that. Their actions indicate a fine disregard of convention, an almost 'heroic' ardour and daring. They are rash, impetuous, apocalyptic in their quest for the divine knower. They shock their peers, and what is worse, usually their lovers as well. They are abruptly brought down.

One of the themes of Ruth Jhabvala's fiction, then, is the clash of inflated expectation and bathetic reality, high-flown idealism and pragmatic self-interest. Yet it would be a mistake, I think, to read her as a chronicler of the comical exploitation of naïve lovers by cynical men. For she paints the desire to be known as an essential human quality, without which one is deeply alientated from oneself.

Scattered through Ruth Jhabvala's fiction are such successful, single-minded businessmen as Mr Gupta, 'Guppy' to his lady friend Etta in *A Backward Place*. They do not suffer in love. Nor do their female counterparts, the successful coquettes, such as Regi, the ice-queen of *In Search of Love and Beauty*. Coquettes, surrounded by admirers as girls, may, if they have been truly clever, be able to continue buying themselves young (homosexual) escorts well into old age, as Regi does. But no joy is to be had from this relationship of instrumentality, advantageous though it may be. It is an empty triumph, unfelt as such; and the capacity to feel is finally the index of value in this moral – that is, fictional – universe. There lies the strength and supremacy of Ruth Jhabvala's passive protagonists.

UNSUITABLE ATTACHMENTS

Jhabvala's passive and mythicising women and men seek transcendence through phallic power: the more powerful the male, the more meaningful a sense of recognition and self-revelation he can bestow. Thus the fatal appeal of the psychologically astute but self-serving gurus and psychiatrists whose ashrams and 'centres' dot her oeuvre. 'Spiritual' or 'psychological' pseudo-healers, these individuals merely fulfil the office sought of them by the vulnerable.

Often, however, for Jhabvala's unconventional and idealistic heroines, this male power is even further mythicised, as they tend to locate it in the wretched and downtrodden, or the socially marginal, who by a quasi-aesthetic sleight of hand, assume in their admirers' eyes a godlike state. The disenfranchised thus reclaim mythic power: in the story 'Passion' (*A Stronger Climate*), Har Gopal (whose name derives from Krishna's), is arrogant and imperious to Betsy. But his arrogance is fuelled by the bitterness of his actual social position, particularly in relation to the (comparatively) vastly privileged Betsy. What is more, he disapproves strongly of her bohemian, passionate ways, while she adores his steely power: alone with her he becomes 'an aristocrat . . . whose right it was to be served by others' (p. 71).

In the same vein, though he is actually an aristocrat, the Nawab of *Heat and Dust* is by the fact of his Indianness socially inferior to Olivia. The distance is greater yet, and the relational dynamics the same, between Sofia, a landowner's wife, and her lover the Superintendent of Police in 'Desecration' (*How I Became a Holy Mother*).

Many of Jhabvala's educated young women have deliberately discarded the privileges and advantages that their university degrees might have conferred – for example, the young Indian narrator-protagonist of 'On Bail' (*How I Became a Holy Mother*), who was supposed to have been a 'new' woman. Ironically, she is undone by foolish love, marrying a charismatic hustler and becoming the cheerful and willing dupe of him and his wealthy mistress. So much for her 'First Class first' exam results that showed such promise.

This character, as we shall see, leads dirctly to that of the aptly named Harriet Wishwell, another smart woman making a foolish choice (in *Three Continents*): Harriet and her twin brother are in a great hurry to rid themselves not only of their substantial inheritance, but of their good educations as well: it is all *neti* – as nothing.

The scenario springs from a deep current in literature: the highborn lady who loves her social inferior is a staple of the European literary heritage. Examples abound in every mode, from pornography to high art: one thinks of Miss July, of Lady Chatterley, of Blanch duBois, to cite the most well known. Genet's drag queens and pimps only exaggerate the dynamic.[2] Archetypally the players are the lady and her gypsy lover, even, on a symbolic level, the frog-prince, whose repulsive exterior hides a noble soul; 'Beauty and the Beast' is another familiar incarnation. In American popular culture, one has the irresistible rebel without a cause.[3]

Perhaps this dyad is an attempt to repair the original fall from grace: the institutions of property, class and caste. Woman may transcend class distinctions to heal through love and to mitigate the social tragedy. But the image also has an 'obscene' side: the lady loves her social inferior for his sexual charisma.

Ruth Jhabvala explores this archetypal dynamic in a cross-cultural setting, where its ironies multiply as each partner even more radically misinterprets the other. Yet, as I have said, she views with sympathy the propensity to mythicise and idealise the beloved. That tendency is an aesthetic dimension without which the individual lacks something essential. The lover is always a mythmaker, an idealiser: and only the lover is fully human, that is, touched by the divine.

For example, Betsy's roommate Christine, in 'Passion', also has an Indian boyfriend: he is suitable and can be safely invited to intercultural parties. Like Har Gopal, he represents to his female lover an image of India. But it is a conventionalised image, a cliché: 'Manny was the India one read about in childhood, coloured with tigers, sunsets and princes; but Har Gopal was *real*, he was everyday urban, suffering India that people in the West didn't know about.' The rather odious Christine has borrowed a flat and ready-made image, but Betsy is the superior artist, with the imagination to love

> his finely drawn features, yes, his dark dreaming eyes, his sadness, his sensitivity; and also – but how could she tell Christine this? – she loved the shabby clothes he wore, his badly cut cotton trousers and his frequently washed shirt with his thin wrists coming out of the buttoned cuffs. She was positively proud of the fact that he looked so much like everybody else –

like hundreds and thousands of other Indian clerks going to
offices every morning on the bus and coming home again with
their empty tiffin-carriers in the evenings: people who worked
for small salaries and supported their families and worried.

As she is the superior artist, she is the superior lover. Christine's
safe and appropriate Indian affair is not 'passion': Betsy's is, though
Har Gopal beats her and curses her.

It is easier to assent to the tendency to mythicise and idealise
the beloved than to countenance the tendency to recreate in him
the image of a punishing deity. Yet it is so. Leo Kellermann, for
example, is as fond of conquest *per se* as he is beloved of many:
'It's no fun unless the fish resists; unless it struggles – flaps and
fights and wriggles for its life until – yupp! you've got it: up in the
air where you want it, dangling there, with all your hook, line and
sinker inside!' (*In Search of Love and Beauty*, p. 32).

Jhabvala's concerns are shared by many current theorists and
writers on the psychology of gender. The problem of 'sado-
masochism' is *the* issue of the eighties for feminists. Much recent
work addresses itself to the enigmas of desire. Feminist conferences
have been devoted to exploring the meanings of sexuality in our
lives, often producing profound disagreements and ideological
rifts: the infamous 1982 Conference on Sexuality at Barnard College,
New York, generated months of debate in such periodicals as *Off
Our Backs*, *Feminist Studies*, *Feminist Issues*, *Sojourner*, *Mother Jones*,
Heresies, *Signs* and others.[4]

One current of ideas assigns the cultural association of female
desire and self-abasement to the conditioning of a diseased society.
For example, Susan Griffin, in her study *Pornography and Silence*,
explores the imagination that associates femaleness with bondage
and slavery.[5] To attempt to sum up her argument in a sentence is
to do it an injustice, but it has to do with the bifurcation of human
experience into two poles, that is, culture and nature, reason
and feeling. 'Culture', which celebrates control and denigrates
spontaneity and feeling, is pitted against 'nature', and man comes
to embody 'culture', woman 'nature'. As culture must control
nature, man must control woman. Within the terms of this
metaphor, it is necessary to punish and control woman for her
'crime' of feeling, thus reaffirming man's invulnerability.

One of the problems with this formulation is that, in concentra-
ting on pornography, a literature designed for and consumed in

the main by men, it conveniently disregards the issue of women's desires as they are revealed in literature and art, high and low.

Literature written by and for women must and does provide a field for the interpretation or even naming of these desires. The dreams and fantasies of women have to be looked at again. As feminist literary critics it is our task to re-evaluate the literature that represents those dreams, on every level of skill or artistry; such a re-evaluation must correct a male-centred view that has until now been the only one. The current interest of feminist critics in romance literature and the 'Female Gothic' (to use Ellen Moers' term) is a response to this question of female desire.[6] Women writing serious fiction – like Ruth Prawer Jhabvala – write within the context of this re-evaluation. Jhabvala's fiction seems to be about India: it is really about the desires of women.

One meets in her fiction unconventional, even marginal, women, who have gone so far as to travel alone in India. They have chosen a daring autonomy. They have an ill-disguised impatience with the forms that other women of their class live by: for example, Asha in *A New Dominion* takes a keen pleasure in scandalising a group of hypocritical committee women – who are, ironically, in the midst of a meeting affirming the rights of women.

Like the women who read Gothic novels and romances, Jhabvala's women seek apocalyptic, transcendent, glorious passion. They seek it in the form of phallic, 'dark', sinister, mysterious men. As an ironist, she shows us the tragi-comic results of this impulse: but as it arises in all her protagonists – including her homosexual male ones – it would be absurd merely to condemn it. Perhaps it would be enough if we could at least understand it.

One of the first critics to write from a woman's perspective about 'demonic' sexuality was Susan Sontag, who in her 1967 essay 'The Pornographic Imagination' ventured to oppose the prevailing idea that healthy sexuality, if we only knew what it was, would be clean, natural and good. Speaking of the branch of literary 'pornography' represented by Sade, Lautréamont, Bataille and the pseudonymous Pauline Réage, she concluded that

> Their assumption seems to be that 'the obscene' is a primal notion of human consciousness, something much more profound than the backwash of a sick society's aversion to the body. . . . Tamed as it may be, sexuality remains one of the demonic forces in human consciousness, pushing us at intervals close to taboo

and dangerous desires, which range from the impulse to commit sudden and arbitrary violence . . . to the voluptuous yearning for the extinction of consciousness, for death itself.[7]

Jessica Benjamin, in a more recent contribution to the debate, takes a position that links the opposing views of Sontag and Griffin, and goes a step further in analysis. Her hypothesis is that civilisation, with its 'individualistic emphasis on strict boundaries between self and others, promotes a sense of isolation and unreality. Violence acquires its importance in erotic fantasy as an expression of the desire to break out of this numbing encasement'.[8] This idea is borne out in Ruth Jhabvala's psychological portraits. Often her wandering women are so understated as to seem numb – the narrator of *Heat and Dust*, for example. In *A New Dominion*, because of her sinister guru's ministrations, Lee is at last able to weep, to break out of her numbness. Only the cavalier Crishi seems to break through Harriet's isolation, in *Three Continents*.

In his study *Deceit, Desire and the Novel* the structuralist René Girard examines the issue of 'masochism' without considering its relationship to gender. His conclusions are illuminating.

A man sets out to discover a treasure he believes is hidden under a stone; he turns over stone after stone but finds nothing. He grows tired of such a futile undertaking but the treasure is too precious for him to give up. So he begins to look for a *stone which is too heavy to lift* – he places all his hopes in that stone and he will waste all his remaining strength on it.[9]

Human beings desire most that which eludes them, simply because it holds out the greatest promise. The treasure that is hidden must be the best. Girard's perspective is refreshingly demystifying. Jhabvala shares with him a sense of the universality of what is generally taken to be aberrant behaviour. Her fiction accords well with Girard's astute observations, and with his commentary on our tendency to distance ourselves from the phenomenon of what he calls 'metaphysical desire' by patholigising it:

To make suffering . . . the actual object of [the 'masochist's'] desire is a particularly revealing 'mistake.' Like other mistakes of the same type, it is not due to an unfortunate accident or to a lack of scientific precautions by the observer. This observer *does not want* to delve into the truth of desire to the point where he himself would be just as much involved as the subject of his observations. By restricting the deplorable consequences of metaphysical desire to an object which the masochist, and he alone, would desire, one makes an exceptional being of him, a monster whose sentiments have nothing in common with those of 'normal' people, i.e., our own. The masochist is supposed to desire the *opposite* of what we desire. The contradiction which ought to be perceived as being desire itself at its most intense becomes an individual's idiosyncrasy; it becomes a barrier between the observer and this masochist whom it would be dangerous to understand entirely.[10]

In Jhabvala's understated comedies, lovers desire what is mysterious and alien and dangerous. They are courageous and rash: they venture where common sense forbids. Their courage is paradoxically in the service of their desire to submit, to be annihilated, to give up their individuality. But giving way to passion usually turns out to be deeply self-destructive. The passionate abandon of the lover becomes confused with the societal enslavement of women, with disastrous results. In the case of the guru and the disciple, yet another inequality is added to the mixture:

> 'Say you're glad I take all things away from you and do what I like and how I like with you.'
> After a longish silence Lee said yes.
>
> (*A New Dominion*, p. 107)

Jhabvala's fiction shows us how the 'search for love and beauty' can backfire and destroy – particularly women. Nevertheless, it does not invalidate the romantic quest itself. The protagonists learn by shedding naïve illusions about men, romance and sex. Their experience yields not cynicism or even renunciation but only a deeper curiosity, which may well persist into advanced age, as with characters such as Minnie, in 'Grandmother'.

Like any quest, the search for love and beauty is dangerous, but it is also compelling. Ruth Jhabvala's fiction affirms the paradox of desire, 'which pleasureably resolved itself for the sake of him who accepted it and gave himself over to it'.

This paradox inheres in Jhabvala's characteristic 'demon-lover' tales. A well-educated woman makes a foolish choice, loving not wisely but too well. Her inappropriate lover is from a social class lower than her own. The foolish choice is made with a peculiar combination of will and involuntariness: she is enchanted, enthralled and hypnotised because she wishes to be. Her inappropriate choice is to some degree a political act, a rejection of the hierarchies of class.

Olivia's story in *Heat and Dust* is a novelistic rendering of the plot; many other stories recast it in other Indian settings. 'The Housewife' (*Like Birds, Like Fishes*), 'Passion' (*A Stronger Climate*), 'On Bail' and 'Desecration' (*How I Became a Holy Mother*): all explore the theme. (All these stories have been reprinted in Jhabvala's fifth collection, *Out of India*, 1986.) Always, the passionate liaison signifies the woman's refusal to comply with the societal imperatives that constrain her – whether Indian or Western – but also her incomplete and naïve notion of her chosen escape route. For the demon-lover, though sexually compelling, may bring to the relationship not only his own culturally sanctioned misogyny – particularly virulent toward an 'adulterous' wife, which she had now become – but class resentment as well. He will hardly bring her relief: all he can do is provide a way out of her unsatisfying life, and a convenient method of avoiding either personal responsibility, or clarity of analysis.

The female protagonist is not solely to be indicted for such an avoidance, for patriarchal systems, Eastern or Western, work to discourage clarity of analysis in any area that concerns the relations of men and women. Like class relations, sex and gender relations are most often not a mystery but a muddle, as Forster saw. What is a good marriage, for example? The marriages described in 'Desecration', 'The Housewife' or *Heat and Dust* appear exemplary: the husband is kind, well-meaning, even adoring. But a closer look shows him to be curiously *absent* – satisified to have his wife care for him, uninterested in and unaware of the self that *she* perceives to be her real one.

Marriage, built on false images, tends to enclose us in hypocrisy. As Mary comments, in the story 'In Love with a Beautiful Girl' (*A Stronger Climate*), 'It's so humiliating to be loved for what one values least.' She is speaking of her possessions, which excite her Indian boyfriends. But the same might be said of marriage as it is portrayed in these pages. Moreover, the very stability of these ostensibly happy marriages creates the guilty need to seek excitement outside them. Antidotes to boredom other than illicit love affairs – creative work, rich friendships, the pleasures of children, for example – are either trivialised, or unavailable. Both Olivia and Sofia are childless, not, at least in Olivia's case, by choice.

In *Heat and Dust*, Douglas thinks it unbecoming for a woman to study Hindi. In 'The Housewife', Shakuntala's musical study is possible only because her husband views it as a harmless pastime. In 'Desecration', Sofia has leisure and education, but no sense that she might be anything other than hostess, companion and audience for her husband's blank verse.

If the woman is cherished by her husband – for assuming an identity not vital or authentic to her – she is despised by her lover, who thus liberates her from her pedestal. Powerful, high-handed and contemptuous, he releases in her the energy that destroys her peaceful adjustment to the dull marriage. The demon-lover plot is a commentary on the self-destructive non-solutions available to a woman who seeks exaltation, transcendence, vitality and spiritual intoxication. These are not options for ladies. *Heat and Dust* ends with Olivia's ruin and enforced withdrawal, a virtual solitary confinement; 'Desecration' with Sofia's literal suicide. 'The Housewife' and 'Passion' end ambiguously: the impassioned women throw everything aside to be with their indifferent lovers. Clearly, their decisions are absurd and unworkable: there we leave them.

Susan Sontag, in the essay just discussed, makes the point more broadly, that is, across gender lines. For her, the 'pornographic imagination' springs from

> the traumatic failure of modern capitalistic society to provide authentic outlets for the perennial human flair for high-tempered visionary obsessions, to satisfy the appetite for exalted self-transcending modes of concentration and seriousness. The need of human beings to transcend 'the personal' is no less profound than the need to be a person, an individual. But this society serves that need poorly. It provides mainly demonic vocabularies in which to situate that need. . . . One is offered a choice among vocabularies of thought and action which are not merely self-transcending but self-destructive.[11]

The analysis can best be applied to women, whose capacity for 'high-tempered visionary obsession', 'concentration' and, for that matter, 'seriousness' is tacitly assumed, East or West, to be less developed than men's. It aptly describes the condition of Ruth Jhabvala's errant female protagonists.

Part Two
To the Ashram

You had Western women, very introverted, vulnerable, sensitive, all carried to the extreme. And you had gurus who seemed to me the epitome of a definite Indian type – charismatic, physically magnetic, deeply intuitive. The meeting of these two was just irresistible to me.

(Ruth Prawer Jhabvala, interviewed in
The New York Times, 1983)

3
Gurus: Short Stories

Ruth Jhabvala's fiction does contain a number of gurus who stand for – or at least on – a path of legitimate spiritual development: there is the smiling guru of *The Householder*, who inspires his band of followers to a blissful ardour that is portrayed without irony. There is the peaceful guru of 'The Old Lady', or Banubai, the elderly female guru of *A New Dominion*, or the music master of 'The Housewife', or finally Maji, whose special powers help the modern narrator of *Heat and Dust*. Though flawed, some more than others, each does represent at least some of those positive qualities that a spiritual teacher might embody: knowledge, wisdom and compassion. Each *is* a real source of comfort and delight to his or her followers. But these followers are almost always Indians.

There is thus the suggestion that only Indians may legitimately enter into a guru–disciple relationship: it has been part of their culture for centuries. But for Westerners it is quite a different matter – as it is for many things. 'This knowledge [the immanence of God – to 'see God in a cow' is Jhabvala's expression] may be true for an Indian, but can never quite become that for me', she remarks in 'Myself in India' (*An Experience of India*). The same is true of the teacher–disciple relationship: Indians *may* be able legitimately to participate in it (even there, her fiction betrays an uneasiness), but European enthusiasm for spiritual quest and involvement with spiritual leaders is always uncomfortably close to feverish eroticism:

> They're always keen on things like that – I mean, bowing down and touching feet – I don't know what kick they get out of it, but they do. . . . When they stumble up again, there's a sort of holy glow on their faces.   ('How I Became a Holy Mother')

Katie, the narrator whose words these are, is acute and dispassionate enough to observe the erotic impulse behind the European disciples' submission to the guru. She is not alone among Jhabvala's Western women tourists.

Katie is one of a number of tourist-heroines, female questers and researchers. Often these observant figures are themselves writers: Daphne, the protagonist of 'A Spiritual Call' (*A Stronger Climate*) is at least a rewriter, while the narrator of *Heat and Dust* and Natasha of *In Search of Love and Beauty* are writers. Whether Daphne (a naïve) or Katie (tougher) or Lee of *A New Dominion* (matter-of-fact), all these young women are intelligent and unconventional. They serve their author well; they are ideal narrators: intensely interested in the culture they pass through, sharply observant, ironically deflating. The last quality gives them a rather anti-erotic force which nicely undercuts the erotic aura that surrounds them for the Indians, for whom they represent Western sexual licence.

They blandly report the transparent sexual manoeuvres of their childlike suitors, and give in not so much out of desire as out of an almost motherly combination of weariness and altruism. Since he is sexually deprived, since he desires it so much, since it is expected of her. So the English narrator in *Heat and Dust*, with Chid and with Inder Lal; so Lee with Gopi in *A New Dominion*. That his passion quickly shades into a predictable misogyny they claim not to take very seriously, having always maintained the invulnerability of distance and a kind of maternality. In this misplaced nurturance, the dispensing of sexual favours becomes a kind of consolation prize for the poverty and powerlessness of their boy lovers.

'AN EXPERIENCE OF INDIA'

One such tourist-heroine explores the connections between sexuality, quest and discipleship. The unnamed narrator of 'An Experience of India', in the collection of the same name, is one of Jhabvala's most blithely unconventional young wanderers, an adventurer in India. Sceptical and pragmatic, she doubts much, yet she is impelled by the underlying conviction that her travels *are* a quest, that is, that there *is* something to look for, and that she may yet find it in India. Her narrative details the progress of her flight from European values, her descent to a kind of madness: she is one of the first to have 'gone too far' – saying an indifferent goodbye to money, comfort and English boyfriend.

The story is clearly preparatory for *A New Dominion*, having to do with lovers and ashrams and the connections between the two. Narrated in a cheerful, diaristic style, it is mostly flashback. 'Today Ramu left', she begins, at the end. The servant Ramu's departure signals her new poverty. She has come to India 'to be changed'; but Henry, her companion, only 'wanted a change'. At first she travels around having 'interesting adventures' – mostly sexual, since 'Indian men are very, very keen to sleep with foreign girls'. Yet no pleasure seems to be exchanged in these encounters, which are furtive and hurried, 'over in a great rush'. Her partner is immediately intent on escaping before being seen.

The only pleasure may be in having defied a repressive and puritanical social system. Her many admirers are trapped in a miserable cycle of crowding, poverty, hopelessness and repression: the last an odd irony in this ancient civilisation of 'the Kama Sutra, and the sculptures showing couples in every kind of position', as she observes. Poverty itself militates against opportunities for sexual expression: one of her lovers recounts that in the early days of his marriage he and his bride slept in a room with the entire family, so that of course they had no privacy. 'I had a strange sensation then, as if I wanted to strip off all my clothes and parade up and down the room naked.'

The Indians, the men who follow her, seem to her to envy her undreamt of freedom to talk and laugh with anyone she pleases. Their eyes seem to her 'the eyes of prisoners looking through their bars at the world outside'. Her pity may be naïve and ethnocentric, however. Her next adventure reveals that such freedom might not always be envied by the Indians. Women's misplaced pity for men is a familiar Jhabvala theme: compare 'The Housewife', 'On Bail' or 'Desecration'.

Ahmed, her beautiful young musician lover, has the emotional delicacy and intuitiveness that her Western boyfriend, with the best will in the world, falls far short of. Where Henry, making a 'sincere effort' to understand, would earnestly enquire after her moods and feelings and still not quite understand, Ahmed is able to feel with her, and, without being told, to sense her changes of mood.

One holds on to such a delightful companion: she persuades Ahmed to leave his crowded family quarters and accompany her to Delhi. But without his large family he languishes, and he 'crumpled up as if he were a paper flower'. He returns to his village, 'and all that was left to me of Ahmed was a memory, very beautiful and delicate like a flavour or a perfume or one of those melodies he played on his sarod'.

So his ways and hers cannot overlap for long. Her explorations continue, and she now encounters a toothless old holy woman who dances with joy and tells enchanting mythological stories. Such ecstasy is a powerful testimonial to holiness, and the encounter leads to the ashram. 'The way she carried on it was as if she had all the looks and glamour anyone ever had in the world and was in love a million times over. I thought well whatever it was she had, obviously it was the one thing worth having and I had better try for it.'

The ashram episode in this story directly foreshadows *A New Dominion*. As in the novel, the guru, a powerful, charismatic figure who uses his huge eyes 'to tremendous effect' eventually rapes the narrator. Foreshadowing Evie, Swamiji's ultra-obedient slave in the novel, is Jean, who praises the joys of submission and 'not having a will and not having thoughts of your own'. She hopes for Lee's sake that she too will abandon her stubborn, 'ego-centred' ways: 'if she could only give me some inkling of the infinite bliss to be tasted in this process – here her breath would give out for a moment and she couldn't speak for ecstasy'.

In the novel to come, a third disciple, Margaret, fulfils the prophecy voiced by the narrator in the preparatory story:

> At such moments I envied her because she seemed to have found what I was looking for. But at the same time I wondered whether she really had found what she thought she had, or whether it wasn't something else and she was cheating herself, and one day she'd wake up to that fact and then she'd feel terrible.

In the novel, Margaret dies of dysentery and jaundice because she refuses medical treatment, in accordance with Swami's philosophy. So she never gets the chance to wake up. Only the Christian burial she is given at the close of the novel symbolically reasserts her Europeanness and her autonomy.[1]

The rape of the narrator by the guru – which he justifies as a necessary step in the 'smashing' of her ego – represents both a relief and a disappointment: his magic and fascinating power is revealed as self-gratifying, loveless sexuality, the mere satisfaction of his physical needs, and thus neither as profoundly menacing, nor as exciting, as she had hoped and feared.

He said he would teach me to obey, to submit myself completely, that would be the first step and a very necessary one. For he knew what we were like, all of us who came from Western countries: we were self-willed, obstinate, *licentious.* On the last word his voice cracked with emotion, his hand went further and deeper. *Licentious*, he repeated, and then . . . he asked 'How many men have you slept with?' . . . But I was no longer afraid; now he was not an unknown quantity nor was the situation any longer new or strange. 'Answer me, answer me!' he cried, riding on top of me, and then he cried 'Bitch' and I laughed in relief.

For those many urban Indian lovers have prepared her for the guru's ritual question:

Always, at the moment of mounting excitement, they ask, 'How many men have you slept with?' And it's repeated over and over 'How many? How many?' and then they shout 'Aren't you ashamed?' and 'Bitch!' – always that one word which seems to excite them more than any other, to call you that is the height of their love-making, it's the last frenzy, the final outrage: 'Bitch!' Sometimes I couldn't stop myself but had to burst out laughing.

The narrator's detachment, like her laughter in both quoted passages, is, I think, less than convincing. At any rate, it is a joyless laughter, for the deflation of guru and lover, while it may be comical, is also bitter. With the disappearance of his mysterious aura, she is thrust back into a state of isolation and boredom. Her search will continue, now even more intensely, and with greater risk to herself, than before. Henry returns to England. By her own choice, she remains in India alone and penniless. What little money she still has, she spends on religious books, the Upanishads and the Vedanta Sutras. Reading them, 'it was as if I were all by myself on an immensely high plateau breathing in great lungfuls of very sharp, pure air'.

These images emerge again in the later novel *Heat and Dust*, when two heroines, half a century apart, make the trek up the mountain to enlightenment. The narrator of *Heat and Dust* sets out to live the life of a wandering religious, alone, without destination and without money. But the line between that identity and that of a female derelict is unclear.

In two day's time I . . . will have to go with my bundle and my bedding. I've done this so often before – travelled here and there without any real destination – and been so happy doing it; but now it's different. That time I had a great sense of freedom and adventure. Now I feel compelled, that I *have* to do this whether I want to or not. And partly I don't want to, I feel afraid. Yet it's still like an adventure, and that's why besides being afraid I'm also excited, and most of the time I don't know why my heart is beating fast, is it in fear or in excitement, wondering what will happen to me now that I'm going travelling again.

The compelling *reality* of her dangerous fugue is convincingly rendered. We understand her view that it is just another, only more exciting, journey, but we also understand that it is exceedingly ill-advised: crazy, in fact. These are the steps, then, leading to a 'ruin' every bit as real as that of the 'fallen woman' in another time. Whether by eroticism or religious ecstasy – or some combination of the two – the woman who strays from sense into an excess of sensibility is greatly at risk.

'A SPIRITUAL CALL'

A number of other stories, particularly those of the sixties collected in *A Stronger Climate*, rework the Gothic theme, that is, the sexualisation of villainy and victimisation. Now the roles are filled by clever male guru (Indian) and unsuspecting female victim (Western). 'A Spiritual Call' tells the story of shy Daphne and gross Helga, and *their* self-interested Swamiji. This tale, set in yet another unprepossessing ashram, where the food is poor and the flies abundant, conveys with masterly economy the precise atmosphere of the little society of European seekers with their Indian guru.

Daphne, like her mythological namesake, is modest and reserved. She is the 'very introverted, vulnerable, sensitive' Western woman referred to in Jhabvala's remarks above. Foil to her is Helga, who suffers from no such refinement: both women, however, will fall in love with Swami.

Helga is described with relish: an 'unreserved' person,

loud and explicit about everything she did, expressing the most fleeting of her thoughts in words and allowing no action, however trivial, to pass without comment. Every morning on waking she would report on the quality of the sleep she had enjoyed, and thence carry on a continuous stream of commentary as she went about her tasks ('I think I need a new toothbrush.' 'These flies – I shall go mad!')

Yet to Daphne's surprise, Swami finds Helga good company. The reader realises what Daphne does not: that Helga shares Swami's bed. Daphne's own sexual feelings become apparent in the course of the story, to her and to the reader, if not to Swami. Ironically, for all his supposed psychological acumen, he vastly misreads Daphne, seeing her as 'cool' when she is burning with desire. His inaccurate perception springs from a certain crudeness of vision. Daphne's 'metaphysical' desire is unknown to him.

If Helga's services are agreeable to the Swami, he can find a use for Daphne's too – but literary, not sexual. She is to rewrite the 'turgid, often naive, grammatically incorrect' and misspelled manuscript that will become a book, to be called *Vital Principle of Living* and 'to be translated into all the languages of the world'. While Daphne, who has been educated at Oxford, recognises its errors,

> she realized that it was not for him she needed be ashamed but for herself. How narrow was her mind, how tight and snug it sat in the straitjacket her education had provided for it! Her sole, pitiful criterion was conventional form, whereas what she was coming into contact with here was something so infinitely above conventional form that it could never be contained in it.

The delicious satire of the Western anti-rationalism of the sixties is developed further in *A New Dominion*. There too the pitfalls of the anti-rational are laid out. In one droll scene the disciple Lee is enjoined to spell 'transience' with an *a* ('transiance') as a demonstration of devotion to her Swami – it is his misspelling. Ruth Jhabvala's own formalism, that is, her seemingly effortless use of 'conventional form' underlies the satire and adds to it another diverting dimension.

Yet Daphne's impulses are correct: there are indeed times when education may corrupt vision, when form becomes formula. The comedy lies in the crudeness and immaturity of Daphne's view, her false application of correct ideas. In this she resembles the heroines of many an English novel, spirited, individualistic young women who think they see beyond – and who do, in fact, see beyond – their more conventional peers, and who make the wrong choice based on their incomplete understanding: Dorothea Brooke, Emma Woodhouse, Elizabeth Bennett, Isabel Archer. Deeply vulnerable, Daphne overestimates a comparatively worthless man whom she sets up – with ample prompting – as a kind of divinity. (But Swami is far more canny than Casaubon, for example, and far more sexually manipulative.)

Daphne herself eventually recognises the erotic nature of her joy in Swami's presence. The scene in which she makes this discovery has a distinctly 'metaphysical' flavour. One is reminded of Lucy Snowe and Paul Emanuel in Charlotte Brontë's *Villette*. Swami gently reprimands her for not attending morning meditation (she has, after all, been up until dawn rewriting his dictations). In response to his 'lower voice' she replies

> 'I was lazy, that's all,' and waited, pencil poised, hoping for a resumed dictation.
> 'Look at me,' he said instead.
> She was too surprised to do so at first, so he repeated it in a soft voice of command, and she turned her head, blushing scarlet, and lifted her eyes – and found herself looking into his. Her heart beat up high and she was full of sensations. She would have liked to look away again, but he compelled her not to.

Her hands tremble. After this contretemps, which fizzles out with his advice that she relax, she recognises the nature of her feelings. Her honesty with herself represents a liability, since she must now admit that her love for Swami is 'very much more personal than she had hitherto allowed herself to suspect'.

If Swami finds her a creature of 'cool and rational mind', she 'knew herself to have become a creature tossed by passion and wild thoughts'. The reader sees why he misreads her so: Helga, loud, boisterous and buxom, is more to his taste. Still, to Daphne's joy, he invites her to accompany him to the United States. A good editor, she represents a real convenience, no less so in her own way than Helga, who will also accompany him. Now her submission is complete. Even as secretary/editor/amenuensis, 'She was completely happy to be going to California, and anywhere else he might want her to accompany him'. With this ending line, Daphne's 'spiritual call' attains its tragi-comic fulfilment.

4

Gurus: *A New Dominion* or *Travelers*

DOMINION: THE POLITICAL CONTEXT

A New Dominion, published in England in 1973, was called *Travelers* in its American edition. The American title has the virtue of stressing the novel's tourist motif, but the British title is, I think, the better and richer one. Just as the simpler American title of *To Whom She Will* sacrificed a key idea, *A New Dominion* refers more directly to this novel's theme.

The word 'dominion' has three senses, at least: 'the power or right of governing and controlling'; 'territory subject to a king or ruler'; and in particular 'the larger and self-governing British dominions'.[1] In all its senses, 'dominion' is the subject of the novel: colonialism, Indian-style, and more generally, power relations based on wealth, class or personality.

The colonial theme emerges from context and setting. The state of India was never, like Canada, Australia or New Zealand, included in the elect 'dominion' category – which was an imperial status reserved for territories in which the relatively sparse and indigenous populations occupied a position of absolute power-lessness *vis-à-vis* the English settlers. The population of the subcon-tinent, of course, always represented a political entity very different, and far more complex than those. The precise nature of India's *contemporary* relationship with England comes up in the novel: it is the subject of some very funny dinner-table conversation. A group of upper-caste and Oxford-educated Indian and English guests at the table of a British High Commission counsellor debate, in 'very English' accents, whether indeed there is some 'special relationship' between England and India (*A New Dominion*, p. 53). 'Oh I *say*,' exclaims the Indian Deepak, objecting that there is none whatever.

Against the backdrop of this colonial theme, the novel inquires into a number of power-unequal personal relationships: that is, dominion created by individual circumstances and personality. These relationships of relatively voluntary dominion and subjection fall into two categories in the novel, though the lines between these categories will blur and finally dissolve: I refer to the arenas of desire on the one hand, and spiritual or religious quest on the other. (Female) disciple and (male) guru are linked in a relationship that is presented as a kind of traditionally sanctioned psychological thralldom whose sexual component is only thinly veiled. Thus Lee, Margaret and Evie, described in the novel's prefatory cast of characters as 'girls on a spiritual quest', are in voluntary thrall to Swamiji, called 'a spiritual guide'.

James Ivory in his account of the genesis of the film *Autobiography of a Princess* has traced the historical and sociocultural connection between nawab and guru. Once, he says, there were ill-fated relationships between Englishwomen and maharajas; now there are ill-fated relationships between Englishwomen and gurus.

> Whereas the followers of the Maharajas used to move from palace to palace in private trains with a trunkful of pretty dresses and evening slippers, the swami's admirers travel from ashram to ashram in third-class cars on the Indian railway, with a bedroll and a knapsack containing a cotton sari, an extra T shirt and some cheap plastic sandals from the bazaar.[2]

So Lee, Margaret and Evie are in a tradition, though not the tradition that they think.

Like colonists, lovers, heterosexual or homosexual, also operate within relationships of inequality, the familiar inequality of desire, in which the one who cares less, or not at all, holds sway over the one who cares more. The novel presents two such relationships: Asha, 'a middle-aged princess', is in love with Gopi, 'a student'; Raymond, 'a tourist', is also in love with him. Handsome and charming, Gopi uses his evanescent power – for, generated as it is by his youth and beauty, it will soon fade – to obtain what material advantage he can: Asha, and even Raymond, a middle-class Briton with a small legacy from an aunt, are fabulously wealthy in comparison to him, son of an ordinary urban Indian family.

The novel also contains two literal servants: Shyam, Raymond's servant, and Bulbul, Asha's maid. Both figure rather importantly in the novel, and function to undercut the romanticised servitude of both lovers and disciples – whose fevered obsessions are shown to have everything to do with each other, yet nothing to do with the dominions created by class, caste and wealth: more cruel because absolutely involuntary. Yet how voluntary *is* the psychological servitude of lover or disciple? That question is the crucial one in this novel: as it is in Jhabvala's fiction as a whole.

BRITONS IN THE NEW DOMINION: RAYMOND AND LEE

Good novelists are always in a sense spies and aliens, reporting on the activities of those whom they silently observe, among whom they pass unnoticed. Marginal and disenfranchised, they may well be women. One thinks of Jane Austen in her drawing-room, hiding her manuscript as it is being written. Ruth Jhabvala has quoted, as being especially meaningful to her, James Joyce's definition of the novelist's art – that it must be carried out in 'silence, exile and cunning'.[3] Her foremost critic, Gooneratne, has taken the felicitous words for the title of her critical biography. *A New Dominion* contains two exiled character-narrators who have this ability to fade into the background. Lee is young and female, given to bright colours and Indian jewellery. Nevertheless,

> No one else [other than an eldery cabinet minister – wearing a revealing *dhoti* – who inveighs against her immodest dress] took any notice of Lee. It was easy for them to see that she was not an interesting personality so they did not waste their efforts in engaging her in conversation.   (p. 16)

Lee divides the narrative with Raymond, who is in many ways a male version of her. He too is intelligent, observant, sensitive and British. He too is alienated even among his compatriots – *especially* among them, it would be more accurate to say. Both Raymond and Lee have a horror of British government functionaries. At their first meeting he endears himself to her by answering an emphatic *no* to her polite enquiry if he is with the Embassy (p. 23). He too is travelling in India without any formal goal.

But his underlying motive is, oddly, a good deal more straightforward than Lee's: he loves Indian boys, and he knows it. That he does not want to talk about it, that he views conversation about his, or anyone's, homosexuality as 'undesirable revelation' (p. 187) is another, not unrelated, issue; whether through reticence or shame, he keeps his silence. But beneath the silence the reader knows him to be formed, integrated, and in possession of a clear sense of himself, his boundaries and his values. The same cannot be said of Lee, whose formlessness gives her a special vulnerability, which the novel will explore. Gender contributes to this contrast: maleness bestows a sense of validity, femaleness detracts from it. Although on balance presented sympathetically, Lee is at times subjected to satire – her faulty grammar, her breathless infatuation with Swami, her admiration of his robotised disciple Evie – but Raymond never is: *he*, not Lee, is the authorial spokesperson. It is far more acceptable to do as Raymond does than to do as Lee does, in the eyes of Indian and Westerner alike.

Raymond and Lee together dominate the narrative structure, which consists of some seventy-five vignettes – V. S. Pritchett commented that many can stand alone as short stories.[4] They are arranged in a larger, tripartite, structure that corresponds to geographic setting: the cities of Delhi and Benaras, and the province of Maupur. Eleven of the vignettes are titled 'Lee', and those she narrates. Most are told by an omniscient narrator in the cinematic manner of Ruth Jhabvala's latest novels, and capture key moments in the progress of the interlocking stories. Six vignettes are called 'Raymond Writes to his Mother'.

These last, of course, are Raymond's own voice, though through a rather distorting filter, since his communication with his mother, chatty and warm though it is, omits the most important thing, the real reason for his being in India. He never speaks to her of Gopi; at one point he begins to, and then checks himself: 'it would be of no interest to her since she had not been kept up on the progress of their friendship' (p. 210). This omission of the unsayable essential is noteworthy in itself. It is very much in the manner of E. M. Forster's letters to *his* mother, which form the bulk of his Indian narrative, *The Hill of Devi*, and to which Ruth Jhabvala turns in her next novel, *Heat and Dust*. Omission as a narrative strategy is particularly congenial to her, and is a characteristic feature of her own relationship to *her* readers; a passionate intensity seems to burn beneath the surfaces of her novels, never revealed but always implied. In this novel about love, for example, no 'love scene' occurs.

A New Dominion details the progress of two major love triangles and several other minor rivalries. The first concerns the two English girls, Lee and Margaret, who love Swami; the next concerns Raymond and his rival, the fiery Indian princess Asha, who love beautiful Gopi. There is an odd symmetry in the fact that Margaret literally dies as a result of her obsessional love for Swami, while Lee reluctantly repudiates him; and Asha, having succeeded in keeping Gopi, retreats into an alcoholic stupor, while Raymond rather reluctantly leaves for England. Both Margaret and Asha get their man, unluckily for them. Both Lee and Raymond do not, and are the more fortunate.

There are other rivals too, for dominion in human relations is made up of, *depends on*, rivalry. If there were no rival, the beloved would be that much less valuable. Gopi is also loved – though how becomes an issue in the novel – by the guru Banubai at her ashram. Sensing a rival in Raymond, she implicitly accuses him of racism and throws him out. Banubai also competes with Asha for Gopi. Both Margaret and Lee compete with Evie, the third English disciple, for Swami's attention. Asha's servant Bulbul resents Banubai's influence on her mistress. Raymond's servant Shyam resents Gopi. Lee sleeps casually with Gopi and thus is a rival to Asha. Even Swami and Banubai resent each other as fellow teachers of meditation, and each subtly undermines the other's competence. Every human relationship bears the seeds of jealousy.

There are, continuing the triangle theme, three major religious centres in this novel (not counting the Dickensian 'University of Universal Synthesis', which is housed in a little room in Banubai's house in Benaras – the founder-president sleeps on a mattress on the floor amid piles of old newspapers and pamphlets). Banubai's house is actually on the shores of the Ganges. Swamiji has his ashram only *near* the holy city, ten miles away: 'This was deliberate policy on Swamiji's part: he did not wish to batten on the holiness of the past but to inspire new souls with a new spirit. It was also convenient that land was going cheap in that area' (p. 65). The third religious centre is in Delhi: Miss Charlotte's Mission, where Lee and Margaret meet, now functions as a sort of youth hostel. It is about to be shut down by the government, which looks unkindly on proselytising missionaries (p. 13) while shrugging its shoulders at the plight of the few wretched families that Miss Charlotte's dispensary has, until now, managed to serve.

The New Dominion replaces all that, for Christian missions are part of the Old Dominion, outright colonial rule, as opposed to the 'new spirit' as it is encountered in Swamiji's sinister ashram.

The New Dominion rejects Western meddling, although Banubai speaks with grudging approval of a German professor who comes to her in all humility, begging – as she tells it – to be allowed to sit at her feet. 'We will do our best with you', she tells him kindly (p. 161).

This is only one side of the 'new spirit', however; it has another aspect, quite opposed to 'the holiness of the past'. That aspect, ironically, is the wholehearted acceptance of Western materialism, as represented by Bob, the 'go-ahead young man' who wishes to buy Asha's father's estate – 'The Retreat' – at Maupur. Ruth Jhabvala has already treated this dynamic with much humour in *The Householder* (in a scene in which Prem, the Indian protagonist, attempts to impress the Germanic Hans Loewe with India's strides forward in industrialisation, while Hans praises Prem for his mystic enlightenment – one of her trademark dialogues at cross-purposes).

Bob, né Harish Chandra, has attended business school at New York University. Once he has acquired The Retreat, he will tear down that monument to self-indulgence and decadence, and set up workshops for the manufacture of spare parts for mechanised drills. (A nice touch, for no product could be further from the effeminised spirit of The Retreat, which is furnished with 'Edwardian opulence', intended only for pleasure, and barely used, at that. The mechanised drills, on the other hand, symbolise the over-masculinised, rapacious – and 'boring'? – spirit of rampant industrialism.) Bob also represents a contrast to Rao Sahib, Asha's brother and spokesman for the Old Dominion: like Raymond, Rao Sahib is a graduate of Cambridge.

Even with his 'devouring' (p. 194) glance, Bob is something of a bright spot in the cast of corrupt brokers of power. Perhaps his factory may, even if coincidentally, contribute to the social good. As such he is a welcome presence in the hopeless poverty and corruption of the barren province of Maupur. True, he is indifferent to the nuances of romantic suffering and joy that are Asha's special territory, but in a place like India, Asha's luxurious sensibilities are deeply problematical.

Ruth Jhabvala has spoken, in 'Myself in India' (*An Experience of India*), of her own sense of guilt at doing nothing directly toward the betterment of the masses of the wretched on whose backs, she says, live all of the moneyed in India. Bob and Asha must be seen in this context, so that if Bob errs in the direction of insensitivity and crass materialism, still he is not lost in a slough of self-indulgence and depression, as is Asha. He may, with his drills, be boring, but at least he is not bored, like Gopi and Asha, whose main pastime apart from lovemaking is playing cards. Of course, Bob is devoid of altruism, the special province of Miss Charlotte. He merely wants to make a lot of money, in the tradition of his caste, the banias (p. 200). Bob's crude self-interest is, sadly, the best of the New Dominion.

As an epigraph to her collection of stories *A Stronger Climate*, Ruth Jhabvala quotes from an unnamed source, 'They came no longer to conquer, but to be conquered'. This socio-historical observation derives from the longest vantage-point. In the waxing and waning of historical energies, the vigorous self-confidence and brute energy of the colonialists has been replaced by their descendents' cultural relativism, sensitivity, self-doubt and romanticism. Whether presented parodically – with Helga ('A Spiritual Call') or Hans Loewe (*The Householder*), the heavy-handed German seekers after enlightenment, or seriously – as with Raymond, or even Lee, the Western visitors now come on pilgrimages, not military forays.

Into the New Dominion come the Europeans. The things they value most about India are often the things that the Indians value least, while the Indians value most the things that the Europeans wish to divest themselves of. Again, 'It's humiliating to be loved for what one values least' ('In Love with a Beautiful Girl', *A Stronger Climate*). The cross-cultural misunderstandings only echo the kinds of misinterpretations we are all heir to, even without cultural differences. What is least valuable is often held in the highest esteem, while what is most valuable is discounted.

NAMES

In Ruth Jhabvala's artfully crafted novels and stories, names are never idly assigned. A look at the characters' names in *A New Dominion* confirms this, while providing clues as to authorial intention. Asha, the middle-aged princess who succeeds in seducing Gopi away from his family responsibilities as a bridegroom, has a name that means 'Hope' in Hindi. No longer young, but still living for love's pleasures, she must be an optimist if she believes they can continue to give her life meaning.

Her maid Bulbul, of the rough and scratchy voice, sings Asha to sleep with epic ballads of love and battle, and is ironically named for the silver-throated 'nightingale'. The nightingale, symbol of love, is also woven into the story with Asha's quotation to Gopi of a lyric Urdu couplet: 'O nightingale, forgive me your death, it was my tears that drowned you' (p. 74). Those, like Asha, who love not wisely but too well, ensure the failure of love; since their amours spring from despair, they are bound to fail. Tears drown the nightingale.

Gopi, the lover, is named for Krishna in his amorous form, 'Gopala', one of the names of God that Lee and Margaret chant at the ashram (p. 66). Ironically, Shyam the servant is named for Krishna in his contemplative and peaceful form – a humorous underlining of Shyam's jealousy and contentiousness.

Raymond is an Anglo-Saxon name meaning 'wise protector'. Raymond attempts several times in the novel to counsel Gopi to return to his family and the advantageous marriage they have arranged for him, and to litigate his acrimonious relations with Shyam. The name may also derive from the Germanic *Rein/mund*, 'clean of mouth', and Raymond is notable for his scrupulosity of word. He carefully considers before making any statement, for which he is roundly criticised by Banubai.

Banubai is a compound made up of two words, one with two meanings: *Banu*, in Urdu 'voice or desire', and in Hindi 'respected woman'; *bai*, a Rajisthan form of respectful address to a woman. Banubai, a woman known for her wisdom, neatly conflates all these ideas. At one point she is heard singing, in a high sweet flute-like voice, a love song to her Lord Krishna, who has come to her in a dream the previous night, as a mischievous boy: 'the more she followed Him, the more she called to Him, the more He hid himself and laughed at her' (p. 140). The dream image, incidentally, accords quite precisely with the structuralist definition of 'metaphysical desire' cited earlier in this study.

'Margaret' derives from the Latin *margarita*, 'pearl', but is also the name of Faust's beloved, perhaps a reference to the Faustian bargain with Mephistopheles that Margaret recapitulates in its feminine aspect.

Lee alludes to Leah, meaning in Hebrew 'weary one', Jacob's first wife, the less-coveted older sister of Rachel. At the close of the novel, Lee is weary indeed, and even more sorely tempted by the allure of Swami's false haven; and all along she has played a part secondary to Margaret or Evie in relation to Swami.

'Bob' is really named Harish Chandra – yet another name of Krishna, this time in his moon aspect – again, an ironic reference to Bob's literal 'nuts-and-bolts' approach to life, so opposed to the metaphysical lyricism for which he is named.

ASHRAMS

The presence in the novel of so many ashrams invites comparison among them. None is altogether lacking in validity: even Swami's ashram has a measure of authenticity. But the evil result of Swami's ministrations – the death of Margaret – far outweighs the good. In contrast to Swami, Banubai at least does no harm, and Miss Charlotte does some good. All three individuals radiate energy, which can be seen in their countenances. Miss Charlotte's face shines with happiness (p. 25), Banubai's eyes are always bright (p. 98), but Swami's eyes glitter in a 'strange, passionate way' (p. 123). The two women alone use their power to the good, which suggests at least a partial endorsement of a female-centred value system. The impulse is more fully worked out in *Heat and Dust* and *In Search of Love and Beauty*.

Here, for example, Banubai counsels a family whose adult son has vanished. After examining his wife's palm, Banubai 'pushed the hand away': '"I can't see anything. I can't tell you anything. Only this I know: that you are suffering. Day and night you are on thorns." . . . A great sigh rose from them' (p. 111). She directs them to imagine the dreadful possibilities: she advises them to submit to the will of God. Unexceptional as it is, this interview seems to help the suffering victims. When they get up to leave they look 'somewhat lightened' (p. 111). Perhaps they have been helped. There are no great claims here. Banubai has listened and that alone has had an effect.

Similarly, Miss Charlotte's faith and human relatedness represents a boon to Lee. At the end of the novel, when Margaret has at last succumbed to dysentery and jaundice and is lying dead in her hospital bed, Lee reports:

They disconnected all the tubes and covered Margaret with a sheet. Everyone was quite businesslike about it. The event had been expected. . . . Evie said we would leave in the evening.

But when Miss Charlotte came into the room, everything changed. Miss Charlotte embraced and kissed me and made my face wet with her tears. She got down on her knees by the side of Margaret's bed and began to pray. . . . tears continued to flow down her face. Then the body on the bed was not only someone who had died and had been expected to die – but was Margaret! Margaret!   (p. 205)

That is the outcome of the ashram story in this novel: the danger that Margaret, Lee and Evie flirt with is, finally, death. It may appear to be spiritual commitment, it may appear to be sexual love: in either case, its point of utmost intensity, its logical extreme, is annihilation. Jhabvala's New-York-based novel, *In Search of Love and Beauty*, is more explicit still in making connections between sexual desire and the desire for death or annihilation, but *A New Dominion* and *Heat and Dust* both make the connection. Such a connection is at the heart of the Gothic novel – to which, I believe, Jhabvala's work is linked, particularly *A New Dominion*, with the sinister and powerful Swami at its centre.

Margaret, disgusted with England, its hypocrisy, its emptiness, its '*nothingness*' (p. 27), has been in India for some time, searching for the right guru. Now that she has found Swamiji's 'Universal Society For Spiritual Regeneration in the Modern World' (p. 116), she shares her excitement with Lee, who follows her there to see for herself. At the ashram, Lee and Margaret share a room with Evie, who, like Daphne of 'A Spiritual Call', is taking dictation for Swamiji's book, to be called *Essence of the Upanishads*.

It's going to be a very revolutionary work because it's the first really serious attempt to fit Indian thought into the framework of Western apprehension in such a way that it's not only with the mind that we shall be able to understand it but with our whole being which is really the only way to really know anything.   (p. 74)

The gushing Lee who writes this passage bears little relation to the Lee who narrates Margaret's death. Yet the novel marks the stages of her growth, and the ingenuousness of her tone is eventually to fade.

Evie is an initiate: she has been in the ashram for three years.

'It's all she wants and all she *is* really', writes Lee approvingly (p. 74). Ruth Jhabvala's careful attention to the names of her characters suggests that Evie is akin to the biblical Eve, first to bite the attractive but forbidden fruit. Evie has succumbed to the serpent-like Swami, who with his 'glittering' eyes has seduced and essentially annihilated her. The suggestion is that *this* is 'the fall', the original sin – this ceding to the power of the charismatic man.

The three women subtly vie with each other for the privilege of serving Swamiji, who is deftly revealed as a master of manipulation. Evie is his silent, obedient slave; in the manner of a pimp, he has already 'seasoned' Evie, already 'turned her out', already 'broken her in'. The language is that of the American street, but Swamiji has his own exact equivalents, which describe a similar psychological process, culminating in the girl's fragmentation of self, complete dependency and severing of ties with the outside world. 'The old Lee must be broken before the new Lee can be formed' (p. 139), he explains. 'She must be mine completely in heart and soul and – yes, Raymond, . . . in body also, if I think it necessary' (p. 123).

When Margaret contracts infectious hepatitis and jaundice, she will not admit it, since, as she explains, Swami believes that such diseases are 'purely psychic. We only get them because we try to resist India – because we shut ourselves up in our little Western egos and don't want to yield. But once we learn to yield, they fall away' (p. 146). In any case, 'Swamiji doesn't like doctors' (p. 136). He believes in 'the ancient form of Indian medicine like it's written in the shastras' (p. 136), as Lee explains, rather exasperated, to Raymond. As often in the work of Ruth Jhabvala, Lee's incorrect grammar is a clue to the incorrectness of her perceptions.

Thus, all action at the ashram takes place in the shadow of Margaret's gradual decline, a physical death which makes even more sinister Swamiji's almost irresistible charisma. The comedy is black. The passages already cited may give a good idea of the author's precise ear and barbed wit, which are very much at her service in the depiction of English girls' various responses to their unspoken and unspeakable competition. In the scene just cited, as Margaret recites Swami's medical philosophy and he smiles approvingly at her, Lee suffers the torments of jealousy. She is 'slumped in a chair', 'silent and listless' (p. 144). Her emotional pain is not as conspicuous as Margaret's physical condition, but just as Margaret's, it must not be acknowledged. Even in the throes of jaundice, 'through her yellow sickness [Margaret] beamed, she glowed' (p. 146). She and Swamiji walk 'rather jauntily' out of the hotel that Raymond has been staying in ('for American tourists', Lee says scornfully, though Swamiji, to her surprise, is delighted to accept Raymond's hospitality there). But Lee 'had her head bent and dragged her feet in misery' (p. 146).

Lee's jealousy is a perfectly reasonable response to Swamiji's precise programme of seductive attention, followed by abrupt withdrawal. At first, the disciple is courted and fêted – just as, in the later *In Search of Love and Beauty*, each new student to arrive at an Esalen-like version of the ashram is given a room on the most comfortable floor, then eventually moved upstairs. Here, at Swamiji's ashram, Lee and Margaret undergo the first, delightful, stage of initiation, in which each feels herself to be the particular object of his concentration; even Lee, who thinks at first she is imagining it. She tests the hypothesis, looking away from him – yet never for long, since she senses him 'beckoning', drawing her back, willing her to look at him: 'And when she did, sure enough, there he was smiling at her – yes! at her alone! – so that she had to smile back and sing the way he wanted her to and cry out "Rama! Gopala! Hari! Krishna!" with as much abandon as she could manage' (p. 66).

In the second phase, Swamiji withdraws his attention, and, for Lee, 'it's as if there's no light in the sun, and those glorious Indian nights, well they too are now dark and drab to me. . . . He ignores me completely' (p. 157). Evie knows that this is merely a phase, though she says 'she couldn't tell . . . anything more' (p. 158). Victim that she is, she is aware of the programme by which she was seduced, but believes it necessary and right.

This arbitrary punishment makes all the sweeter its eventual cessation, which coincides with Swamiji's decision to 'make her his in body'. As it happens, the event, for which she had hardly dared hope, falls far short of her dreams and imaginings. A rape, and not a rapturous one, it is far from the transporting spiritual– erotic experience for which she longed. In fact, the encounter passes from terror, which might be considered the obverse of desire, into a kind of numb boredom yet further removed from feeling. He strokes her somehow unpleasantly, so that the 'thrill consisted mainly of distaste' (p. 169). She feels herself not a person, only an 'awful sensation', 'wriggling in the dark'.

He was the only person there. He was terrible, terrifying. He drove right on into me and through me and calling me beastly names, shouting them out loud and at the same time hurting me as much as he could. . . . I loathed him. He revolted me. . . . The strange thing was not only did I suffer but I got bored too because it went on so long and wouldn't stop. I even began to think my own thoughts. . . . The hutment was dense with a greasy hot smell like of a goat, and the only sounds were my funny whimpering and his animal breathing.   (p. 169)

The recurrent animal imagery represents a stark contrast to Lee's expectations, and reveals Swami as a sort of beast or satyr. The 'dark' side of his radiance is foremost now, and it is neither sensual nor sexual, only loathsome and revolting.

The episode is reminiscent of the sexual encounters described in 'An Experience of India' (there too abuse was shouted); it represents the same kind of disappointment. Such a culmination to the nuanced and thrilling emotional build-up serves to underline the oft-noted disparities between (female) romantic expectations and (male) sexual rapacity. But Swami has used his knowledge of psychology, more subtle than is customary, to further a banal seduction ending in an expression of degradation, contempt and conquest.

This instrumentality is played out to its conclusion at Maupur, the setting for the ultimate submission, that is, Margaret's death due to medical inattention; but a prefiguration of Swami's cold misuse of the Buddhist ideal of detachment occurs during the chapter 'A Reading in the Ashram' – from Swami's work-in-progress. The episode, read 'joyfully' by Evie, concerns an injured dog found dying near the ashram. Lee had begged for it to be put out of its misery, but Swami had not allowed it, pontificating that 'there is sunshine and gentle breezes, and there is rain and bitter storms' (p. 159), and acceptance is our lot. Again, the inelegant grammar signals the failure of values.

Fleeing the ashram in 'rage and disgust' (p. 170), Lee goes to the provincial village of Maupur, the site of Asha's family palaces, to join the other principals of this story: Raymond, Gopi and Asha. There at Maupur, Margaret and Evie eventually reappear, having made their wretched way, on third-class railway cars and bullock carts, to fetch Lee back to the ashram: but the 'tummy trouble' has finally progressed too far, and Margaret is taken to die in the local hospital.

'GOTHIC' ASPECTS

Like other Jhabvala works, *A New Dominion* explores the similarities between spiritual/religious quest and erotic obsession. Although the dénouement – Swami's rape of Lee – was revolting, what led up to it was compelling, spiritually, psychologically and erotically. In one encounter he is able to 'penetrate' an emotional numbness to which Lee has hitherto resigned herself; because of him, she is able to weep. The dynamic accords precisely with Jessica Benjamin's thesis discussed earlier (p. 31): the intensity of emotion overcomes a kind of psychic anomie.

Lee sits with him under a tree (the only tree in the ashram!); he has sent everyone else away. Why is she angry with him, he enquires. Her reason is excellent. She resents his abuse of Margaret: denying Margaret's state of health, he insists that she cook for the ashram. 'You *bullied* her', Lee dares. 'Bullied . . . Bullied . . . I like that word. Do I do it to you also? Tell me' (p. 105). She turns away, and 'Look at me', he insists, 'lightly'. Still she looks away. He turns her face toward him. She cries out at his touch. His eyes appear to burn with 'a supernatural power'. As she watches in 'fear and fascination', he slowly touches her face with a forefinger. She experiences 'something like an explosion in her mind and circles of light sparked and revolved within its pitch-black night'. She hears 'a voice' calling her name and only later realises it is his. She denies weeping, yet she wipes away tears, the first in years – she is 'amazed and ashamed'. ' "Now you will say that I'm bullying you also." He smiled gently. "But you like it when I bully you. Isn't it?" ' (p. 105).

In the New York-based novel *In Search of Love and Beauty*, Natasha – another Lee-like young woman – looks at Leo Kellermann, the Viennese guru who shares some of Swamiji's charisma, also with 'fear and fascination'. The exact repetition of these words, in works ten years apart, is a clue to their importance in Ruth Jhabvala's fiction; and of course, not only in her fiction. The dynamic they describe has its psychic roots, as it were, deep in the literary imagination, particularly, I believe, the female literary imagination, and springs from the same soil that nourished, and continues to nourish, the Gothic novel.

In literary terms, 'Gothic' refers to two distinct schools: the eighteenth-century novelistic mode, which relied on ancient castles, ghosts, moving statues and the machinery of the horrific and the grotesque. Horace Walpole, and later Mary Shelley, are its most well-known exemplars. The latter-day descendent of that genre, known as 'Modern Gothic', also a formulaic popular mode, enjoyed a vogue in the mid twentieth century, and is now rather passé, having been supplanted by the formulaic Romance – which is, of course, proving to be an unprecedented gold-mine in the publishing industry.

The modern Gothic, or 'Female Gothic'[5] accentuates the extreme vulnerability of a heroine by placing her in mysterious or frightening circumstances, in which she must interpret an ambiguous set of messages from a sinister but attractive male. *Jane Eyre*, and the Brontës' work in general, is non-formulaic reordering of the modern Gothic plot. Throughout its history, however, the Gothic, whether historical or modern, has been a woman's genre: written and read almost exclusively by women.

Ruth Jhabvala's fiction refers to the Gothic: it incorporates elements of it, reinterprets it and explores its meaning in contemporary and cross-cultural terms. Since her 'field' – her literary territory – is the psychology of women, this is not surprising. Gothic horror is, after all, one fictional reordering of the very real risks embedded in the polarities of masculinity and femininity. The vulnerable heroine, the powerful and attractive stranger or even intimate: these are the players in the modern Gothic, which repeats the crucial drama of *right interpretation* of deceiving appearances. Trusted husband, boss, psychiatrist, lawyer or any male authority figure, may be the one who is trying to murder us.[6]

While interpretation, that is, the examination of life, is *the* literary activity, Ruth Jhabvala's novels in particular hinge on the pitfalls of interpretation, set as they are in an alien world, in which it is difficult to read correctly. Moreover, her ironic, understated tone and her mastery of telling omission as a narrative technique *compel* the reader to interpret from clues. She supplies the important detail, we, it is to be hoped, draw the correct conclusion. We are not told, for example, that Lee is jealous to the point of illness, but we are given the significant clues – the sigh, the migraine headache, the petty argument. So as readers we recapitulate the author's process of meticulous observation.

This is a peculiarly novelistic skill. If the novelist must be one on whom nothing is lost, Ruth Jhabvala is that novelist. Her readers are required to be alert to implication and suggestion: the text will not spell out what we must know. There is comic disparity between Lee's conscious presentation of herself, and what *we* see, her unconscious body language. There is pleasure in our apprehension of that disparity, with the prompting of the novelist.

As novel-readers, of Jhabvala in particular and of novels in general, we delight in our discovery of the significant detail and take pleasure in our alertness to the telling clues that the novelist places in our path. Such literary pleasures are particularly available to women, who like any sub-central class, are required to *read* carefully. Perhaps this is one explanation of women's taste for novels, which, whether serious or formulaic, generally turn on the business of making correct interpretations of the drama of daily life. Susan Brownmiller in her discussion of 'women's intuition' – one name for expertise at interpretation of human behaviour – points out that 'that sentimentally valued characteristic may be nothing more than a defensive watchfulness, a picking up and putting together of verbal and nonverbal cues as a strategy of survival, as the subordinate animal is sensitive to the sounds and movements of the dominant animal, which does not need to think before it acts'.[7]

The Gothic is a fictional reordering of women's reality. Whether in past centuries or contemporaneously, women are at risk in a society built on feminine dependence on male power, a society that glorifies masculine combativeness and feminine compliance. The effects of this vulnerability are pervasive and ubiquitous: for example, in the institution of marriage – whether in the West, where families no longer arrange marriages, or traditionally, where they do. In the West, a young and inexperienced woman is expected to make a lifetime agreement which will place her and any children that she may have in a position of real dependency on a man who is always somewhat unknown, always seen through the filter of media-supported romantic mythology, usually physically stronger; whose potential for violence, also encouraged by the ubiquitous media, must remain an unknown. Battered-women's shelters, child-abuse statistics, rape crisis centres all attest to the real-life Gothic. But family involvement in the choice of a partner is hardly a guarantee of better treatment. In the India that Jhabvala writes of, 'dowry death' is an established social reality.[8]

Early in this novel Lee, in the course of her travels, witnesses the funeral of a young woman whose neighbours know her to be a murder victim, in fact a victim of 'dowry death' – and who cover up the crime. 'They shrugged. "What can be done? It's too late." They shook their heads in sorrow. It was such a pity. She was so young, she had only been married seven months. But her dowry had not been very big; her father had not been as generous to the son-in-law as he might have been' (p. 12). The police, the inquest that Lee asks about, are out of the question: the body is being cremated as they speak, although before the funeral procession 'women were screaming inside and outside the house' (p. 11). The arguing men prevail, and though 'the women redoubled their cries', the poisoned body is borne through the streets (by the men) and burned.

It is a staple of the popular 'thriller', whether literary or cinematic, to place the vulnerable heroine in a situation in which the audience knows, but she does not, that the man whom she thinks is her protector is actually a dangerous and violent murderer. The popular modern Romance plays with the same concepts: mistaken identity, the misapprehension of evil for good and of good for evil; but in this mode the heroine discovers to her delight that the dark, scarred desperado is actually kindly and domesticable: husband material after all. She can have her cake and eat it too. The 'Romance' performs the function of reaffirming and upholding the myths that the daily newspapers threaten to dissolve.[9]

The drama of Lee, Margaret, Evie and the other disciples of Swamiji thus has its roots in the Gothic novel. Though Ruth Jhabvala's ironic understatement is diametrically opposed to the intensely unhumorous melodrama of the Gothic, modern or historical, she shares with her less literary sisters the territory of misapprehension, delusion, and 'fear and fascination' in the realm of sexual love.

Despite the satiric thrust and the cool humour with which the deceitful villain Swamiji is dispatched, this novel among others of Ruth Jhabvala's tends to validate the perverse attraction he engenders. Its subtext is an investigation of that edge of self-awareness which the (female) lover walks, revelling in her attraction to 'dark' forces and pushing away consciousness of its implications. Acknowledging the attractiveness of evil brings it that much closer. Not the demon-lover, but ourselves now engender 'fear and fascination'. To that awful pause Lee is brought at the end of *A New Dominion*, whose plot resolves on the note that is, as I have mentioned, a trademark of Jhabvala's novels: we leave the female protagonist on the brink of a momentous decision, one which will determine her future. Her 'heart' goads her to surrender, while her 'head' knows better.

In this case, Lee considers what to do next: should she travel? Return to England? Return to the ashram? That she has the liberty and the privilege of creating her own life in this way is a luxury unprecedented in history. However, this freedom brings an existential burden to bear on her actions. This burden is closely linked to, in fact is repeated by, her emotional conflict, which turns on the burden of consciousness. She is conscious enough to see Swamiji's appeal for what it is: but now she must choose not to be swept off her feet by it. She does not *want* to so choose. Whatever she does, even should she decide not to return to the ashram, she wants to go back: that wish is bad enough. The repulsive Swami is thus desirable enough to tempt her to sacrifice her very life – for Margaret's illness might well attack her too. And even should she remain 'healthy', Evie's robotised obedience is another kind of suicide.

She cannot choose to return to the ashram: she is repelled by the idea of returning to her meaningless job in London; she no longer wishes to travel aimlessly. Faced with three untenable possibilities, she momentarily retreats to daydream a return to Swami. And there the novel leaves her. That is her condition.

Raymond's Indian experience in many ways parallels Lee's. Like Lee, he loses to a rival – Asha. Like Lee, he nourishes his obsessive love with the poison of rejection. Gopi cares as little for him as Swamiji cares for Lee. Like Lee's, his is a love that dares not speak its name and grows in secret, in marked contrast to Asha's careless, earnest frankness, or even Evie's self-avowed devotion.

But, although Raymond is homosexual, at least he is male, and as I have noted, his maleness confers on him dignity, value and weight – in the eyes of other characters and even, perhaps, in the eyes of his creator. Like Banubai, who jokes about her preferences ('You're not a pretty little son, like he is', she jokes to Asha, p. 125), Ruth Jhabvala favours males. Raymond abandons his dream of love to return to a key position in his uncle's publishing firm – while Lee is awaited only by another meaningless job in London.

Raymond's mother, his faithful correspondent, also anxiously awaits his return. But Lee is strangely without family or friends. These inequities are repeated by Ruth Jhabvala's own attitude toward the two characters: Raymond is given weight and serious-ness, while Lee is held at arm's length and treated by turns sympathetically and with satiric distance: 'Of course she *was* intense, but that wasn't all, she liked to think' (p. 23).

In her next novel, *Heat and Dust*, Ruth Jhabvala will create a female protagonist with the same weight that Raymond is given here. Interestingly, she is several times compared to a eunuch, and set as foil against a more conventional 'romantic' heroine. Moreover, she will be oddly silent whenever the text moves into matters of love or sexuality, despite her sexual freedom – she sleeps with two men during the course of her narrative. Finally, she will never be given a name, an omission that suggests a certain lack of integration.

For any serious woman writer of fiction, femaleness contains profound dilemmas and contradictions, paradoxes that are continu-ally being worked out in the sphere of the fiction itself, as in these novels and stories by Ruth Jhabvala. In each successive setting, the vision is both broadened and refined. What more can one ask of a storyteller?

Part Three
The Demon-Lover

5

'The Housewife'

In the 'ashram' fiction just discussed, the guru was the willing repository for fantasies of the divinely powerful, all-knowing, demon-lover. But the demon-lover comes in many forms. In the next novel, *Heat and Dust*, and in the stories that lead up to it, one meets him in less unusual guises – though he must, by definition, be somehow extraordinary. In 'The Housewife' (in *An Experience of India*) art is the demon-lover's powerful lure.

Shakuntala, the housewife, is another bored wife, vulnerable to the temptations of another false escape route. As if to underline the incongruity between her role and her subjectively experienced self, she – this passionate musician – is a not only a housewife but a grandmother, married for twenty-five years to a good provider. Quite like Sofia's husband in 'Desecration', Shakuntala's 'wasn't interested in her secret thoughts'.

If the title of the story assigns her one role, though, her name alerts the reader to recall another, that of the eponymous heroine of the renowned Sanskrit drama, *Shakuntala*, by Kalidasa. Before looking at Kalidasa's Shakuntala, however, let us stay for a while with Jhabvala's.

Shakuntala lives two lives: an outer one, comfortable and dull, and an inner, *real* one, in which she is a devotee of art. Initially, her marriage suits her well enough: she feels it her 'mission in life' to see that her husband is 'always entirely comfortable', 'But when she fell asleep herself, she slept badly and was disturbed by garbled dreams.' The husband's aunt Phuphiji is something of a surrogate mother-in-law, exacting from Shakuntala the most she can of female respectability and duty to the husband's family. For her, singing in public is disreputable, and singing lessons themselves, while permissible, are suspect, especially if taken seriously. She 'hinted that it wasn't seemly for a housewife, a matron like Shakuntala, to take singing lessons'. She turns out to be right. Music, like any art, and like any avenue to transcendence, is inappropriate for bourgeois matrons. Shakuntala is dimly, unwillingly, aware of the uncomfortable fact that her act means more to her than anything – even her family. With music 'she lived in a region where she felt most truly, most deeply herself. No, not herself, something more and higher than that. By contrast with her singing, the rest of her day, indeed of her life, seemed insignificant. She felt this to be wrong but there was no point in trying to struggle against it.' For the woman artist, the practice of art is something to be fitted with difficulty into the life that she is expected to lead. Its priorities clash with those of her conventional life. Its demands test her loyalties by competing with her real concerns for the well-being of her family.

There is a further difficulty. Shakuntala's music is not purely abstract but identified with her singing teacher. So the fascinations of art are complicated by the fascinations of love. Like Swamiji in *A New Dominion*, the singing teacher is an unusual object of desire. Wiry, aged and wizened, he also looks forward to Marietta's Indian love Ahmed, in *In Search of Love and Beauty*. His physical presence underlines the idea that Ruth Jhabvala's romantic women are not impressed by youth and good looks. What is striking about the singing teacher is his competence and his artistic mastery. With these qualities come his arrogance – in his case, perhaps, merely the pride of achievement.

Never named, almost mythic, he embodies threat to domestic order. He has the indifferent confidence of 'one who has no particular destination'. Like Indian classical music itself, which, though requiring the greatest technical mastery, is improvisational, he eschews a fixed routine. He fails to show up for lessons, as the spirit moves him. Yet he commands special respect. If he misses his morning appointment and arrives in the afternoon, he is waited upon with fried delicacies for which he shows no appreciation. He is contemptuous. He treats Shakuntala and Phuphiji shortly; he usually wears 'an expression of distaste'. He lives 'in great disorder' and is supported by his wife, 'a bedraggled, cross woman' whom Shakuntala glimpses at work sewing – very much as Sofia in 'Desecration' in turn calls on *her* lover and finds *his* bedraggled wife.

Yet when he does speak, his monologues fascinate: he provides, both for Shakuntala and for the reader, a glimpse into a way of life devoted to art and pleasure. Its meaningful values contrast with the empty materialism of Shakuntala's domestic life. Her initial pride in her 'blue rexine-covered sofa-set' will give way eventually to a sense that 'it [her jewellery] was just things, metal'.

The intensely social cameraderie of his way of life only underlines Shakuntala's isolation 'alone in the silent bedroom beside her sleeping husband'.

Describing his years of study with his own teacher, a 'very great and famous and temperamental musician', her teacher recalls the old house in Benaras where all the disciples had lived with their guru: each was expected to rise before dawn and spend the day practising technique. Yet 'their way of life was entirely without constraint': they ate, slept, loved and formed friendships, chewed opium when and as they liked; they travelled with their guru when he was invited to perform, and 'they were equally happy wherever it was'.

Shakuntala longs for such a life. Unable to attend concerts without a chaperone, and unable to find one who will go with her, she can only imagine from her bed, 'beside her husband who had been asleep these many hours', the shared joys that her teacher knows:

> She wondered what raga was being sung now – Raga Yaman, serene and sublime, Raga Kalawati, full of sweet yearning? – and saw the brightly lit stage on which the musicians sat . . . all of them caught up in a mood of exaltation inspired by the music. Their heads slowly swayed, they exhanged looks and smiles, their hearts were open and sweet sensations flowed in them like honey.

When the teacher finds Shakuntala's singing worthy of an audience, she is 'triumphant with joy'; she longs to 'give another dimension to her singing by performing before strangers'.

> But she also knew it was not to be thought of. She was a housewife from a fine respectable middle-class family – people like her didn't sing in public. It would be an outrage, to her husband, to Phuphiji, to [her daughter] Manju's husband and Manju's in-laws. Even little Baba would be shocked, he wouldn't know what to think if he saw his granny singing before a lot of strangers.

The tension between Shakuntala's two lives – housewife and singer – grows untenable. She gives away a valuable pair of earrings that her husband gives her. She disdains 'all the shiny furniture'. At the same time, her art and her teacher become confusingly intermixed.

For his part, he grows increasingly impatient with her, perhaps for her refusal to sing in public, and her adherence to convention. 'He said what did she expect, that he came here to waste his time on training *housewives*?' Yet he demands more of 'her husband's money', the fruits of that adherence. Increasingly he fails to appear for the lesson, even walking out before she has finished singing. She suffers. 'She breathed heavily as if in pain, and indeed her sense of unfulfilment was like pain and stayed with her for the rest of the day.' Phuphiji enlists Shakuntala's daughter Manju as a domestic spy. The gifts to the teacher are noticed. Scandalised, 'they both looked up at her as if she were someone remote from and dangerous to them. Shakuntala hardly noticed them' (p. 156).

Now Shakuntala 'did not hesitate any longer'. The next time her teacher fails to show up, she goes to his house; finding it padlocked, she seeks him out in a disreputable neighbourhood. She is insulted by men lounging in the street full of prostitutes: again she fails to notice. She finally locates her teacher in a shabby restaurant.

When Shakuntala stepped up to the table, the other men sitting with him were astonished; their jaws stopped chewing betel and dropped open. Only he went on swaying and drumming to the tune in his mind. He let her stand there for a while, then he said to the others 'She's my pupil. I teach her singing.' He added 'She's a housewife,' and sniggered.

But she follows him to his rooms, where he

wasted no time but at once came close to her and fumbled at her clothes and at his own. He was about the same age as her husband but lean, hard, and eager; as he came on top of her, she saw his drugged eyes so full of bliss and he was still smiling at the tune he was playing to himself.

Intimacy brings Shakuntala to a state of telepathic awareness, which underlines the identity, for her, of her teacher and his art. She is able to enter into him as he enters her.

And this tune continued to play in her too. He entered her at the moment when, the structure of the raga having been expounded, the combination of notes was being played up and down, backwards and forwards, very fast. There was no going back from here, she knew. But who would want to go back, who would exchange this blessed state for any other?

This question, which is the final line of the story, presents a number of disturbing ambiguities. But before any further commentary, let us turn to Kalidasa's *Shakuntala*, and ask whether her story sheds any light on this one.

The full title, in translation, is 'Shakuntala Won by the Sign of Recognition'. The play is not just any play: it is generally held to be the masterpiece of Indian drama, as Kalidasa is considered the greatest poet and playwright of Sanskrit literature, the Shakespeare of India. (Though even less is known about Kalidasa, who is thought to have been active somewhere between the second century BC and the fourth century AD.)[1] Like *King Lear*, then, or *The Odyssey*, Kalidasa's *Shakuntula* is a literary touchstone.

As always with Ruth Jhabvala's allusions, investigation is rewarded. The story, drawn from the ancient Sanskrit epic, 'The Marhabharata', and based in turn on even more ancient legend, goes as follows: the god-King Dushyanta, straying into the forest on a hunting expedition, meets and falls in love with Shakuntala, the foster daughter of the hermitage guru, actually the daughter of a sage and a divine nymph. Shakuntala and the King are married in secret, but the King returns to his capital, leaving his ring as a token and promising to send for his bride. Deep in a dream of happiness, Shakuntala is visited by a notoriously irascible old ascetic, and neglects to receive him with due courtesy. He casts a curse on her: the King will forget her. As luck would have it, she loses the ring that alone would jog his memory. When she presents herself at his court, he does not know her. After much lamentation, the play ends in harmony as the ring is found by a fisherman, and the little boy who is the product of their union eventually succeeds in bringing about a recognition.[2]

It is clear, I think, that Ruth Jhabvala's story alludes to Kalidasa's. Though hers stands well on its own, it is enriched by a parallel reading. The elements of the modern story acquire new depth, and the tale becomes almost allegorical. Thus the modern Shakuntala, inwardly devoted to art and beauty, serves a 'departed king'. But the realm of art is effectively closed to her, for as a woman and a lady, she is barred from the public practice of her art: the 'King' has 'forgotten her'. In such a reading, the gender codes of patriarchy and respectability become the 'curse'. The 'ring' of connectedness between artist and divinity is lost. The 'foster daughter' of divine birth is kept from her rightful place as artist and musician who might one day equal her teacher in stature. If it is 'her husband's money' that pays for Shakuntala's singing lessons, how can she disregard these stultifying codes? She is, as the title reminds us, a housewife.

The earrings that the modern Shakuntala gives away, though functioning differently, serve as a textual echo of Kalidasa's lost ring. They may even suggest the modern Shakuntala's dilemma: in spurning *her husband's* regard she may be in error, may have jumped, as they say, out of the frying pan and into the fire. Poor Shakuntala is damned if she does and damned if she doesn't.

The singing teacher is a witty conflation of King Dushyanta and the irascible old ascetic. Presenting herself at his table in the sleazy modern café, the modern Shakuntala echoes the ancient Shakuntala's appearance at the King's throne – a crucial scene of non-recognition. The modern Shakuntala's singing teacher represents, in my reading, two opposing figures: the King who 'recognises' her – he deems her art worthy of public performance – and the maleficent old man who 'curses' her: 'That's the only thing old women are good for, burning.' This offhand insult, intended for Phuphiji, actually applies to her too, or at least it soon will. It is not mere hyperbole, for widow-burning is still venerated in traditional Hindu society. But Shakuntala accepts the 'joke': her 'mouth corners twitched with amusement'.

It is worth noting that the myth of Shakuntala warns that if a woman neglects a minor act of courtesy to a male superior, the oversight can have tragic consequences. In Ruth Jhabvala's story, women hasten to fulfil the obligations of courtesy – but still things go awry.

The gifted, arrogant singing teacher is the embodiment of ambiguity. How is one to read his contempt: is it merely a reflection of the customary distance between master and disciple? In describing his own training, the teacher has stressed the disciples' obedience and servitude to their guru: for example, he himself paid for the sin of forgetting to light his guru's hookah by sleeping three nights on the doorstep and being fed on scraps!

The fact that Shakuntala is female, however, is paramount. In this light, one wonders whether her choice could have any validity, in reality: that is, what would be Shakuntala's options now, after leaving her husband? 'Who would exchange this blessed state for any other?' An Indian audience might have a clearer idea. It is difficult for the Western reader to judge the viability or the folly of Shakuntala's action – though one would guess that it looks bad.

Has the author begged the question with this ambiguity? The entire validity of Shakuntala's act rests on the success or failure of her attempt to live a life of greater authenticity. The other 'demon-lover' stores are clearer in their outcome. In *A New Dominion*, Margaret pays with her life, and Evie with her humanity, for following Swamiji; in 'Desecration', Sofia will kill herself; in 'Passion', Betsy has made a big mistake by giving up her job and her social position to be with Har Gopal (*he* certainly thinks she has); Olivia's withdrawal to the mountains, at the end of *Heat and Dust*, is solitary and essentially tragic. But there is the chance that Shakuntala has made a right decision, and that the reader is intended to approve of her flight and its object.

By identifying the supremacy of artistic creation and the supremacy of a (male) individual, Ruth Jhabvala has made it difficult to endorse or condemn Shakuntala's act. Yet this very ambiguity repeats a central difficulty even for Western women, so much freer in their options than Shakuntala. It happens that art and maleness *are* connected. Most recognised and practising artists *are* men. For the woman who wishes to make art a central focus of her life, that fact is bound to make for a number of obstacles.

Certainly it has in the well-documented lives of women artists in the modern West: one thinks of the many difficult relationships of men and women artists, in which the man achieved recognition and the woman did not. Or, in which the pair both put the man's career above the woman's. As teacher, mentor *and* lover, he must embody a power that is overwhelming and eventually destructive.

The scenario of male artist and female aspirant, the latter admitted to the circle of artists only because of her (sexual) relationship with the former, is a familiar one. Shakuntala and her teacher shed light on a very Western phenomenon. The tale is a commentary then, not only on the dangerous allure of the demon-lover as a convenient escape from an untenable though ostensibly happy marriage, but on the many obstacles that beset a woman artist. These obstacles emanate first from a society in which, as in the nineteenth century in the West, respectable women were not performing artists. But even when that is not the case, as today in the West, the subculture of artists themselves is often open to women only on certain (sexual) conditions. Shakuntala's dilemma speaks to all women who (like Ruth Jhabvala herself) wish to combine the creative impulse with a life lived in the world of men, children, and family.

6

'Desecration'

Oh, if thou didst but know what it is like to live in hell the
way I do!
('Desecration')

The last two stories in Jhabvala's 1976 collection, *How I Became a Holy Mother*, foreshadow the next novel, *Heat and Dust*, in which the demon-lover theme is treated again. *Heat and Dust* consists of two chronological settings of the same story, two treatments which stress, respectively, the tragic and the comic aspects of eros. As my discussion will make clearer, the 'old' story emphasises the tragic, the 'new' the comic. And as if to prepare for this double vision, the last two stories in the collection immediately preceding the novel deal, respectively, with the same issues. Thus 'How I Became a Holy Mother', foreshadows *Heat and Dust*'s 'new story' – the absurd comedy of erotic connections. The heroine emerges triumphant, as the title indicates. 'Desecration' foreshadows the 'old' story in the later novel, the tragic illicit affair of a married woman.

In 'How I Became a Holy Mother', Katie is the breezy, cheerful narrator, a model, who goes to India to see the world and ends up in an ashram, enshrined as the 'Mother principle (which is also very important)'. Young and beautiful, she engages the affections of the Master's chosen 'senior swami', a young man named Vishwa. Of course her 'holy Motherhood' is a public relations game, and the story is pitched in a satiric and comic mode: a comment on the Westerner's India of the sixties. Models and descendents of European royalty – such as the Count – were the first, élite, wave of what was to become a flood of middlebrow Western truth-seekers. According to Gita Mehta, 'The first wave of disciples was really top-drawer. They were the nobles of meritocracy and they were looking good. The women were models, the men were stars. . . . There followed the new untouchables, the anciennes royales. Dispossessed monarchs, some related to every regent in Europe, as well as Counts, Dukes and Ladies – nobles all.'[1]

Katie's comic monologue foreshadows the comedy of *Heat and Dust*, particularly the novel's contemporary sections. Katie herself resembles the narrator of *Heat and Dust*, with her breezy, anti-romantic air. On the other hand, 'Desecration' is a compressed version of the tragic or dark portions of the novel, that is, Olivia's tale. There are clear stylistic similarities in the narrative: for example, the first sentence of 'Desecration' contains the story's dénouement – in a subordinate clause. We shall see that this is also the case in *Heat and Dust*. 'It is more than ten years since Sofia committed suicide in the hotel room at Mohabbatpur.' (Mohabbatpur is an invented place name meaning, in Hindi, 'the place of love'.)

It is notable that the suicide is not referred to again, just as the first sentence in *Heat and Dust* will supply information which is not referred to again, and which will round out the story. The whole tale is flashback. A mystery is being investigated, and we will see how love led to self-annihilation for Sofia. Her name – the Greek personification of wisdom – suggests an allegorical dimension, and directs the reader to consider a whole set of meanings: of wisdom; of its opposite, what used to be called 'folly', or madness, of which suicide is the ultimate expression; of the transformation of wisdom into madness, of love as the transforming element.

The scandal is all but forgotten, and the past takes on a sinister mysteriousness by being compared to a benign or anti-romantic present: 'The present Superintendent of Police is a mild-mannered man who likes to spend his evenings at home playing card games with his teenage daughters.' *Heat and Dust* also investigates an obscure scandal of the past, also is told in flashback and also more fully contrasts two modalities: the tragic/romantic past and the comic/anti-romantic present. Again, as in *Heat and Dust*, past and present are linked by buildings that remain. The seedy hotel in which Sofia died has been torn down 'to make way for a new cinema' which will 'back on to the old cinema, which is still there, still playing ancient Bombay talkies'.

The architectural motif appears often in Ruth Jhabvala's work, and the Western reader learns from her work that it is a conventional image in popular Indian poetry. In fact, throughout her Indian tales, characters from all walks of life are fond of quoting, at appropriate moments, lines of poetry which lament a vanished past, and draw on the Indian equivalent of the European Romantics' love of ruins. For example, in 'Picnic with Moonlight and Mangoes' from the same collection of tales, a character comments on

> the passing away of all earthly things, the death of kings and pariah dogs alike. He waved his hand toward the abandoned pleasure palace, he said, 'Where are they all, where have they gone?' . . . These reflections were perfectly acceptable – probably at this very moment Sri Prakash's friends were making the same ones at their picnic in Moti Bagh.

That 'Desecration' takes place in a recent, yet almost-forgotten past is in itself a literary *Vanitas*, a reminder of the evanescence and illusoriness of experience. This world of people and things to which we give such importance is soon forgotten: it is merely one of the snares of Maya, Goddess of Illusion. But within our illusory matrices of time and place, we live enmeshed in further illusion: the tangled web of erotic fantasy. This story details the workings of that particular trap.

The 'ancient Bombay talkies', whose distorted sound-tracks serve as background to the lovers' trysts, are both models and context for their distorted affair. Occasionally the sound-track actually breaks through to their consciousness, and is reported by the narrator. Rather in the manner of a Greek chorus, it provides ironic clarification of and commentary on the events of the story itself. For both the old and the new cinema exist solely to provide for collective celebration of illusion and erotic fantasy. Like Hollywood, Bombay turns out a stock of dreams ready-made for the consumer: dreams of comfort, to soothe, to make bearable a wretched present. (Jhabvala refers repeatedly to the power and importance of the cinema in her Indian characters' lives: see, for example, the story 'Like Birds, Like Fishes', a poignant tale of two young dreamers.) That the lovers meet literally in the shadow of the cinema illustrates with witty precision the relationship between experience and myth.

The tale is almost a fable; it springs from traditions deep in the European past. Wronged husband, bored wife, caddish seducer: we know them all. They are archetypes, references particularly to the art of nineteenth-century Europe: novel, drama, even opera and melodrama form the backdrop for this tale. Sofia resembles Anna Karenina, Emma Bovary, Madame Butterfly, and a host of other suffering heroines of European vintage who are seduced and abandoned.

For all its traditional lineage, however, the tale is of today. Its territory – the gap between innocence and experience, between the ideal and the profane, between 'femine wisdom' and 'masculine knowledge' – is better charted with the insights of feminism. As its title suggests, it describes a process of 'de-sacralisation', by revealing the multilayered misunderstandings behind the arche-typal images of romantic seduction.

The plot is simply told: Sofia is a young, educated Muslim, married to the Raja Sahib, an aristocratic Hindu landowner and amateur playwright more than thirty years her senior. She has an affair with the village Superintendent of Police, the 'S.P.' As he becomes indifferent, her ardour increases; she pursues him, she casts caution to the winds, becomes the subject of public mockery; finally she commits suicide.

Sofia's obsessional attraction to a worthless and brutal character is the puzzle of this disturbing story. The same puzzle is at the core of the novel – *Heat and Dust* – that it prepares for, and again, of Jhabvala's tenth novel, *Three Continents*. The S.P. is recast in *Heat and Dust* as the Nawab, another man known by his title rather than his name. (Both are products of male 'culture' rather than female 'nature' – to use Susan Griffin's terms.) The S.P. is to Sofia and the Raja Sahib as the Nawab is to Olivia and Douglas: their social inferior, though possessing greater local power than they. In both cases, the wife's affair is an inarticulate, half-understood and doomed protest against the terms of bourgeois marriage, in which she is essentially an ornament.

The S.P. is much cruder than the Nawab, though: he is an 'entirely self-made man' whose brutality is close to the surface indeed. He is 'known as a ruthless disciplinarian. But he had a softer side to him. He was terribly fond of woman and, wherever he was posted, would find himself a mistress very quickly – usually more than one'. Nothing succeeds like success, and the Superintendent's reputation as a womaniser is itself a part of his attractiveness. At a dinner party that she and her husband host, Sofia's first interest is aroused by actually seeing, almost voyeuristically, the developing relationship between the S.P. and a prostitute-singer.

Like the novel that follows it and like 'The Housewife', just discussed, this story probes both a marriage and the adulterous affair that destroys it. In all three cases the husband is ambivalently characterised. Like Douglas, the Raja Sahib is all solicitousness and indulgence to his young and 'highly strung' wife. The condescension of this posture changes in the course of the story to an anguished, and completely sympathetic, stoicism when he learns of her affair: if his lordly complacency is irritating, his solitary suffering is tragic. Like his wife, he cannot reveal its source.

At the end of the story, Sofia, with a guilty pang, comes upon the outcry in the latest of his romantic verse-dramas: 'Oh if thou didst but know what it is like to live in hell the way I do!' Her own hell of unrequited love is too overwhelming for her to respond: in her desperation, she lacks the ability to attend to his suffering: 'If thou didst but know!' By the end of the story, she does know, for she herself is suffering from the same malady. But the essence of that malady is alienation from all but the infinitely attractive love object: others are irrelevant. While she may now *know*, her obsessive attraction to the S.P. blocks everything else out, and the knowledge becomes meaningless. The married pair remain in this absurd alienation from each other until she opts out of it by suicide.

KNOWING AND BEING KNOWN

To transcend individuality, to attain revelation and to be revealed, to know and to be known, is to abandon the illusion of separate individuality – Maya. One might say that such revelatory, transcendent knowing approaches what we think of as wisdom – 'Sofia'. Clearly, knowledge and wisdom are related. Perhaps it is the difference between them that constitutes the territory of this story. Sofia, who functions for her husband as an icon of wisdom, supremely 'feminine', mysterious and enigmatic, during the course of this story takes matters into her own hands, and crosses over into the realm of *knowledge*, off-limits to women. The text plays repeatedly with the idea of 'knowing', as I hope to show. Not only is Sofia's story a meditation on the hell of separateness, the difficulty of either knowing or being known by the desired Other, but it also recounts a woman's discovery of the *social* realities that deny her the power to know, rather than merely to 'be known', in the sexual sense.

In our quest to actualise the yearning to know and be known, a state which, in its deepest sense, confers and implies divinity, we most readily take the path of eros, Jhabvala's fiction says. And eros implies the irrational, that which contradicts our felt and reasoned values. For Ruth Jhabvala's lovers, eros is thralldom – always deeply disquieting, since they, like Sofia, are intelligent, independent of mind, refined and sensitive. Often she knows, uncomfortably, that he is rather a brute, an exemplar of what gay male slang calls 'rough trade'.

Love is dangerous, love is exciting. Like God's, the beloved's attitude tends to range from indifference to direct hostility. The romantic leads into the Gothic, which leads in turn to the pornographic. With its archetypal plot, this tale alludes to a spectrum of fictional genres portraying love. Set in the 'exotic' Orient, containing a ruined fortress and a mysterious heroine of uncertain nationality, it seems almost to parody what is thought of as 'romantic'. Like the current heroines of Harlequin romances, Sofia is entirely dependent on her much older husband. Virtuous and delicate, convent-educated and full of 'tender pity', she is ineluctably drawn to the brutal S.P., and the Sadean overtones of the tale become unavoidable.

There is even an aspect of Sofia's passion that might be termed 'fetishistic': policemen's uniforms are, after all, favoured garb among the (mostly male homosexual) 'erotic minorities' seen in the streets of New York, Paris, London and other capitals in the eighties. In the context of Jhabvala's later fiction, that set in the West, which includes so many male homosexual characters (sympathetically presented), and which indicates close observation of the contemporary male homosexual milieu, that policeman and his uniform must reverberate with allusions.

In her germinal essay on pornography already referred to, Susan Sontag writes that the essential quality of the pornographic heroine is that she never learns.[2] Instead, she persists infinitely in her provoking and provocative innocence, clearly an invitation to be violated. Jhabvala's story is literature, and Sofia does learn: in fact, her movements toward knowing – not just being known – mark the progress of her tragedy. On a certain realistic level, it is dangerous, even somehow inappropriate, for women to know, when men define knowledge. In taking for herself the freedom to choose an unsuitable but sexually compelling lover, and in actively seeking to know a sexual dimension that excludes 'ladies', Sofia ventures beyond the pale. And she learns, not only about herself, but about herself as a woman in her society.

Romances, those best-sellers which have been aptly called 'pornography for women', also contain heroines who never learn.[3] Here, I would argue, ignorance does not stop at the heroine, but is offered to the reader as well, who must accept the inexplicable transformation that occurs at the conclusion of the romance: the quasi-satanic figure cast in the male lead is conveniently sanitised. His dark, brooding, snarling, 'undersocialised' maleness was only a silly illusion.[4] Really, he is and always was, despite appearances to the contrary, kind and gentle and good. Does not this invitation to ignorance confirm the notion of romance best-seller as another kind of pornography – 'pornography for women', another face of the pornographic imagination, where women never learn, and are victimised for their ignorance/innocence? Innocence is a product of the cultural separation, even opposition, of head and heart: as 'heart', women should remain ignorant. In popular romance, that ignorance is offered to heroine and (female) reader alike.

'Desecration' is a response to both 'hard-' (i.e. male) and 'soft-' (i.e. female) core pornography, in that its subject is a woman's passage from innocence to experience, from romance to pornography. Sofia rejects her symbolic role as icon of wisdom, and ventures to pursue knowledge of the world and of sexuality. Not content to stand on her pedestal, she descends to seek to be known, and to know. However, she is not known – she is only misconstrued again, now as whore, not angel. And what she comes to know causes her to take her own life.

The danger inherent in sexual knowledge, for women, is an ancient and archetypal theme. Persephone consigns the earth to a cycle of darkness and light by her wish to know. In the biblical myth, Eve's foolish desire for knowledge leads to a fall greater still, and all are thereby condemned to suffer for all eternity. Pandora, Lilith, the Sirens: all repeat the association of woman with forbidden and dangerous sexual knowledge, and all bear as a corollary the imprecation against *good* women's seeking that knowledge.

Jhabvala's 'Desecration', this small tale set in an Indian village, reverberates with associations reaching into the roots of literature itself. One of the great themes of all literary narrative is the uneasy intercourse between what is seen and what is unseen: the dark, inchoate dreamworld that we attempt to hide – from ourselves, and from others – is always threatening to impinge. *The lady is always in danger of becoming the whore.* The human condition, the narrative art tells us, is both to want and not to want to succumb to the temptation proffered by the subversive and erotic world of unconscious desire. A rich and eloquent tradition of ballad, folk-tale and fable prefigure modern literary treatments of the great Gothic theme of the demon-lover. 'Desecration' looks back to these traditions. It even refers to pre-literary ballad and folk-tale, with its use of the repeated 'refrain': 'Sofia, Sofia, what are you thinking?'

Sofia's pursuit of sexual knowledge leads to madness and suicide: an archetypal progression. The story, told from the wife's point of view, is an explication rather than a proscription. Sofia's self-destructive fugue becomes, if not the only possible course of action, at least one which follows from the circumstances of her life. Her flight from boredom is a violation of the social code: as wife of the most highborn aristocrat in the village, Sofia is particularly under scrutiny, in a place (the Hindu village) where women's freedom of movement is already severely restricted. Her tragedy unfolds on two fronts: on a personal level, she is degraded – 'desecrated' by her lover. In relation to the village, she is 'ruined' and cast out. Having crossed over into ground that is taboo to women – the active pursuit of sexual experience – she is no longer entitled to full humanity. She becomes virtually a whore. Her suicide is a conventional response to the 'shame' of her fall.

Even more irrevocably than the marginal women wanderers and tourists of Jhabvala's cross-cultural stories and novels, Sofia becomes in the course of this story a marginal, sacrificeable individual – a whore. The S.P. treats her as one and gradually she comes to be seen as one by the villagers. As I have mentioned, a prostitute sparks the first encounter between Sofia and the S.P., at the Raja Sahib's dinner party. After the party, Sofia falls into one of her moods: dreaming of some different and distant landscape, aimlessly wandering about and 'idly kicking' at pieces of stone. And now appears the first balladic refrain, her husband's question, 'What are you thinking?' If the story is a compressed meditation on the tragic impossibility of *knowing* or *being known* – when that is the human spiritual imperative – this unanswered refrain is paradigmatic.

Sofia cannot tell what she is thinking for a number of reasons. Clearly, one does not confide in a partner one is about to betray; but even if she were not contemplating an affair, the distance between her and her adoring husband is too great. For him she is the innocent child-bride. For her to admit to an autonomous erotic appetite would shatter his image – in itself 'pornographic' – of her innocence. The Raja Sahib only half-heartedly wishes to know what Sofia is thinking. His real need is to preserve for himself her mystery, her unattainability, her distance. Part of her Otherness is her 'convent manner': when she so much as uses the word 'mistress' she shocks her husband.

This emotional distance of his is variously presented as a defect and a quality. At first it seems a diguised condescension; later it is a genuine and 'tender respect that would not reach farther into her than was permissible between two human beings'. Always it is contrasted to the S.P.'s desire to 'expose' her 'mystery' – a menacing intent to which she responds with interest. For the S.P. seems, at first, authentically to wish to know women and to feel with them. Sofia sees that he is moved to tears at the prostitute's singing.

It might then appear that there is real parity in the S.P.'s relationship with the singer-prostitute. On a personal level there may be. But there cannot be that parity on a sociopolitical level, for she is disreputable while he is not. She is so disreputable, in fact, that Sofia's presence in the same room with her is unusual: 'The ladies had been sent home in motorcars. It would not have been fitting for them to be present, because the musicians were not from a respectable class. Only Sofia was emancipated enough to overlook this restriction.' The restriction applies not only to class, of course: ladies do not know about, let alone associate with, prostitutes.

In his study *Violence and the Sacred*, René Girard suggests that both aboriginal and 'civilised' societies maintain themselves psychically by deflecting violence on to surrogate victims, who are then sacrificed, whether by traditional rites or judicial systems. The process, he says, 'constitutes the major means, perhaps the sole means, by which men expel from their consciousness the truth about their own mimetic relationships: the crimes attributed to the surrogate victim are the hidden desires of all men, the secret source of human conduct'.[5] The prostitue is 'marginal' and sacrificeable, but her male client is not. This well-established social dynamic, common to East and West, is an illustration of the functioning of taboo and sacrifice in Girard's analysis. Though he does not emphasise gender, his thesis works in the context of feminism:

thus *women* are cast in the role of sacrificial victims to men: *women* act out 'the hidden desires of all men, the secret source of human conduct'. *Women feel*. The truth about their own mimetic relationships, the hidden desires of all men, the secret source of human conduct – what might these be? One set of answers might be the particular skills generally allocated to women: feeling, expressiveness, nurturance – and the vulnerability that goes along with these.

The crucial and useful distinction between lady and whore blurs the dynamic of this sacrificial victimisation and allows it to continue, since 'ladies' are given a spurious and superficial exemption from their profane womanhood, that is, their biology and their feeling. What then is the function of the lady? Sofia in this story illustrates it: she exists *to not know* about the whore. At the other end of the spectrum, the whore exists to be wholly sexualised and then declared non-human. The lady, as an upholder of the social order, must never see the whore: must not see what is being made of femaleness.

Just this is expected of women, even today, even in the West: passing by the adult bookshop, we are expected not to see the clear evidence of the violation and sexualisation of ourselves. The lady's role is to remain in ignorance, or failing that to pretend ignorance, of the sexual victimisation of women. When, twice in the course of this story, Sofia puts her hands over her ears, she images the lady's role. But she also oversteps its limits with her opposing wish to know.

She begins her descent with participation in an activity generally taboo to ladies – listening to the musicians – and ends it with the sacrifice of herself. Similarly in *Heat and Dust*, Olivia witnesses a taboo entertainment – eunuchs dancing – and after this fateful witnessing falls prey to the Nawab.

The repeated use of this mytho-symbolic motif is noteworthy. To look upon taboo objects is to become sacrificeable oneself. One thinks of aboriginal societies in which certain taboo objects are never revealed to women, whose viewing of them would subject all to danger. One thinks of the strange Gothic ballad of Christina Rossetti, 'Goblin Market', in which Laura proceeds from first *looking* at the goblins, to tasting and finally becoming addicted to their poisonous fruits. There are things that ladies must *never* see.

Wearing psychic or even literal blinders, the lady risks a fall at every step. There is so much to be protected from! Even her clothes, at various times in history, have literalised this idea. The cherished daughter/wife must be kept from knowledge of the world; to be safe, she must be isolated. 'Inside their big house, the Raja Sahib and Sofia had led very isolated lives. This was by choice – his choice.' Imprisoned not in the usual tower but on a plain, symbolic of the flatness of the marriage, Sofia quite naturally seeks any avenue of escape. 'Restless' after her first encounter with the S.P., she wanders around the parched garden, aptly symbolic of her condition, and shelters in a 'little ruined fort' near the big house. 'It was very dark inside there, with narrow underground passages and winding steep stairs, some of which were broken. Sometimes a bat would flit out from some crevice.' In this rich image are melded together multiple and interlocking layers of significance. Proceeding inward, so to speak, from the literal plane, one remarks first that a fort, normally a place of defence or advantage in battle, now no longer offers either: Sofia is vulnerable even from within her husband's protection, which is based on a past rapacity. The sociohistorical background emerges that the village landowner's estate, seized 'during a time of great civil strife some hundred and fifty years before' is founded on greed and pretence. The family had 'built themselves a little fort and had even assumed a royal title'. Draining the improverished villagers through the imposition of high taxes, they had squandered the funds on the big house, only to live elsewhere, Bombay, Calcutta and London. The Raja Sahib is the pampered son of a line of privilege, one who plays at being a peasant as his ancestors played at being nobles.

The role to which he has consigned his wife – 'he had carried her away to this spot with the express purpose of having her to himself, of feasting on his possession of her' – impels her escape to something more authentic. Conveniently, the S.P. will soon appear on the roof of this little abandoned fort offering an avenue of erotic escape, and symbolising his dominion over her damaged marriage.

Apart from the social context, the image of the fort functions to evoke Sofia's psychic and spiritual condition. The hidden and secret passages within it allude symbolically to her solitary inner life: 'very dark', even mutilated and difficult of access: 'winding steep stairs, some of which were broken'. The narrow crevices evoke female sexuality, and the bats that are liable to flit out from within, the frightening and unpredictable aspects of desire itself.

On the most profound level this image may be read as an emblem of the predicament of women in the society of patriarchy, that is, in a society that isolates and separates them from an autonomous self, from other women, from meaning, wholeness and centrality. On this level, the fable becomes an explication of the psychology of the alienated woman. As the quintessential alienated woman, Sofia is herself, like the little ruined fort, only a symbol among her husband's possessions. From deep within the 'narrow stone passages' that image her system of defences and the deadened sexuality within it, she – woman as victim – moves upward, as it were, from the underground passageways to the cruel light of the social world, from the inner world to the outer, from the inarticulate visceral to the speaking world of mentation: the voices of sado-masochistic and violent fantasy that will penetrate her numbing system of defences are heard on the 'roof', that is, the level of conscious thought. 'Something terrible' seems to be going on. The noises that she hears are those of the S.P. in the act of disciplining one of his underlings. He punches the unresisting man, kicks him when he falls, then hauls him up to beat him some more – at which Sofia cries out. The other policeman runs away sobbing as the S.P. calmly and carefully adjusts his clothing.

That this encounter should lead to Sofia's erotic obsession with the S.P. is deeply disturbing. Yet it matches a scene in *Heat and Dust* leading up to Olivia's rape-like encounter with the Nawab. Olivia will succumb, almost swoon, on hearing the Nawab recount with relish and approval the story of his ancestor's sadism. Horror is associated with sexual arousal. 'There is blood on your hand', Sofia says to the S.P. Then, in answer to his question, she tells him that she visits the fort every day. '"You come here all alone?" he asked. "Aren't you afraid?" "Of what?"' Sofia's remarks are intended, and received, as tacit invitation. Just as ladies do not attend gatherings at which prostitutes are present, they do not venture alone into isolated places – to do either is to confront one's vulnerability. Without answering, the S.P. mounts his horse and 'lightly flicked its flanks, and it cantered off as if joyful to be bearing him' – even the animal seems to repeat the eroticisation of submission.

'Desecration' illustrates the dangers of half-consciousness. Sofia is deeply ambivalent – as well she might be – about 'knowing'. She seeks out forbidden knowledge, but she also 'covers her ears' when told of evil, as we shall see. More than knowing, Sofia wishes to be known. Her fall is the result of that desire – which is actually desire itself.

A feminist critic writes perceptively of *The Story of O* that O's

> great longing is to be known, and in this respect she is like any lover, for the secret of love is to be known as onself. But O's desire to be known is rather like that of the sinner who wants to be known by God. Sir Stephen thrills her, in part, because he knows her, from the moment he meets her, to be bad, wanton, 'easy', reveling in her abasement.[6]

The same may be said of Sofia, who has been obliged to retain her seductive 'mystery', but who would just as soon let it go.

It is inappropriate for Sofia, as a lady, either to know or to be known. (There is so much that is inappropriate!) As a lady, however, she may intercede – unsuccessfully – in the cruel functioning of the socioeconomic machine. At one point a drunken servant in the big house creates a disturbance and shouts obscenities. Here Sofia 'covers her ears' so as to avoid the 'obscene' language that makes explicit connections between violence and sexuality. But when the Raja Sahib has the servant sacked, the man's wife and many children plead at Sofia's feet for his reinstatement. She in turn prostrates herself at her husband's feet, crying '"Forgive! Forgive!"' . . . as if she were begging forgiveness for everyone who was weak and had sinned . . . trying over and over again to bring out the word "forgive" and not succeeding because of her sobs.' Her intercession turns out to be worse than useless: her husband 'was so enraged by the cause of her attack that the servant and his family had to leave immediately'. Thus, *in her name* the servant together with his large family are rendered destitute by the absolute authority of the landowner, who emerges here as a 'stern and unforgiving', 'gaunt and bitter' old man. For all his 'tender respect' and artistic cultivation, the Raja Shabib is guilty of a fundamental failure of humanity.

The configuration to which Jhabvala draws the reader's attention is familiar: in the name of womanhood, war is waged – war in which the enemy's women are booty. The failure of compassion and a humane morality is camouflaged by a sentimental elevation of womanhood. Sofia lies prostrate at the feet of her husband, pleading fruitlessly for compassion, exactly as, later in the story, she will lie prostrate at the S.P.'s feet, playing out the second scenario of desecration. The first scene points the way to the second. Indeed, the narrative only now begins to show us the relationship of Sofia and the S.P., whose coarse power is contrasted with the Raja Sahib's ostensible delicacy and underlying callousness.

The S.P. wishes to 'expose' Sofia's mystery. This wish seems to coincide with her passionate wish to be known. But the reality is that he wishes only to know her in the biblical sense – which, in keeping with the underlying patriarchic biblical assessment of women as inferior – is to violate her.

His impulse to violate her mystery, like the Nawab's in *Heat and Dust*, is grounded in class resentment; the transaction is not so much between him and her as it is between him and her rich husband, or alternatively, between him and her Muslim 'brothers'. The fact that he is a Hindu is, of course, crucial to their affair. It illustrates Lévi-Strauss's formulation that men use women as verbs with which to communicate with each other. The men of a conquering tribe signal victory to the men they have conquered by raping 'their' women. If a Muslim woman is raped by a Hindu man, the act has a political meaning; if a lady is raped by a man of an inferior class, that act does as well. Conveniently, Sofia is both a lady and a Muslim, so that the S.P. may vent his rage on her on two counts.

In a richly ironic exchange, the S.P. reveals his anti-Muslim prejudices and their importance for him in his relations with Sofia. He holds a queasy 'fascination' for Muslim rituals and mores, particularly circumcision, 'the eating of unclean flesh', or 'what Muslims did with virgin girls' – showing a preference for motifs that lend themselves to eroticisation. His barely disguised disgust recalls, I think, the more familiar phenomenon of Western anti-Semitism, the effects of which had such devastating consequences in the author's early life. In the same way, the descriptions of Sofia's outsiderhood, and even some of her physical attributes, match up with those of Ruth Jhabvala herself: 'It was generally thought that she was partly Afghan, perhaps even with a dash of Russian. She certainly did not look entirely Indian.'

Within the same scene comes another, further, confusion, quite typical of popular attitudes and misconceptions, whereby the women of a given group are blamed and even punished for the misdeeds of its men. The S.P. blames Sofia for Muslim atrocities toward Hindu women, all in jest, of course. As she begs him not to go on, as she 'put[s] her hands over her ears, pleading with him', he recounts the horrible details in full. 'He laughed at her reaction. "That's what they did," he assured her. "*Your* brothers. It's all true." And then he struck her, playfully but quite hard, with the flat of his hand.' As before, Sofia puts her hands over her ears, wishing *not* to know. It is too late to ignore obscenity, however: she is already 'ruined'. And despite his slap, the violence of their relationship is not only, or not mainly, physical. Power has always rested with him in their relationship, because it was she who first showed interest; besides, as a lady, she stands to lose far more than he. As he says, 'people talked enough about him anyway; let them have one more thing. What did he care?' She could hardly have made the same remark.

Power in love rests with the one who cares less. Indifference itself represents godlike power, in the context of a love affair.[7] The S.P.'s indifference, and, from Sofia's point of view, his power, increase directly with her passion, and her powerlessness. Their relations illustrate, like so much of Jhabvala's work, the diabolical arithmetic of erotic attraction, recalling LaClos, Stendahl, Proust – and even 'Pauline Réage'.

The next time they meet 'she had to wait for him in the hot little room' for two hours (clearly an assertion of his power and her powerlessness). When finally he arrives, and she clings to him 'crying and laughing and trembling all over', the film at the neighbouring cinema gives out with a popular song 'that had been on the lips of millions'; the S.P. recognises it and sings along: '*O my heart, all he has left you is a splinter of himself to make you bleed!*' Sofia draws away, and in the face of his odious, good-humoured indifference, she cries 'Oh, you pig!', an uncharacteristic outburst, which is quickly attributed to the ever-present heat.

The sadism, or wilfully controlled cruelty, that the song celebrates is, of course, thematic: the phrase also exactly portrays Sofia's state of being. She is hardly alone: the song is loved by millions. But the S.P., as the tale makes clear, is *not* 'a sadist', though Sofia's obsession with him is 'masochistic'. He cannot be called a 'sadist' because his indifference is real. He derives no great pleasure from the relationship, except for its political meaning. His affections, it is implied, lie rather with the prostitute from Mohabbatpur: it is with her, the reader guesses, that he spends those hours that Sofia begrudges him. Sofia is too easy: the prostitute, one gathers from her initial appearance, exercises her own personal power and is not so easily conquered.

THE 'UNKNOWN WOMAN'

There is one character in this tale who is unnamed and mute: we do not hear her speak, though we meet her once. Yet she represents a crucial index to Sofia's progression toward knowledge. Sofia will make the connection between herself and this unknown woman, as she will discover the 'unknown woman' in herself. She must recognise her role as victim before her terrible knowledge can be complete.

This character, the S.P.'s wife, images women's servitude, even slavery, in very literal terms. This wife's suffering is generic. 'It is a woman's fate to suffer', sigh the wives and daughters in *Amrita* (p. 81).[8]

It is worth noting that Jhabvala gave the wronged wife a chance to speak for herself in the uncollected story 'Better than Dead', published in the *New Yorker* in 1958. This is a Hindu village woman's account of her husband's affair with 'Fatima', a neighbouring Muslim lady much more worldly than either the wife or her comparatively well-educated husband. The affair begins when, in Delhi, where the couple live, Fatima cures their sick child with a homeopathic remedy (shades of Sofia's intervention). The story is a compassionate glimpse into the wife's anguish, but also the husband's, for his cry seems to echo well beyond the confines of the story: '"Always tears," he said, and his voice was not like his at all but that of an angry stranger, "wherever I go, there are your tears!"'[9]

The conditions of the S.P.'s wife's oppression are so widely accepted that they escape notice. Indeed, they are invisible to Sofia at first. But the image of this woman, we are told, stays with Sofia, and undergoes a gradual transformation, until in the last passages of the narrative Sofia comes to understand the full horror of the wife's condition, the condition of women in general, and of course, her own condition. This 'unknown woman', as she is called, is a metaphor for an aspect of Sofia's own being which has hitherto remained unseen and unacknowledged. As Sofia passes from lady into whore and outcast, her awareness encompasses this servant-wife; and 'her heart aches for her as if it were for herself'.

In 'Desecration', Sofia's class and privilege allow her to separate herself from women who are overtly victimised. The lady (Sofia included) blames other women for their victimisation. The lady (Sofia included) identifies with a masculine ethos – after conveniently sanitising and sentimentalising it, very much in the style of the heroines and readers of popular romance. The lady adopts the reasoning of the masters and blames the victim: 'La Raison la plus Fort est Toujours la Meilleure' [the reasoning of the strongest is always the best], in the words of de la Fontaine in another fable of another time.[10] Our own contemporaries continue to uncover the workings of this principle,[11] and feminism has clarified it still further.

Sofia forfeits the comfort of sanctimonious victim-blaming by choosing to know. Her departure into Mohabbatpur is a journey into painful awareness: she confronts her own unaccountable appetite for humiliation at the hands of the S.P., and she then confronts the condition of wives in general, including herself, in the person of the S.P.'s neglected and wretched wife. At first, she blames the wife for slovenliness, and pities the S.P. (just as in 'The Housewife', Shakuntala blames her teacher's 'bedraggled' wife and pities him, not her). But as the love affair progresses, she comes to identify with the 'unknown woman', and even, on a deeper level, to recognise that she herself is 'unknown'.

Sofia first seeks out her lover's wife simply to ascertain whether she has any cause to be jealous of her. 'Mad with excitement', she orders her chauffeur to turn in to the lane of residential houses beyond the Police Headquarters, the street in which he lives. The impulse is ineluctable: 'she could not turn back, *she had to see* [my emphasis]'. Furtively, in the manner of a girl detective, she poses as someone looking for another man.[12] Her curiosity is slaked, and she gets a close view of the wife, the wretchedness of whose condition is briefly and succinctly drawn. In contrast to the S.P.'s fine military uniform, which he constantly adjusts 'in order to look smart', his wife is dressed in a dirty cotton sari, and resembles 'his servant rather than his wife. She looked older than he did, tired and worn out. . . . She told one of her children to point out the right house, and turned back into the kitchen with no further curiosity. A child began to cry.' So apathetic that she lacks even a primal human curiosity at the presence of an elegant lady in her 'derelict rooms', this wife, as it turns out, represents no occasion for jealousy. Instead, she elicits Sofia's 'indignation', which we understand as self-serving camouflage for her guilt. Rather than face our own failure toward another, we prefer to vindicate it by finding a pretext for blaming her: blame-the-victim working now on the personal scale.

The S.P. is clearly accustomed to this mode of self-justification toward the wife whom he has been betraying for years, as Sofia discovers, when she inquiries for the first time about his marriage.

> he shrugged, bored by the subject . . . it was all right; they had children – sons as well as daughters. His wife had plenty to do, he presumed she was content – and why shouldn't she be? She had a good house to live in, sufficient money for her household expenses, and respect as the wife of the S.P. He laughed briefly. Yes indeed, if she had anything to complain of he would like to know what it was.

Sofia joins in the comforting accusations, and, as a lady, she pitches her criticism in the feminine arenas of grooming and personal appearance:

> She agreed with him. She even became indignant, thinking of his wife who had all these benefits and did not even care to keep a nice home for him. And not just his home – what about his wife herself? When she thought about that bedraggled figure, more a servant than a wife, Sofia's indignation rose – and with it her tender pity for him, so that she embraced him and even spilled a few hot tears, which fell onto his naked chest and made him laugh with surprise.

The S.P.'s womanising is his wife's fault, since 'he could not be expected to waste himself there'. To bolster the fragile case for blaming the victims, it is necessary to shower their oppressors with extra sympathy. In this manner, typically, men are seen as victims of women, or, failing that, of their own mysterious drives. In weeping for the S.P., Sofia dramatises the sentimental fallacy of women's pity for the 'fragile male ego' – so often conjured up to justify preferential treatment for men in any sphere.

Sofia gives the familiar dynamic a further twist in the direction of transparent self-delusion when she begins to perceive that his interest in her is waning. This situation is one of Jhabvala's specialities: it illustrates the state of interested self-delusion; and how we arrange our perceptions to coincide with our wishes. Sofia decides that, in order to protect him from his compelling sexual needs, which lead to his propensity to wander, she 'had to arrange to be with him more often'.

At their next meeting, she suggests that they meet more often: he hedges; she insists. Before giving his final decision, he interrupts their discourse to draw attention to the voice in the next room, an old Muslim man at prayer. He is then inspired to demand that she recite the prayers in concert with the overheard voice, while he 'mounts her' from behind. This is the descration referred to in the title, an image of violation, in which the S.P. utilises the Islamic prayer extolling the greatness of God and the posture expressing submission to God's will. (The word 'Islam' means 'submission'.) 'Never had he had such enjoyment out of her as on that day.'

That she complies with his demand, even though 'pretending it was a joke' is partially due to his excellent timing. As the act occurs in the midst of negotiations about future meetings, Sofia still believes he may accede to her wishes: she is even less likely than she might have been to deny his whims. But her attempt at appeasement is futile, for after the scene just described 'he still wouldn't agree to meet her more than once a week', and Sofia has sunk to a further level of degradation.

Only now do her thoughts turn to 'that unknown woman'. She is on her way home from Mohabbatpur, after a visit with the wives of the town gentry, from whom she can expect no sympathy:

> She wasn't sure whether it was her imagination or whether there really was something different in the way they were with her. Sometimes she thought she saw them turn aside, as if to suppress a smile, or exchange looks with each other that she was not supposed to see. And when the gossip turned to the S.P., they made very straight faces, like people who know more than they are prepared to show.

Her car, by now familiar, is actually cheered by the policemen lounging in underwear outside their quarters. To escape full awareness of this nightmarish public humiliation, she must break with her own consciousness: her reasoning now takes on the flavour of madness: 'She didn't trouble herself much about that either. There were so many other things on her mind.' Now, she *deliberately* instructs her chauffeur to enter the gate of the officer's quarters, and *impulsively* changes her mind, which represents a reversal of her first drive to his quarters, when she had given in to the obsessional voice despite her reasoned awareness that it would be imprudent to do so. Such is the progress of her delusion, which paradoxically represents both knowledge and the refusal to know. Now, the self-destructive imperatives of obsession have the upper hand, while the voice of self-preservation is experienced as afterthought. The shift signals a break with a reality that is too painful to bear:

> She did not want to see his wife again; it was almost as if she were afraid. . . . She had never ceased to think of that sad, bedraggled woman inside. Indeed, as time passed the vision had not dimmed but had become clearer. She found also that her feelings toward this unknown woman had changed completely, so that, far from thinking about her with scorn, she now had such pity for her that her heart ached as sharply as if it were for herself.

'Ma semblable, ma soeur', she might have said.

Her heart, as if to fulfil the image of the popular song sung by the S.P., has literally begun to ache. She thinks that if only she could tell someone, her pain might lessen; but there is no one to tell. The stolid, impassive chauffeur, whom she has been bribing to keep silence, now seems like her closest friend, but it is only his back that she can see. In fact, to him she speaks in a voice calculated *not* to communicate: 'She had a special expressionless way of giving orders to the chauffeur, and he had a special expressionless way of receiving them.' Like a mythic ferryman, he conducts her back and forth between the socially sanctioned prison of boredom that is her marriage, and the shameful prison of erotic obsession that is her 'affair', between her isolated home, and Mohabbatpur, where live her lover and the women mentioned in the text: the S.P.'s wife, the prostitute and the ladies that Sofia visits with such discomfort. There is no place for her in town. But she will not return to the isolation that the Raja Sahib has chosen for himself and for her. Her erotic quest, her longing to know and be known, has hardly brought her fulfilment; rather it has forced upon her a series of revelations with which she cannot live.

Paradoxically, her husband has by now become aware of her affair, and her betrayal has heightened his desire for her. With his silent suffering the infernal circle is complete, and gender divisions dissolve. He ceases to regard her with the odious condescension that he showed earlier: in fact, he becomes something of a normative 'woman', while she plays the male role in their relations.

He 'trembles' and 'clings' to her, while she indifferently supplies him with reasonable explanations for her absence. His next verse-drama contains 'something different', the motif of this fable: 'Oh, if thou didst but know what it is like to live in hell the way I do!' But the real existential hell is the inability to share our individual and private hells, that is, to authentically *know* an Other.

At least, the reader's sympathy is with both partners equally. The Raja Sahib has redeemed his earlier mercilessness. Paradoxically, the couple, while profoundly alienated, each caught in the grip of unsatisfied desire, are now more alike than ever. If this alienation is the existenial hell, the existential 'desecration' is not the profanation of Sofia's ritual prayer, or not that alone, but the metamorphosis of the erotic impulse, spiritual at its core and aimed at infinitely heightened consciousness, into, literally, 'desacralisation' and pornography. While most of Ruth Jhabvala's work delineates, with a humour just this side of bitterness, the comic deflation of grandiose self-delusions, this powerful, almost mythic, tale is pitched in the mode of tragedy.

7

Demon-Lovers and Holy Mothers: *Heat and Dust*

Heat and Dust (1975) is at the time of writing probably Jhabvala's best-known novel; it has been available in a paperback edition ever since the appearance of the film version of the novel in 1977. It contains Jhabvala's most characteristic techniques – filmic flash-back, using a combination of first- and third-person narrative, and themes – the dangers of sexual passion, Westerners in India, heterosexual women in relation to homosexual men. Again, the work is constructed, magically, it seems, on the fine line between the comic and the tragic. The two factors of the novel's availability and its centrality, I offer to justify the disproportionate amount of space that it occupies in this study. In fact, it is a rather short novel, almost a novella, and its spare, compressed prose has almost the effect of poetry, reverberating with meanings and significations that seem to lie just beneath the surface – another quality that may explain my fascination with it.

Heat and Dust is a double-layered novel about two women in India, fifty years apart. Two plot lines echo and double each other, their similarities and differences revealing and resulting from the similarities and differences between the two women, one a romantic idealist and one an anti-romantic observer. The stories are linked through their teller: the 'I' of the modern story is also the narrator of the first story, which takes place in 1923. Because of this conceit, the novel may be seen as an exploration of the process of storytelling itself.

While my reading takes note of this 'literary' aspect, I am more interested in a feminist reading: the novel as a study of the options available to women *searchers* – searchers after wholeness, meaning, transcendence and exaltation: qualities that convention and society seem to deny. Sexual adventure, one possible escape route, is considered and rejected by the novels.

In *Autobiography of a Princess*, James Ivory, Jhabvala's collaborator in Merchant–Ivory Productions, writes about the British or American women who lived with Indian nawabs or maharajas in the early part of this century – and there were many, he says, commenting upon their lively faces looking out of old photographs:

> Any European woman who lived with a Maharaja was asking for trouble sooner or later. She got it from his wives and old female relatives, who schemed for her removal. She got it from the official British, who snubbed and despised her, and tended to regard her as an unsettling influence, a threat to stability in the state. And sometimes she got it from her protector, who might turn out to be an opium addict, a drunkard, or a brute. Their stories would make good films, good period pieces. These young women are still around today – no longer following Maharajas, but swamis.[1]

Heat and Dust concerns the trouble Olivia was 'asking for'. It contrasts a male-centred tragic romanticism, essentially barren and destructive to women, with a female-centred comic realism, informed, despite its comedy, by a vitality that is spiritual and aesthetic in essence. The novel represents the transformation of the romantic heroine Olivia, a naïve and innocent victim: as the modern narrator recreates her we come to accept her as a kind of beatified foremother. But the transforming power is the modern narrator's art.

The novel is rich in nature imagery. It contrasts the heat and dust of the plains – which signify at once an obsessive sexuality and the absence of feeling – with the life-giving moisture of the Himalayas. Throughout, water – rain, fog, springs, an 'oasis' – represents relief, real or imagined. Overarching both plots is the same Muslim/Hindu festival day and holy place: the 'Husband's Wedding Day' and the 'shrine of Baba [Papa] Firdaus'. Important and pivotal events take place on that day years apart in time, and at that shrine, which *is* an oasis in a parched landscape: its spring is thought to be a miraculous cure for female infertility. Through the use of these motifs and images, Jhabvala weaves into her novel a multiplicity of overlapping references: to the patriarchal institution of marriage, Hindu- or Western-style; to the societal derogation and psychic mutilation of women, Hindu- or Western-style; to a subversive yet vital strain of resistance, Hindu- or Western-style, resistance both to the institution of marriage and to the romanticism that elevates and deifies maleness.

The unnamed narrator has come to India to search out a literal 'herstory', an almost-forgotten family scandal. Namely, the story of Olivia Rivers, the wife of a British colonial administrator. (Douglas Rivers' name has two functions. It is part of the imagery of water, and it alludes as well, I think, to another notable literary Rivers, St John, Jane Eyre's missionary suitor. Like St John Rivers, Douglas Rivers is fair and gentlemanly, and bearer to the heathen of the British code of honour.)

As a young bride, Olivia adores Rivers' gentlemanly idealism, but with the passage of time and the closer perspective of wifehood, her ardour fades. She allows herself to be drawn into a liaison with a powerless minor prince of the neighbouring province of Khatm (the Hindi word *Khatm* means 'finished'). If Douglas Rivers recalls St John Rivers, the Nawab recalls Rochester: he is dark, mysterious and worldly; he has a mad wife. As the affair develops, Olivia becomes pregnant, probably with his child, though perhaps with her husband's. An abortion is performed by Indian midwives, but it is discovered by a strait-laced British physician whom Olivia of course knows socially. 'Ruined', she flees to the Nawab's palace, and lives out the rest of her life in a solitary retreat high in the Himalayas.

Douglas remarries, and his *second* wife becomes the grandmother of the young woman who will tell Olivia's story. Thus Olivia is not, as some reviewers have mistakenly stated, the modern narrator's grandmother.[2] She is, rather, the outcast foremother, in the manner of Adam's first wife Lilith.[3]

The modern narrator has come into possession of a number of old letters from Olivia to her sister Marcia, in Paris, which recount the tale. She is so fascinated by the story that she makes a journey to India in order to better understand and write it: the fruits of her labours are her novel and her journal, which details her own experiences in the provincial town of Satipur (the Hindi word *Satipur* means 'the place of suttee').

Satipur is quite different now from what it was fifty years before. For example, the building that Douglas and Olivia occupied now houses 'The Water Board, the municipal Health Department, and a sub-post office': the rather chaotic juxtaposition of dreary offices underlines the contrast between the genteel colonial privileges of the past and the bureaucratic and absurd present. That the 'Water Board' is located there is significant: just as 'Baba Firdaus', the Muslim holy man, is beatified by the spring that flows from the place of his devotions, Olivia's beatification is lightly foreshadowed in this passing detail – typical of the densely organised structure of this short novel.

The narrator's stay in India develops along lines parallel to Olivia's. She too forms a liaison with an Indian (Inder Lal) and with an Englishman ('Chid'). She too becomes pregnant and considers an abortion, although she decides to keep the pregnancy. She too ascends to the Himalayas – but she does so autonomously, and voluntarily, whereas Olivia's ascent was, at least initially, an exile. But Olivia stayed in her mountain bungalow until her death decades later: she could have left. Why did she stay? Why did she leave her husband? Who was she, and who was her Indian lover? Writing Olivia's story, the narrator experiences her own 'new' story, and at the same time sees into the 'old' one – the past out of which the present emerges.

From the combination of the narrator's reconstruction of Olivia's story, and her journal, another novel emerges, which is the one called *Heat and Dust*. History, circumstance and the mysterious quantity of personality have freed the modern narrator from the need to sacrifice all for love, and be sacrificed herself. Thus she is free – even to a fault – of the romantic idealism that entrapped Olivia. By entering into Olivia's world as fully as she does, the modern narrator suggests that she and her subject are 'sisters under the skin'. Yet her own tale is curiously unemotional, though there is no shortage of sexual encounters. She would seem to speak for the contemporary woman who, having discarded the old, unsatisfactory patterns of relations between the sexes, finds herself facing an emotional void.

Though just about every plot element in the 1923 story has its analogue in the modern one, even to the repetition of lines of dialogue or scene settings, it is not a case of 'plus ça change, plus c'est la même chose'. Time has passed, and with it the Edwardian values of the Anglo-Indians of 1923. 'Everything is different now', the narrator says simply. Sexual mythology has been challenged and no longer possesses the power it once had – at least for the narrator. The political reality, too, has undergone a profound shift. The quintessential Briton in India is now not a colonial administrator, but a drugged-out, quasi-schizophrenic teenager – his guru has renamed him 'Chidananda' and he is, improbably, one of the modern narrator's lovers.

So, woven though the novel are the twin themes of sexuality

and colonialism. Clearly, these themes have much to do with each other, relations between men and women being an analogue of colonialism, as John Stuart Mill and Harriet Taylor first pointed out.[4] Moreover, sexual polarities repeat a host of other dualities contained in the ethos that informs colonialism: male is to female as white is to black, as occidental is to oriental, as active is to passive, mind to body, control to spontaneity, rational to irrational, conscious to unconscious, coloniser to colonised. But modernism, together with political movement, has thrown into question these signifying polarities by the time the modern narrator undertakes her researches. Even in the collective Western imagination, the first term of the polarity is no longer automatically viewed as superior. And these dualisms, once named, have been challenged: in the disciplines of linguistics, psychology, politics, history, physics, in literature and in the arts.

Certainly, the modern narrator does not endorse such polarities: for one thing, she is both a woman and a writer, ostensibly two mutually exclusive identities. She represents the breed of modern women writers who have observed and challenged the assumptions of patriarchism and colonialism. She is there, in India, to report and uncover. Unobtrusive, anonymous, even unnamed, she is the observer par excellence. One never learns who she was in England, what she did there: she is a voice, almost disembodied. She reports to her journal, and to us, her impressions of India today: tremendously intriguing, gorgeous and repellent. She focuses on the women around her, reporting the limits of their lives and their various escape routes.

The narrator herself, of course, is a fictive creation, and it is Jhabvala who has forged the old story, the new story and the links between them. This novel, by means of its peculiar structure, raises questions about the act of writing novels, and, for that matter, of reading them. It is composed of *texts*: Olivia's letters and the narrator's reading of them, and the narrator's journals themselves. It is a novelist's *tour de force*, recalling the literary giants through its use of the story-within-a-story to plumb a forgotten mystery: one thinks of James's *The Turn of the Screw*, Conrad's *The Heart of Darkness*, and, most notably, of Forster's *A Passage to India*. But in *Heat and Dust* the story is told from a woman's perspective, with an emphasis on women's options, women's expectations and women's solutions.

'GOING TOO FAR'

Beginnings being crucial, let us take a close look at the first sentences of the novel:

> Shortly after Olivia went away with the Nawab, Beth Crawford returned from Simla. This was in September, 1923. Beth had to go down to Bombay to meet the boat on which her sister Tessie was arriving. Tessie was coming out to spend the cold season with the Crawfords. They had arranged all sorts of visits and expeditions for her, but she stayed mostly in Satipur because of Douglas. They went riding together and played croquet and tennis and she did her best to be good company for him. Not that he had much free time, for he kept himself as busy as ever in the district. He worked like a Trojan and never ceased to be calm and controlled, so that he was very much esteemed both by his colleagues and by the Indians. He was upright and just. (*Heat and Dust*, p. 1)

If one reads carefully, one finds the entire plot of the 1923 story. In the very first line of the novel is its dénouement, tucked into a subordinate clause: 'Shortly after Olivia went away with the Nawab'. So the mystery that the narrator's novel seeks to explicate is *'Why* did Olivia "go away" with the Nawab?' *That* she did it we know from the outset.

From the start, the modern narrator seems oddly detached. Her flat style suggests, paradoxically, an emotional weight behind the blandness. Olivia's actions are so outrageous as to be unsayable for two generations. Even the modern narrator glosses over them euphemistically, quickly passing to chatty fillers, 'keeping busy', even as Douglas did.

Douglas's qualities of character (his 'Character') are, in contrast to Olivia's, named immediately. Like the Anglo-Indians, the narrator appears to respect her grandfather's stoicism. Olivia's name is no more mentioned. Even the modern narrator seems reluctant to speak directly about Olivia, who stepped beyond the pale when she left Douglas and the Anglo-Indians. Olivia went too far – which is why she is so fascinating.

Olivia's lover, the Nawab, inhabits a palace of innumerable corridors and passageways, in which Olivia at one point in the novel literally loses her way. The symbolism is felt by everyone in

Olivia's world. Beth Crawford knows that one does not venture into 'oriental privacies', dark regions that are outside her ken – 'as was Olivia once she had crossed over into them' (p. 169).

The syntactical and narrative obscurity in the novel's first paragraph suggests the obscurity of Olivia's story. The words of the title, *Heat and Dust*, in addition to describing the climactic conditions in which Olivia's story is set, signify the largest literary themes: love and death, passion and the obscurity of the past. The novel's bitemporal structure allows us to see a little more clearly into that obscurity, to brush away the dust. Even in the present, the modern narrator can now venture into an India that was closed to Olivia: she risks less. Olivia risked all for love – like others of Ruth Jhabvala's bored and lonely women who run off with demon-lovers, lovers who are socially inferior, dangerous and exciting. Risking all, she loses. The modern narrator, cool and anti-passionate, is relatively invulnerable. Yet, as she records the past (dust), she researches 'heat', and the 'nature of passion' emerges. Though, perhaps necessarily, passion itself eludes the modern narrator – she is an analyst, not a participant – she follows Olivia up the mountain, so that in the end both protagonists are lost in the mists of the Himalayan peaks. Both have sought, and found, the same 'peak' of transcendence, extremity, vivid experience; both have chosen to go too far.

What *really* was going on in the paradigmatic seduction? As the novel develops, we learn the ironic truth that deflates the drama and the high passion of what has become the family legend of Olivia. The Nawab had his own reasons for wanting Olivia; and they were mostly political. Olivia had a lively imagination, a susceptibility to good looks and charm, and a quite laudable disdain for the banality and racism of her community of Anglo-Indians. She took sexual freedom for herself. She was 'caught' in a peculiarly female dilemma, brought about by the combination of biology and patriarchal rule. She became pregnant at the wrong time, by the wrong man. Hence, she was compelled to leave a less than perfect marriage. Having left, she chose to stay alone in an alien place: to take that freedom even further? To live out a penitential solitary confinement? To turn her back on human society? Her final motivation remains obscure, despite the narrator's researches.

The modern narrator also takes sexual freedom and freedom of movement for herself. But she is more cautious: her emotional detachment is the polar opposite of Olivia's passionate abandon.

Throughout the novel, the modern narrator resists the shocked voices that predict danger for her; in a stance of stubborn, almost ostentatious, carelessness, she goes where she pleases. The earliest passages in the modern narrator's story play with the notion of risk-taking. After the telescoped plot synopsis that has just been discussed, the modern narrator quotes a passage from her own journal describing her arrival in Bombay. (Somewhere in the course of the novel this past catches up with the present of the journals, so that by the end her journal records events as they occur.)

The narrator's first act on arrival is to head for 'the dormitory of the S.M. hostel'. Society of Missionaries, she supplies in a parenthesis. One must wonder whether Ruth Jhabvala has intended the sly pun. Can anyone hear the initials 'S.M.' without thinking of the 'erotic minority' ('sadomasochism') so crucial to contemporary advertising and image-making? Whether the association is intentional or not, there are certainly links: this novel, like virtually all of Ruth Jhabvala's work, touches on the commonalities between obsessional religious devotion and obsessional romanticism.

At any rate, having arrived at the hostel, the narrator puts her watch on top of her suitcase and falls into an exhausted sleep. Awakening in darkness, she gropes for the watch, finds it missing, and is already lamenting its loss when 'a voice from the next bed' admonishes her tartly: 'Here it is, my dear, and just be more careful in future, please.' This disembodied voice belongs to a Christian missionary, who for thirty years has been tending the souls of poor Indians. Now she attends to her compatriot with advice and warnings. Wearing 'a white nightgown that encases her from head to foot', she is compared several times to a ghost. Indeed, she points out to the narrator, very much in the fashion of a Dantean angel, the various rings of Inferno that can be seen from their windows in the S.M.: the Indian street-scene below, bright as day with naptha flares though it is half-past midnight, crowded with the wretched: crippled children, a legless boy, scavengers of the leavings of hawkers of food and their customers. Yet the narrator observes that the beggars seem 'lighthearted, even gay'.

If the wretched seem lighthearted, the privileged vacationers are wretched, as we see next. Another aspect, this time literally on their own spatial level, through the windows of 'A's Hotel', reveals a crowd of 'our own': derelict Europeans, mostly young. 'Who are they, where do they come from?' demands the ghostly guide rhetorically, and then relates the story of a young German or Scandinavian whom she has seen being deloused, in the street, by a monkey! Looking into his face, the missionary sees 'a soul in hell' (p. 5). And the narrator concurs: the hippies across the way look to her too like 'souls in hell' (p. 6). There is much to fear in this India, which has so reduced her compatriots.

The watch is a neat symbol for European rationalism, efficiency and temporal linearity, which the narrator's neighbour is at pains to remind her to hold on to; and she is there too to warn her of the consequences of abandoning these values. More than this, of course, she particularly embodies the ethos of Christianity, having lived in India as its emissary and sustained herself inwardly by her faith. Jesus is with her every moment.

The elderly missionary functions to charge the atmosphere with a certain consciousness of risk, which the modern narrator blithely ignores. This is the traditional Gothic beginning: a young woman arrives in an exotic place, naïvely fearless; she is warned by one who knows more; she scoffs. However, the novel departs from the formula, in which the heroine–victim discovers, to her chagrin, that the warnings were correct. Instead the contemporary Ms Rivers – as her name may be reconstructed – is correct not to be terrified. The warning voice represents a past system of values no longer necessary or applicable to her.

A thematic verbal motif emerges here, that is, a play with images of standing up or lying down, resisting or submitting to the seductions of India: a name that can represent sensuality, chaos and the non-rational. The narrator calls the missionary 'tough', like any survivor: 'a ghost with a backbone'. In the history that the modern narrator researches, the British administrators too have 'backbone', which keeps them from going 'too far in'. Douglas is 'upright' and the Anglo-Indian ladies of Olivia's acquaintance are 'bright', 'practical', 'straight and steady'. Major Minnies has a number of theories about the influence of India on the European temperament: he has even published a monograph on the subject, at his own expense. His theories reveal his European horror of the non-rational. One must resist, 'withstand' the force of India, which always

finds out the weak spot and presses on it . . . this weak spot is to be found in the most sensitive, often the finest people – and, moreover, in their finest feelings. It is there that India seeks them out and pulls them over into what the Major called the other dimension.   (p. 171)

The missionary derives her backbone, however, from a paradoxical self-abnegation: she has no will of her own, she says, only the will of God, in which she has lived for thirty years. 'When she says that, her voice is not a bit ghost-like but strong and ringing as one who has been steadfast in her duty' (p. 4).

The rather comical paradox is thematic. For the strength and vitality that can paradoxically accompany absorption into the will of another, are to entice Olivia into her affair with the Nawab. This paradox, of strength through submission, underlies the kind of romantic love to which Olivia falls prey twice during the course of the novel: first in relation to Douglas, then in relation to the Nawab.

PARALLEL STRUCTURES

The structure of this double-layered plot is fugal and antiphonal: past and present echo each other as subject and counter-subject in a fugue. There is hardly an element of plot that is not repeated in the bitemporal structure. Olivia has two lovers, one Indian and one British; so does the narrator. Olivia twice visits the shrine of Baba Firdaus, the first time among a gay party of the Nawab's attendants and companions, the second time alone with him – it is then that he seduces her; the narrator also pays two visits to the shrine of Baba Firdaus, first among a gay party of Inder Lal's mother's friends ('the merry widows') and the second time alone with Inder Lal – it is then that *she* seduces *him*. The Nawab has a mad wife ('Sandy') from whom he lives apart. Inder Lal has a mad wife (Ritu) – unfortunately for her, they live together still. The Nawab's mother, the Begum, dominates the palace behind the scenes: Inder Lal's mother dominates *his* humbler household. Beth Crawford and Mrs Minnies take a trip to Simla, leaving Olivia and the Nawab to each other's company: Inder Lal's mother, his wife Ritu and the lodger Chid take a trip to Simla, leaving the modern narrator and Inder Lal alone under the same roof. Olivia becomes pregnant and considers abortion; so does the narrator. Olivia ascends to the Himalayas; so does the narrator.

From the outset, ironic parallels direct the action. For example, the narrator describes Olivia's obligatory social call upon the ladies of the Nawab's family, in the palace at Khatm; and then her own social call 'on the two ladies of the Inder Lal family' in their impoverished rooms. The stark contrast between 1923 and 1973 occurs throughout, as the colonial past is set against the grubby present, its golden patina now tarnished to reveal the reality underneath. Occasionally, the comedy lies in the persistence of cultural misunderstandings, across half a century: to take the same example, during both social calls, the unconventional English-women would have preferred to sit Indian-style on the floor, but on both occasions, special chairs are provided for them, which they reluctantly occupy.

The novel has been faulted for its unusual structure: John Updike objected that the constant cross-cutting prevents either story from fully engaging the reader.[5] While the weaving together of two or more plot lines is a time-honoured novelistic technique, a classical device in the history of the novel, it is, admittedly, rare that the action repeats itself in two different time settings. Novel-readers, well-accustomed to shifting focus from one set of characters to another and back, are brought up short by this repetition of events, by which Ruth Jhabvala's novel calls attention to its form. My own sense is that the unusual structure works, so that the novel's subject in a way becomes the process of novel-making itself, that is, the search into and recreation of an imaginary past. Uncanny links connect the researcher–novelist and her subject. A reciprocal shaping takes place: as the narrator shapes Olivia's story, *it* shapes hers. She actually lives it out, modifying it in the new context of enormously increased freedom.

In the same way, there exists a reciprocal relationship between collective myths and images – of which novels are only one example – and individual lives. By virtue of its interesting and innovative conceit, this novel touches on epistomology. It shows how we find meanings in nature, in the world of experience, in history, in texts, and, at the same time, how those meanings create their own reality in our lives. In this way, the novel's structure is of the late twentieth century, a commentary on, even an illustration of, the reciprocally dependent relationships of myth/history and experience; moreover, it is particularly rich for feminist criticism. The novel's plots, which have to do with romantic flight and options and expectations for women, are explicated by its very structure. The construction of literature from a set of imaginary texts (Olivia's letters, the narrator's journals) echoes the process by which the female protagonists construct their lives from, or in spite of, the myths they have received.

OLIVIA AND THE ANGLO-INDIANS

Olivia arrives in India, like her creator, because of her marriage; like Ruth Jhabvala she is at first intensely enthusiastic about her new surroundings. But unlike her creator, Olivia needs to confront a set of nasty political realities: she is a member of a hated ruling presence.

The postwar years were times of particular ferment in Indian and Anglo-Indian politics: there was a growing political consciousness among the colonised to which British response was two-fold. First, it was thought advisable to implement more liberal and conciliatory relations with high-caste Indians like the Nawab. 'Dyarchy', or the sharing of government between Indians and British, was recommended by one faction.[6] Princes of the native states were now enlisted as allies, to a point, in the British struggle against emerging Gandhism.[7] Thus Mr Crawford and Douglas, as colonial administrators, are at pains to maintain good relations with the Nawab, and to overlook as much as possible his ties to the dacoit bandits and, worse, his pivotal role in the yearly ritual slaughter of Hindus by Muslims, on 'the Husband's Wedding Day'.

Because of the growing Indian nationalism, the British implemented repressive legislation for 'sedition', and resentment among Indians – particularly Muslims – was intense. In 1920, Gandhi had announced a policy of 'non-cooperation' with the British.[8]

Olivia's seduction by the Nawab must, of course, be seen in the light of these political realities, in which it emerges as an elaborate stratagem, politically motivated. Olivia takes the most naïve view possible of the Nawab, in contrast to the other Britons, who see 'our Friend' as a rogue or worse. The possibility, so clear to the others, that he seeks to use Olivia to humiliate Douglas and the British community in general, seems never to cross her mind. Nor does she question Harry's presence in the palace, which certainly has its sinister aspects. Like Olivia, Harry is a weak link in the British chain. Both Harry and Olivia are vulnerable to the Nawab's seductive advances; both can, in the realm of realpolitik, be used against the British. The homosexual Harry represents 'a living exemplar of all the possibilities of Englishness that the British in India would rather deny existed', in the words of R. J. Cronin.[9]

Critics are quite divergent in their readings of the Nawab. Cronin takes a very dim view of him, in contrast to Gooneratne, who finds some laudable qualities in him.[10] Shahane praises his generosity, which he appears to accept as sincere.[11] The Nawab's creator herself is characteristically ambivalent toward him. He is one of a long line of charismatic, seductive men in her fiction who, while they cannot be trusted, represent vitality, intelligence and a certain very welcome force of opposition to the hypocritical and suffocating dullness of the world in which the female protagonist finds herself. Shakuntala's music teacher, Betsy's Har Gopal (in 'Passion'); the odious Swami of *A New Dominion*, even the S.P. (of 'Desecration') are a few; in Jhabvala's next two novels others will emerge to disturb their willing prey.

As if to echo the novel's ambivalence toward the Nawab, Olivia voices the ultimate in romantic idealism in her comments on the institution of suttee. The voluntary self-immolation of the widow on her husband's funeral pyre, and a well-known aspect of the Hindu tradition, suttee is a thematic element of some importance in this novel. Suttee is woven into the name of its setting, 'Satipur', or 'the place of suttee' as I have mentioned.

In the 1923 story, Douglas attempts and fails to interrupt a suttee, which was outlawed by the British as early as 1829, as the narrator thoughtfully reminds us (p. 55). His attempt to stop the widow's 'sons, brother-in-law and a priest' from pushing her into the flames is hotly resented by the Indians, and becomes the cause of an outbreak of anti-British riots. Like the chador in present-day Iran, suttee became a rallying point for Indian autonomy.

Widow-burning was not always voluntary on the part of the widow. Dorothy Stein reports on a variety of physical coercions such as 'scaffolds constructed to tilt towards the fire pit', and so on. 'If all else failed and the woman escaped from the burning pile, she was often dragged back by force, often by her own son.' Stein also notes the economic and social advantages that the widow's in-laws derived from her suttee.[12] Certainly in the case that Olivia refers to, the woman is burned against her will.

The British administrators at dinner in the novel discuss the actual case of one Colonel Sleeman of Jabalpore. Here, too, the British officer had failed to prevent the suttee, but this time his failure was due to the widow's own determination: clearly, that too is a possibility.[13]

Olivia takes the most romantic view possible of the widow's self-sacrifice: thinking it 'noble' to 'want to go with the person you care for most in the world' (p. 55). Though her compatriots as politely as possible let it be known that they think her a fool, the novel does not condemn her for this sentiment, just as it does not unambiguously fault her for falling in love with the Nawab. Part of her regard for him is a by-product of her rejection of the British position as colonialists.

Two generations before the modern narrator does so, Olivia questions the axioms of her peers: the inevitability of colonialism and even the primacy of the Western mind-set. She may be a naïve, but she is on the side of the angels. Like many another female protagonist, she is at once too smart and not smart enough. In the style of Emma Woodhouse, Dorothea Brooke and Isabel Archer, to name a few, she is too smart to accept the conventions of her peers, but not smart enough to understand the dangers to which she exposes herself. All of these presumptuous young heroines take a stance of assertiveness in a society hostile to women's individuality. All are endangered by this rash stance.

Olivia – unlike these heroines, already wed – chooses the wrong lover through an excess of spirit and feeling. But like these other presumptuous heroines before her, she believes her lover to have special qualities of character not perceived by her insensitive peers. For that matter, she had over-romanticised her husband as well, and is learning to her chagrin that the very qualities that had dazzled her in Douglas as a suitor are the things that now grate on her the most. Thus, his chivalry turns out, viewed through the close-up lens of marriage, to be a naïve and sentimental paternalism; his steadfast uprightness entails 'genuine respect' for his dull superiors; he shares their condescension toward their Indian subjects, whereas Olivia is enlightened enough, in 1923, to be repelled by their paternalism, their smiles of 'tolerance, of affection, even enjoyment . . . like good parents, they all loved India whatever mischief she might be up to' (p. 58).

As the novel unfolds, Olivia comes to see a connection between Douglas's racist paternalism and his sexist paternalism. For example, in an early scene she overhears as he receives the respects of some local landowners, and thinks that 'it was almost as if Douglas were playing a musical instrument of which he had entirely mastered the stops'. As he comes in, smiling, he shakes his head in 'benign amusement' and remarks on the 'pack of rogues': 'They think they're frightfully cunning but really they're like children.' Olivia objects: 'Oh really, darling.' But her meaning is lost on Douglas, who thinks she means he's made a mess with his pipe – of which more, later. The conversation then turns to 'Hindustani', which Olivia feels she '*must*' learn. (It is worth noting here that two generations later, in the modern story, Olivia's counterpart does study Hindi.)

Douglas is unenthusiastic, though he allows that '"It's the only language in which you can deliver the most deadly insults with the most flowery courtesy. . . . I don't mean you, of course." He laughed at the idea. "It's a man's game, strictly." "What isn't?", Olivia said.'

Olivia's ironic question indicates her growing recognition of her essentially decorative function. To Douglas, the idea that men, colonised or colonisers, make the rules and play all the games is less disturbing: 'He sucked at his pipe in a rather pleased way which made her cry out sharply: "Don't do that!" He took it out of his mouth and stared in surprise. "I hate you with that thing, Douglas," she explained' (p. 39). Only lately, she had loved Douglas's eyes, 'the eyes of a boy who read adventure stories and had dedicated himself to live up to their code of courage and honour' (p. 40). But the gentlemanly code has palled, and she has grown weary of her pedestal.

Although she tells herself that 'really everything was quite easy to bear and overcome just as long as she and Douglas felt the way they did for each other' (p. 61), her words are empty. They echo those of other naïve protagonists of earlier Jhabvala works: there is starry-eyed Amrita, for example, in love with a good-looking boy several classes beneath her and sure that 'everything – life, everything – was suddenly very simple' (p. 85). Or foolish Naraian, of 'The Young Couple', who exclaims, 'What does it matter, Cathy . . . *where* we are as long as we are together?' (*A Stronger Climate*, p. 64). With such clichés do lovers delude themselves. When Ruth Jhabvala puts them in a character's mouth, the fall from bliss is imminent.

Olivia is further disappointed by the provincial society of the Anglo-Indians, to which Harry and the Nawab represent a most welcome contrast. The three of them together constitute a kind of mini counter-culture of their own. Witty, intelligent, attractive, they are the Bohemians of the Satipur 'Civil Lines' (British residential area). Harry's homosexuality represents a further – and welcome – alienation from an unattractive society. Olivia's sister Marcia (to whom her letters are addressed) is a similar Bohemian figure, offstage, in Paris, where she lives 'in a series of hotel rooms', with 'some rather difficult people' (p. 48). (The brief reference recalls Jean Rhys's novel *Quartet*, which Jhabvala was to adapt for the screen in the Merchant–Ivory production of 1981.)

As a critic of Anglo-Indian paternalism and racism, Olivia is particularly vulnerable to being charged with it herself. Jhabvala ironically marks the manner in which Olivia's principles are used against her. Shortly before the final consummation of her affair with the Nawab, Olivia calls on Dr Saunders's wife, a rather déclassé Anglo-Indian, who tells her the story of the lady from Somerset and her dhobi (washerman), who attacked her while 'ironing her undies'. Not surprisingly, this was 'too much for him'. Mrs Saunders wonders whether the spicy food has anything to do with the Indians' excitable 'constitution' – but of one thing she is sure: 'they've only one thought in their heads and that's to you-know-what with a white woman' (p. 119).

Olivia is appalled by her vulgarity. As if to continue the exposé of Anglo-Indian attitudes, later that same day, the Nawab draws Mrs Saunders's foolish husband into an unwitting comedy, treating him with exaggerated courtesy – his method of expressing contempt. He elicits from the Doctor such lines as 'They [Indians] haven't got it here, you see, up here, the way we have' (p. 120). After a while, the joke palls, and the Nawab, Olivia and Harry send him away. There follows a scene of recognitions, worth quoting for its revelations. The Nawab expertly utilises Olivia's sense of collective guilt. Harry is given the opportunity to take sides and to display his real allegiances – which are to the Nawab, rather than to Olivia. This is unexceptional, as Harry and Olivia are rivals. Olivia urges the Nawab not to 'judge' by Dr Saunders.

> The Nawab looked at her rather coldly. 'Don't judge what by him?'
>
> 'All of us.'
>
> 'Who's us?' Harry asked her. He too sounded hostile. Olivia felt herself floundering – it was the same sensation she had had at the Crawfords' dinner party [where she had manoeuvred

herself into a defence of widow-burning] of not knowing where she stood.

'I don't know how you feel about it,' Harry pursued, 'but please don't lump me in with all that lot.'

'But Harry, the Crawfords – for instance – they are not like Dr Saunders, you know they're not. Or the Minnies. Or for that matter Douglas and –'

'You?'

'All are the same,' the Nawab said suddenly and decisively.

Olivia had a shock – did he mean her too? Was she included? She looked at his face and was frightened by the feelings she saw so plainly expressed there: and it seemed to her that she could not bear to be included in these feelings, that she would do anything *not* to be. (p. 122)

Colonialism is not *her* game, as she has said. Yet like Sofia, she is to pay for it, though the Nawab eventually assures her that she is exempt. She is not. At the close of this scene, the Nawab brings on the male-only entertainment of the eunuchs (it is here that he compares Mrs Crawford to one), as if to reassure Olivia that she is an exception. Yet the dancing hijra signal not benign fun, as he pretends, but a sinister trap into which Olivia is being subtly drawn. Ruth Jhabvala's language indicates this by its very flatness: 'It was then that he called his attendant young men and ordered eunuchs to be brought to sing and dance. And for the rest of Olivia's stay that day she had a very enjoyable time.'

Olivia is enlightened enough, in 1923, to be a cultural relativist, one of *us*! But she is liable to some confusion: she believes the Nawab to be 'almost like one of us . . . so entirely *emancipated*' (p. 69). Olivia sees in the Nawab a contrast to all that is unattractive and dull in her compatriots, very much as Ruth Jhabvala's contemporary English and American girls see India as a relief from the empty materialism of the West.

The narrator delineates the progress of Olivia's attraction to the Nawab in the subtlest of signs: her vulnerability to his 'bad mood' and relief when he is 'nice again' (p. 43); her embarrassment at his 'intense gaze' (p. 47); her own compulsive gaze toward the palace (p. 118); her gaiety and her despondency which gradually come to revolve around the Nawab's mood. And all the while Harry is clearly in thrall, so that an atmosphere of charged emotion is created and maintained around the Nawab. Then, when he takes her to the shrine of Baba Firdaus for the second time, they come upon a band of dacoits (bandits), dangerous and armed, who fall at the Nawab's feet. The dacoits stand humbly before him with a look of 'adoration' on their 'desperado faces' (p. 133). The Nawab's power is underlined, and so is its eroticism. He is well aware of the eroticism of power, for he chooses this moment to recall the exploits of his ancestor, the Amanullah Khan, who murdered an entire party of guests to avenge a rather minor slight. As he concludes his tale of violence, rather horribly referring to 'the blood . . . so fresh and new', Olivia is as if mesmerised by his Gothic tale: 'She could not escape him now, even if she had wanted to' (p. 137). Olivia is as fascinated as Harry was, and for the first time the seduction is consummated.

MOTIFS: GRAVEYARDS, HUSBANDS, PIANOS, HIJRA

Like suttee, other plot elements are multi-layered, and accrue new levels of significance as they are used again and again. I have already spoken of the repeated use of the shrine of Baba Firdaus, which figures as a trysting place in the old and the new story. To take another example, graveyards figure prominently in both the old and the new story. By an Italian statue marking the grave of the Anglo-Indian Saunders's baby (Mrs Saunders never ceases to grieve for it) Olivia and Douglas discuss Olivia's pregnancy, which she too is to lose. At the very same graveside, the modern narrator decides *not* to tell Inder Lal that she is pregnant, which decision underlines a new female autonomy. Both Olivia and the narrator read to their companions the same, significant text, a gravestone inscription: '*As a soldier ever ready where Duty called him, a dutiful son, a kind and indulgent Father but most conspicuous in the endearing character of Husband*' (p. 105). Each then flatteringly compares her companion to the remembered soul. But the thought is more a wish than a reality, for *neither* is a good husband: not Douglas, who idealises and neglects Olivia; not Inder Lal, who derogates and neglects Ritu. The novel may be taken to ask, indeed, what *is* a good husband, and can there be one? Not when the sexes misconstrue each other as Douglas and Olivia do, as the Nawab and Olivia do, as Inder Lal and Ritu do. The modern narrator, whose vision is clearest, has no husband.

Taking up the idea, the 'Husband's Wedding Day' figures importantly in both plots. It is the cause of violent rioting between Hindus and Muslims in the 1923 tale; it is a lively women's holiday in the new story; again underlining the ascendency of women in the modern plot. However, there is rich irony in the motif, for the 'Husband's Wedding Day' is, we are told, a Hindu festival day on which it is customary to make offerings 'to cure childlessness' (p. 66). The full story is instructive and significant: a childless wife had been driven out of 'her husband's home' to permit him to marry again. She comes to the shrine of Baba Firdaus to 'hide her shame and grief'. She prays for help, and help is given: she conceives. Thenceforth the shrine is known to be particularly powerful for the misfortune of childlessness.

One learns from this story that in the Hindu tradition, as in others, a woman is liable to shame and even divorce – an economic catastrophe – if she does not bear children. On the other hand, if she does – at the wrong time – there are also problems. And even if she conceives at the *right* time, things can go badly. For example, at the shrine of Baba Firdaus (sacred to Hindu women only on the 'Husband's Wedding Day') the narrator recounts a story told by one of the 'merry widow' friends of Inder Lal's mother: a young woman who is intending to have 'an operation on her fallopian tubes' is saved from this fate by the timely intervention of her mother-in-law, who brings her to the shrine and succeeds in bringing about conception. But the widow adds, as an afterthought, that the young woman in the story was driven from her home: since the husband (her son) had 'a spell put on him by another woman and this made him drive his wife and her new-born child out of the house' (p. 67).

Black humour, this. (Suddenly the sought-after offspring is *her* new-born child.) The little story neatly demonstrates, first, the powerlessness of women in the traditional society, and next the habit – which crosses gender lines, and, of course, is entrenched in the West as well – of attributing magical evil powers to them; in short, of blaming them for everything.[14]

But Ms Rivers is unmarried. 'Everything is different now', she says. Though the parallels of the dual plot invite us to mark what has not changed, they force the recognition of difference. The contemporary limits of behaviour for European women have vastly expanded, to the point where the narrator is able to create her own mores as she goes along, working on her writings, casually sleeping with two men, neither of whom is her husband, and deciding to keep the pregnancy that results.

Another significant repeated motif is that of pianos. Pianos connote the best of European values. Olivia plays the piano in her drawing room, and Harry loves to come and listen to her play. He calls the room 'The Oasis'. She plays Schumann, whose lyrical, nostalgic pieces suggest the most refined middle-class domesticity: 'Kinderscenen', perhaps.[15] Harry is entranced. 'Lovely', he says, 'like a man being given a cool drink' (p. 72).

By contrast, the two pianos in the Nawab's palace are decaying homes for small rodents, though the Nawab shows interest in sending for a tuner (he thinks it is a machine) from Europe. There is a piano in the mountain retreat in which Olivia ends her days – 'she still played the same pieces of piano music' (p. 180). And years later, when the Nawab comes to London to try to get an increase on his government retainer, and visits Harry and Harry's lover Ferdie, the motif makes a final appearance. The Nawab spends his afternoons in a popular London restaurant, with marble pillars 'not unlike the Palace at Khatm', and there 'a lady in a long teagown' plays musical selections on 'a multi-coloured organ'. The Nawab listens with pleasure, and remarks to Harry on her resemblance to Olivia. The narrator comments, 'He had always been quite unmusical' (p. 117).

Like the modern narrator – a writer – Olivia participates in acts of aesthetic creation, however secondary: she plays the piano and does embroidery. The arts she practises are domestic: traditionally considered to be feminine and hence trivial. Neither she nor anyone else takes them very seriously. Still, she persists in them, and presumably they give her satisfaction.

But the Nawab's rotting pianos signify his empty appropriation of the Western symbols of leisure and class. His unmusicality, furthermore, indicates a fundamental lack of sensibility. For Jhabvala, musical acuity usually stands for emotional understanding or at least sexual and sensual awareness. (Compare the music master in 'The Housewife', or Ahmet, the playful and sensitive musician-lover, in 'An Experience of India', or another Ahmed, Marietta's musician-lover in *In Search of Love and Beauty*. Even the S.P. in 'Desecration' is musical.) Particularly by the end of the novel, we see the Nawab without Olivia's romantic lens. In the London setting he is middle-brow and effeminate – a kind of

Liberace figure – yet oddly endearing: a far cry from Olivia's dark fantasy.

In the early passages of the novel, the modern narrator introduces the 'hijra' motif, which also appears as part of the 1923 story. 'There is one word that is often called after me: *hijra*' (p. 9). It no longer surprises her to be called after in the street, marked as an outsider and a curiosity. She knows the meaning of the word, since it has been used in Olivia's letters. The Nawab had compared flat-chested Mrs Crawford (the narrator's great aunt) to one; to demonstrate, he had had a troupe brought in. He 'made them sing and dance for Olivia in their traditional style' (p. 10).

Hijra are eunuchs, men who as boys have been deliberately castrated so that they can derive a living from their disability; they are disreputable singer-dancers. The traditional practice apparently still continues, a reminder to the reader of the abysmal poverty that is part of Indian life. Worse handicaps (crippling, maiming and blinding) are deliberately inflicted on children by 'beggar masters', to enable them to beg to greater advantage. Such are the realities of Indian economics. Be they tourists, wanderers or colonial administrators, Westerners must be shaken by the stark reminders of their vast privilege compared to others.[16]

A number of issues, then, are conflated in this one image. The narrator, tall and flat-chested by Indian standards, strikes the Indians as masculine, or at least as an embodiment of an ambiguous and freakish sexuality. As a young woman travelling alone she is viewed with deep suspicion and stigmatised more than a male tourist would be. When little boys run after her shouting the comparison to hijra, their invective is as significant and intuitively precise as a graffito, and the aural equivalent of one. Graffiti say the unsayable things that everyone knows: as 'everyone knew that Western girls were brought up on sex, lived on sex'.[17] As usual, national and class resentment is channelled on to women.

As the modern narrator strolls through Satipur with Inder Lal, they hear singing. Inder Lal is reluctant to accompany her to its source but she insists. Deep within a series of arches and court-yards, they come to the troupe of eunuchs 'smirking' and making suggestive gestures to the amusement of a group of spectators. All the while, she notes, they bear the 'worried workaday' expressions of those who 'are wondering how much they are going to be paid for the job' (p. 10).

The awful reality behind each man's personal story (each was once a normal boy, each suffered the mutilation with the knowledge of his family) is smoothed to normal ordinariness. It is the same with the other reminders that half the world's people are hungry all the time. But as our guide in India, Jhabvala places these reminders deliberately in our path.

Oddly, the hijra are not viewed as asexual, as one might assume, but, on the contrary, are objectified and sexualised to the point of parody. Like the effeminate homosexuals of Genet, their existence serves, at least partially, to bolster and support established male and female roles.[18] They parody women, and at the same time flatter men by the comparison. For the Western reader, as for the European characters in the novel, they shock: they are troubling human symbols of a cruel and nightmarish sexuality.

Like effeminate homosexuals in the West, hijra are stigmatised. The stigma that attaches to them is related to the stigma that attaches to marginal women, such as the narrator in this novel, or Margaret and Lee in Jhabvala's previous one. Western women wanderers – especially lone ones – are, like the hijra, at once desexualised and hypersexualised: they are not *women*, exactly, yet to them are attributed the most spectacularly sexual appetites and behaviours. Furthermore, the narrator has taken for herself what even we in the West view as male privilege: to wander aimlessly, to explore the world. A young woman walking by herself is, in most places in the world, a puzzling sight. No wonder she is viewed as half-male.

This is the context of the narrator's story, and even of Olivia's. While the notion that 'Western girls were brought up on sex, lived on sex' cannot have attained its contemporary popularity and scope as early as 1923 (the post-Second World-War influx of Western travellers had, of course, not yet begun, nor, indeed, had the postwar Western sexual revolution) still, by the early twenties the Nawab's notions about Englishwomen are not unlike Inder Lal's. The Nawab jokes that Englishwomen love not sex but horses (p. 45): one sees that the notion of English sexual inadequacy has already taken hold. The Nawab scoffs at, and dismisses, the idea that Douglas may have caused Olivia's pregnancy.

Western women, third-world men; white women, black men; they constitute a dialectic about which much can be, and has been said, and much of what has been said is the worst combination of sexual and racial stereotype. Certainly racism, that is, the hatred, devaluation and utilisation of darker peoples by lighter ones, is always connected to obsessive sexual notions: fear of 'miscegenation', the ostensible elevation of some women to the status of totemic untouchables, and the degradation of others. Racism is always associated with fascism and exaggerated patriarchism: women are objects to be fought over, 'protected', or raped.

Jhabvala's fiction takes as a starting point the defiance of the racial and patriarchal taboo: not only do her wandering women exercise sexual freedom, but they do so with Indian men. But though their actions defy Western patriarchy, they invite loud disapproval from non-Western patriarchal society as well (including women, of course).

Sexuality brings into focus the strife between classes, nations, races: 'Desecration' illustrates the dynamic; so does *Heat and Dust*. The Indians think Western 'girls' are oversexed, the Westerners think Indian men are oversexed. The phrase 'They only think about one thing' is said of each group by the other.

So when the little boys run after the narrator calling her a hijra, all these ideas are telescoped. The scenario is extraordinary and unprecedented: never before have substantial numbers of young women, travelling alone, ventured casually to explore the realities of the world Out There. The young woman wanderer, as she confronts the urban populations of Mexico, Morocco or India, has not left those places unchanged, as she has not remained unchanged by them. And the myths on both sides are never absent from her experience in these places: 'They only think about one thing.'

The narrator, like Olivia before her, enters unknown and dangerous territory. There are no models for what she does, though her *raison d'être* is to research her predecessor Olivia. The modern narrator will go much further than Olivia could. She will wear Indian dress, because it is cooler and cheaper (the only sandals that fit her are the men's sizes – again, the eunuch association). She will live in the Indian section of the town – indeed, in Satipur there is no other. And, as I have said, as a woman – in her sexual liaisons, in her choice of bearing a child – she will exercise an autonomy unavailable to Olivia.

Heat and Dust attempts to capture a subject for which no forerunner exists, simply because the subject itself is so new: the unattached, non-aristocratic Western woman in the third world. In this it is a sort of *Heart of Darkness au féminin*. It is a pleasing coincidence that, like Conrad's, Jhabvala's first nationality was

Polish. (Although to describe her background as 'Polish', as does the jacket copy of her earlier novels, is quite misleading, and later it is more accurately identified as 'Polish-Jewish'.[19]) Certainly this novel echoes Conrad's, as it echoes James's mystery tale within a tale, and as it echoes *Passage to India*. Moreover, as with Conrad, James and Forster, we never do learn precisely what happened: but now sexual mystery, while powerful and potentially destructive, is finally seen as benign, at least in the modern story. Olivia's misadventure leads to her withdrawal, which may have led, the novel suggests, to a joyful affirmation.

We do not know, finally, what becomes of Olivia. Did she pass her last years gazing at a joyful vision of beauty that 'suffused her soul'? The narrator suggests this as a possibility. Once installed in her Himalayan retreat, she chooses to remain: she could have left at any time. She is, as far as we know, largely alone there: the Nawab divides his time between her, his mother and his wife. Olivia outlives him – and still remains. She even specifies that she wishes to be cremated, in the Hindu manner, rather than buried. That choice is a major clue to the mystery of her life.

The narrator offers the view that while it seems 'ludicrous' to compare Olivia to the other Europeans who lived out their lives in India – 'religious seekers, adventurers and Christian missionaries' – like them, she did stay on; and that the only way to find out what became of her is to follow her: 'that is, stay on' (p. 159).

Like the shrine of Baba Firdaus, Olivia's mountain cottage becomes a sort of shrine for the narrator, and Olivia beatified – *perhaps*. The olive tree for which she is named connotes peace and victory. One recalls that the Rivers's cottage is now the Water Board, a witty repetition of the miraculous-spring fable told about Baba Firdaus's shrine. But Olivia's story has an ambiguous ending, still shrouded, as it were, in mystery and mist. Like the peaks of the Himalayas, which are 'blotted out' by mists, Olivia's story remains unclear.

NATURE IMAGERY

Mountain peaks, particularly, of course, the Himalayas, connote spiritual awakening and heightened knowledge. The descriptions of their beauty certainly suggest that in this novel the various ascents to the mountain tops are presented in a positive light. Olivia's flight, however, is deeply ambiguous, because not wholly voluntary. It is at once an ascent to integrity, representing the withdrawal of the artist, and an admission of failure to live on the plains of human intercourse.

Throughout Jhabvala's novels, religious experience is associated with beauty, nature and withdrawal. Gurus may be bogus, but contemplative connection with nature is not. The Nawab may be a manipulative charlatan, but the Himalaya's promise of beauty is real. The narrator imagines the highest of mountains, topped by the whitest of snows, luminous against a sky of 'a deeper blue than any yet known to me' (p. 180). And this, she guesses, Olivia saw, this was the 'vision' that 'filled her eyes . . . and suffused her soul'. The mountains will offer direct, unmediated communion with the blue skies – even if now those skies are full of rain clouds. But those rain clouds signify a relief from the heat and dust – the obsessive sexuality – that plagued Olivia: a real relief, rather than the false hope represented by the Nawab, who plays on Olivia's obsession by using water as an image. For example, at the Shrine of Baba Firdaus he makes much of this 'little spring which came freshly bubbling out of a cleft between some stones' (p. 46) – the language is clearly sexual.

Squatting by the water, he invites Olivia to dabble her fingers in the spring, looking at her 'intensely'; she looks down at her own hands, covered just barely by the fresh, fast-running water. As shallow as the spring, the relief he seems to offer is illusory.

The dry, parched plains, void of moisture, represent in the language of images, a landscape of maleness. It is noteworthy that Olivia's seduction and 'ruin' are accomplished in an exclusively masculine society, in the absence of the colonial wives: Mrs Minnies and Mrs Crawford have gone up to the mountain resort Simla to spend the hot months. (The term 'grass-widow' actually derives from this common convention in Anglo-Indian life: husbands stayed on the plains, wives ascended to Simla or other hill-stations.)

Exceptionally, Olivia chooses to brave the summer heat, thought too harsh for the delicate English ladies – even though they call themselves 'tough old hens'.[20] She cannot bear to be separated from Douglas, her newly wedded husband. But the novel shows her rapid disillusionment, as Douglas's administrative duties take up his time and energy, and leave her constantly at a loose end.

The heat and the dust parch and scorch the landscape, generating a yearning for escape and relief that is identified with sexual longing: Olivia is now particularly susceptible to the fascination of the Nawab. The narrator stresses the alienating and dangerous exclusive maleness of the society. Like Sofia, who was present where no ladies would venture, Olivia rejects the Westernised 'purdah' of the Anglo-Indian lady, and places herself in jeopardy by this action alone.

As if to underline the breaking of that taboo, Major Minnies now expounds what one might call his 'heart of darkness' theories – at a dinner party at which Olivia is the only lady present: it is dangerous to go too far, one must hold back, with a 'virile, measured, *European* feeling'. 'One should never . . . allow oneself to become softened (like Indians) by an excess of feeling', he warns (p. 171). Of course, it is precisely that apocalyptic abandon that Olivia wants. Major Minnies gives himself as a negative example, confessing that he himself has 'stepped over too far' into 'the other dimension' that is his emotional response to India. He recites the Urdu poetry of the Nawab's ancestor ('the old Nawab'). There had once been a yearly symposium of poets at Khatm. What a contrast to the philistinism of the colonialists: 'Are those dew drops on the rose, or are they tears? Moon, your silver light turns all to pearls.' The romantic lines evoke the theme of this novel: *Heat and Dust* too addresses the ambiguity of eros. One cannot know whether the erotic impulse (again, imaged by water) is to lead to relief (dew) or sorrow (tears). But at this point Olivia has little patience for literary ambiguity. She is caught in an exclusively female dilemma: pregnant at the wrong time, by the wrong man. Major Minnies may think he has gone too far, but how much further she has gone!

The mountains that Olivia, and the narrator after her, ascend represent an opposition to the heat and dust of the plains. They give relief both from boredom and from the obsessional sexual yearning associated with the flatness and the summer heat. As the plains represent a threatening and violent masculine world, the world of patriarchal society, which confines and derogates women, the mountains represent, particularly for the modern narrator, an escape route to a mythic, sybilline nurturance, which is associated with archetypal femaleness. Having left the parched plains, the narrator tells us that she rarely looks down, revelling instead in the air of the mountains, 'so drenched with moisture that the birds seem to swim about in it and the trees wave like sea weed' (p. 180).

Its imagery suggests that this novel may be read as a female-centred reworking of Conrad's – and Major Minnies' – 'Heart of Darkness' theories. The Western horror of abandonment to the irrational – the non-Western – is reversed. In nature and the non-rational (as opposed to the irrational) lies a spiritual relief. (Patriarchal) societies, Indian or occidental, embody horror: certainly it is real. But a joyful or beatified vision *is* available, and should be sought: all human beings need the freedom to seek it, through whatever means. Olivia tried one route (sexuality) but was led, perforce, to another (withdrawal). The women in the modern story will offer other possibilities of quest.

THE 'NEW' STORY: HOLY MOTHERS

Male-Centred Past and Female-Centred Present: The Begum and Maji

The 'old' story has Olivia rejecting the confines of her role and casting herself adrift in a dangerous and exclusively masculine world. The Anglo-Indian ladies' departure exaggerates the masculinity of that world, but even in their presence, the colonial India of 1923 glorifies 'masculine' virtues of heroism, courage and honour. Nor is this confined to the colonialists, for the Nawab, like Douglas, dreams of the exploits of his warrior forbears. Both idealise their ancestors: the Nawab compares himself unfavourably to the Amanullah Khan, and Douglas admiringly recalls the various Rivers officers 'lying in graveyards in other parts of India' (p. 154). While there is one powerful female presence in the old story, the Begum, she is very much behind the scenes, scheming and plotting for the advance of her son. It is a society in which men and masculine virtues are all-important.

The modern India of the 'new' story is peopled by women; women are visible and important in the plot. The modern narrator who comes there has, of course, rejected the traditional female role as her culture defined it. Perhaps because of this alone, she finds in modern India a society of women, a world in which women exercise a certain amount of autonomy. It is a colourful, chaotic, unpredictable world, built around an ethos that seems the polar opposite either of the colonialists' military dutifulness or the

Nawab's aristocratic heroism. In this world, humane practice takes precedence over inhumane theory. Women use their power to the good, of others, in addition to themselves. Good humour and cheerfulness are elevated, the allure of romance is downplayed. The modern narrator guards and insists upon her still-limited freedom to explore the *experiential* world.

The reader encounters the Nawab in the modern story, but it is a very different Nawab who visits London and calls upon Harry (and Harry's current companion, Ferdie). Now effeminised, he is so fat as to appear 'womanly', and he embraces Harry in a 'womanly' way, holding him against his 'plump chest' and keeping him there 'for a long time' (p. 175). He is 'softer and milder' and he had 'got into the habit of eating a great number of cream pastries' (p. 176). We learn that at last he meets his death in New York, 'in the Park Avenue apartment of the ancient Begum and in her arms' (p. 177). The slightly ludicrous yet amiable fellow hardly seems the same person who had held Harry and Olivia in thrall.

Each story contains a powerful, even mysterious, widow, and it is useful to compare them. The Begum is dangerous if crossed: she is not above ordering poisoned garments (p. 151) or smuggling jewels (p. 177). It is she who engineers Olivia's futile abortion: she must have known that it would be likely to lead to discovery and ruin. After all, Olivia was not the first woman to be found out by Dr Saunders, who had, the narrator points out, 'extracted many such twigs' from other women wanting 'miscarriages', and then had had them 'thrown out' of the hospital, after giving them an outraged lecture (p. 169). The dénouement – Olivia being found out, the Anglo-Indian community being shamed, and there being no issue, either black- or tow-headed – would exactly suit the Begum's purposes. Though the suggestion is not explicitly made, it seems probable that the Begum knew very well what would become of Olivia.

In keeping with her *modus operandi*, the Begum rarely appears 'onstage' in the novel, though her malevolent, watchful presence is felt everywhere in the royal palace. But after Olivia's first, formal meeting with her, with Mrs Minnies and Mrs Crawford, she sees her only once more, at the moment of her abortion: as the midwives bend over Olivia, one inserting the pointed twig into her body, the Begum is present. She too bends over Olivia. When Olivia cries out in pain the Begum looks into her face: 'She seemed as interested to study Olivia's face as Olivia was to study hers.' Olivia inwardly marks her resemblance to the Nawab. 'For a moment they gazed into each other's eyes and then Olivia had to shut hers, as the pain down below was repeated' (p. 168). It is a macabre confrontation, fraught with overtones of sexuality and violation, yet at the same time almost friendly. The two women are interested in each other and gaze into each other's eyes. In the context of Jhabvala's other fiction, in which there is an underlying theme of longing for, yet flight from, connections with other women, it represents a nightmarish fulfilment of women's distrust of other women: the intimate female Other as evil stepmother and malevolent rival who has the power to destroy one.

In contrast to all this, Maji, the equivalent mother-figure of the new story, is cheerful, radiant and benevolent. Beginning with her name – 'Honoured Mother', she is a touchstone of nurturance. In contrast to the Begum, Maji is an earthy peasant woman. Far from causing the loss of another woman's baby, Maji is instrumental in preventing the narrator's abortion – although certainly not for ideological reasons. Like the midwives of the earlier story, who may well have been her grandmothers, she knows how to perform an abortion since in some cases it is 'the only way to save people from dishonour and suffering' – an attitude noteworthy for its eminent tolerance and good sense (p. 139). She will do whatever the narrator wishes. Thus it is she who forces the narrator to confront and acknowledge her wish to keep the pregnancy 'and the completely new feeling – of rapture – of which it was the cause' (p. 165).

As the descendant of a long line of midwives, and heir to a tradition in which women healers and practitioners dealt with birthing, Maji has access to the privileged phenomenon of entrance into the world. The narrator feels her to be 'a supernatural figure with supernatural powers' (p. 173), or even 'some mythological figure: one of those potent Indian goddesses who hold life and death in one hand and play them like a yo-yo' (p. 164).

Maji is an adept practitioner of yoga, and easily enters and leaves the ecstatic contemplative samadhi state. In samadhi, the adept enters a higher level of consciousness and is 'submerged in its bliss', as the narrator explains (p. 163): she describes Maji's lotus pose, her open eyes with pupils rolled up, her regular, peaceful breathing. She speaks too of Maji's easy, casual re-entry into ordinary consciousness, her welcoming smile to the narrator, 'as if nothing at all had occurred'. The ecstatic state is compared to 'a revivifying bath' – again, water represents spiritual renewal. Maji's easy transitions between states of consciousness echo her ease and familiarity with the crucial transitional points of the life-cycle, birth and, as we shall see, death.

After this meditation, Maji gives the narrator a massage that could, if she wished, lead to abortion. The scene echoes Olivia's abortion, yet now there is no pain, but a 'soothing quality' in Maji's hands. As those hands 'pass slowly down my womb' they seek out and press certain parts within, imparting to the narrator 'the waves of energy that had come to her from elsewhere' (p. 164); the narrator has the feeling that she is 'transmitting something to me – not taking away, but giving' (p. 165). Whatever she transmits enables the narrator to acknowledge a completely new idea – the 'rapture' of her pregnancy.

If patriarchal systems punish women with shame and pain in sex and childbirth, as Eve and her daughters are punished, Maji, and through her the narrator, taps into an all-but-forgotten matriarchist tradition, restoring female sexuality, of which birth is an aspect, to its proper, sacred, place.

Reassuring the narrator in general, and later particularly approving of her plan to 'go further, up into the mountains' (p. 173), Maji gives the lie to Major Minnies's patriarchist theories that India always finds out and presses on one's weak spots: for doing exactly that, Maji's hands have a benignant power.

WIVES AND WIDOWS IN SATIPUR

The theme of suttee, which figures so prominently in Olivia's story, is taken up again in the modern narrator's sections, in which widows predominate. Maji and all her friends, that rollicking band of companions, are 'merry widows'.

In 'The Widow' (*Like Birds, Like Fishes*) the traditional view is set forth: the widow is 'the cursed one who had committed the sin of outliving her husband and was consequently to be numbered among the outcasts'. Her relatives should 'shave her head . . . reduce her diet to stale bread and lentils, and deprive her from ever again tasting the sweet things of life; condemn her to that perpetual mourning, perpetual expiation, which was the proper lot of widows'. Such vicious hounding would seem to call for some explanation; the traditional rationale seems to have been fear of the voracious, untrammelled independent female sexuality, for widows might 'feed their own passions too, and that which should have died in them with the deaths of their husbands would fester and boil and overflow into sinful channels'. Perhaps, however, one might explain such attitudes as representing a measure of insurance against wives ever toying with the idea of murdering their husbands! At any rate, the ideas that emerge in 'The Widow' indicate something of the official status of widows in traditional Hindu village life.

How does one reconcile these notions with the descriptions of Maji and her friends, such as, for example, Inder Lal's mother, who knows that now is the best time of her life, and has not a very 'high opinion of married life' (p. 53). Inder Lal's mother is fiftyish; she is healthy and 'full of feminine vigor' (p. 53). In contrast to her daughter-in-law, she leaves home often, to go on outings with her many friends, also 'healthy widows'. They 'roam' quite freely around the town, with a fine disregard for modesty, not caring if their saris slip down to reveal their heads or even their breasts. Like schoolgirls, they joke and giggle – 'very different from their daughters-in-law who are sometimes seen shuffling behind them, heavily veiled and silent and with the downcast eyes of prisoners under guard' (p. 54).

Officially, the Hindu tradition, like the Judeo-Christian one, stipulates a life of meek servility for women. Luckily, women have ways of circumventing, subverting or mocking the code, even while paying lip-service to the official code: Inder Lal's mother 'seemed regretful – this merry widow! – that [suttee] had been discontinued' (p. 55). If religion and tradition assign widows one role, circumstances permitting, they take another. These widows, luckily able to make the most of their independence, triumph over the patriarchal marriage system in their husbandless days. Their lives represent the welcome triumph of practice over theory: and practice, with its unexpected particularities, its arena for the force of personality, its quirks of circumstance – real life – is the stuff of which comedy is made. The band of merry widows and the narrator now picnic gaily and make risqué jokes at the shrine of Baba Firdaus, where Olivia was seduced: a spot which seemed, in her portion of the story, to reverberate with mystery, danger and a Gothic sexual excitement.

Another widow, however, is not so lucky. Leelavati the beggar-woman illustrates the cruel workings of the system. The unfortunate combination of widowhood and ordinary ill-luck have brought her to the wretchedness of her present state: after her husband's death she had been 'driven out' of her father-in-law's house (no further explanation is offered, or deemed necessary); then an epidemic of smallpox had carried off her parents and brother. And so the narrator encounters her, dying alone and unnoticed in the middle of a village not her own.

Even through Leelavati's wretchedness is stressed, the goddess-like Maji manages to turn her dying from an occasion of horror to a privileged moment. Unlike the caste-bound, indifferent Indians, Maji, who as a midwife is probably an Untouchable, does attend Leelavati. As she has assisted so many times at the passage into life, Maji now stands guard over the passage out. Taking Leelavati's head in her lap, she gazes at her and strokes her face. Suddenly Leelavati smiles a baby's toothless, blissful smile – a smile that indicates her recognition of Maji's 'love and tenderness', a smile that seems 'a miracle' to the narrator. Maji praises the old woman for her hard work: 'now it is time. Now she has done enough' (p. 115). Again, water is used as a rich image of the continuity and nurturance of life, even, or perhaps especially, at this moment. 'As the glow faded and sky and air and water turned pale silver and the birds fell asleep in the dark trees and now only soundless bats flitted black across the silver sky: at that lovely hour she died' (p. 115). Maji says she has done well and has been rewarded with 'a good, blessed end' (p. 115). To her the Hindu ethos yields meaning: one accepts one's preordained lot, one's Karma, and does the best one can.

The widow Leelavati provides one contrast to the powerful Maji. The wife Ritu represents another. Ritu illustrates the enslavement of women in a society as relentlessly patriarchal as contemporary India: if female infanticide and suttee are disappearing, 'dowry death', the murder of young women whose dowry payments are deemed insufficient, is widespread enough to have a name. One recalls Ruth Jhabvala's reference to it in *A New Dominion*.

Although it is not the province of this study to discuss the social and economic realities of contemporary India, a few global realities may be mentioned: starvation is the foremost, and after that the evils of illiteracy and destitution, which affect women more than men in the vast societies of privation of which India is but one. The traditional violence of female infanticide and suttee, though outlawed, are thought to continue today in India in remote villages – and most of India consists of remote villages.[21]

One gathers from Jhabvala's fiction that there exists an oppressive weight of Indian social violence against women, however it may be circumvented or subverted. Because of the dowry system, a daughter represents an economic liability no matter how much she may be loved (Jhabvala's short story 'Sixth Child' in *Like Birds, Like Fishes* tells the tale).

Child-marriage may be illegal, but girls must still be married by their mid-teens, and the idea of female input in the choosing of a mate is traditionally regarded as a social evil. *To Whom She Will*, Ruth Jhabvala's first novel, is built around this theme, as I have mentioned. Worse still, by tradition a girl is expected to leave her parents' house in her early teens, for the harsh rule of the mother-in-law, and not until the birth of a son is her place assured. Thrust into an alien household where her position is absolutely the lowest and her worth adjudged by factors beyond her control (good looks and light skin raise her value), her situation seems truly bleak. Traditionally the women of the husband's family resent her and her relationship with their son/brother. With these enemies she must reside, often at a prohibitive distance from her own family. No wonder that psychological studies of Indian women have shown that 'a common theme of their personalities is a sense of standing alone among unfriendly forces of nature'.[22] One is given glimpses of the domestic battle-ground in many of Jhabvala's works (such as *The Nature of Passion* or *Get Ready for Battle*).

Even Western commentators generally fail to take into account the position of Hindu women when lauding the Indian family system. For example, the editors of the US *Area Handbook for India* write: 'Although strong ties of loyalty bind son to father and brother to brother, the strongest ties of sentiment are those binding son to mother and brother to sister.'[23] The subject is assumed to be male. What of ties of loyalty between daughter and mother or between sisters?

The global disenfranchisement of women, then, and the patrilocal marriage-system in particular, form the backdrop for *Heat and Dust*. Ritu and the Nawab's unseen wife Sandy are the only two Indian wives in the novel: both are mad. The narrator is not at first aware of the extent of Ritu's desperation. With unintentional irony, she wonders at Ritu's state of mind – does she not 'get tired' of the two rooms in which she is shut up all day and every day, with three small children and a mother-in-law? It is not long before we appreciate the dark humour, for Ritu is literally mad with being tired of it. Even her mother-in-law admits that 'it is difficult to get used to the new family and to the rule of the mother-in-law' (p. 53). Inder Lal gives his own assessment: she had cried, he says, all the time during the first years of their marriage, for homesickness – even though he and his mother 'tried to explain matters to her' – one can imagine! It was, he recounts, Ritu's fault that their child was born weak, since she had wept and refused to 'be happy', for 'an intelligent person would have understood and taken care' (p. 50).

Ritu is 'frail, *weak*' (p. 51). So 'shy' is she that at the narrator's approach she flees to the malodorous bathroom. The wild fits to which she is subject are treated by the application of red-hot irons to her arms and to the soles of her feet – an old remedy which her mother-in-law orders. Eventually she too ascends to Simla to take the cure of the mountains, and disappears from the narrator's life and from the novel. Yet her desperation and madness indicate Jhabvala's horror at the lot of the young wife in a traditional patrilocal marriage.

On a more psychoanalytic level, one may read Ritu as a 'madwoman in the attic', to use the term coined by Susan Gubar and Sandra Gilbert.[24] Ritu embodies an hysteria which symbolically balances the detached coolness and flatness of the narrator's voice, perhaps giving vent to a despair at once suggested and denied by her quiet calm. Certainly, Ritu's fits at once convey the inarticulate anguish of women in wretched circumstances, and symbolically release the emotions that the narrator's flat tone leaves out.

DISREGARDING POLLUTION TABOOS

Of the Indian characters, Ritu and Leelavati on the one hand, and Maji and her 'merry widows' on the other, represent submission and resistance to the politics of gender. Another way in which the modern story illustrates humane non-adherence to inhumane theory is the modern narrator's penchant for disregarding the pollution taboos of the traditional systems of caste.

The results of Hindu pollution taboos seem to strike the Western visitor with particular immediacy. Many contemporary travel

accounts refer to the shock of finding human excrement plainly
visible, even in well-travelled public places. V. S. Naipaul, for
example, must remind himself that 'it was unclean to clean; it was
unclean even to notice. It was the business of the sweepers to
remove excrement, and until the sweepers came, people were
content to live in the midst of their own excrement.'[25] In the
narrator's rooms in *Heat and Dust* the sweeper is a little girl, who
'is not too good at her job' (p. 51). Caste dictates that the task be
alloted to an Untouchable, the pariah caste that continues to exist
(despite the Gandhian offensive), and of Untouchables, the lowliest
are female.

Three times in the modern tale, the narrator comes to the aid
of someone lying in his or her own excrement, usually in full
view of others who cannot or do not consider helping the
unfortunate. The first time, she finds Chid groaning with fever
inside one of the royal tombs; Inder Lal has warned her not to
investigate the groans, but as usual she disregards him. They
eventually take 'the white sadhu' home with them to recover in
the narrator's rooms.

The second time, the narrator finds Leelavati dying 'on the
outskirts of a mound of refuse'. There is a 'terrible smell'; her eyes
are open and she too is groaning. The washerman's wife and the
coalman who live nearby have no time for the woman; nor indeed
does the administrating physician in the Satipur hospital: beds are
scarce. I have already referred to lyrical passages in which Maji
comes to her aid, unimpeded by the pollution taboos.

The third instance occurs at the Satipur hospital (the very same
hospital that Dr Saunders directed in the 1923 story). Chid's illness
has progressed. He now sits among the rows of destitute patients
holding out bowls into which will be 'thrown lumps of cold rice
and lentils'. This food, says the narrator – with what restrained
bitterness! – is 'served up with the contempt reserved for those
who have nothing and no one' (p. 157).

Bringing food to Chid, the narrator notices an old man whose
most immediate difficulty is that he cannot pay the sweepers to
remove his bedpan. Finding him 'in great distress because he had
been left there for several hours' she herself does the job, thus
effectively taking on the status of an Untouchable. Sickened by the
task, she politely tries to hide her disgust 'so as not to hurt anyone's
feelings' – but she has, it appears, already 'done enough'. People
are shocked; she has offended by the commission of an act of

pollution – and the man himself refuses to accept the food she offers!

The narrator's repeated disregard of the taboos of caste and pollution work to underline the theme of the modern story: the triumph of the anti-idealistic, in this case as a corrective, however partial, to the dictates of ideology. It does not seem insignificant that women (Maji and the narrator) break the inhumane pollution taboos, and a man upholds them – even against himself.

ANTI-ROMANTIC LOVERS

As the modern narrator has taken the male privilege of wandering, so too she gives herself the male privilege of the casual erotic encounter. Her two lovers, one dark and one light, but both comic figures, are foils to the tragic romantic heroes, one dark and one light, of Olivia's story. Chid, the English boy with his enormous erections, his illiterate and unintentionally funny letters, and his crazy grasp of pseudo-Vedic philosophy, certainly poses a contrast to noble Douglas. His name is drolly ironic: 'the Bliss of Mind' when his mind is virtually gone.

In contrast to the Nawab's fascinating power, Inder Lal has a childish charm. He is younger than the narrator: she relishes 'his affection and playfulness' (p. 140). At the shrine of Baba Firdaus, where the Nawab seduced Olivia, the narrator seduces Inder Lal: 'It was my idea' to go there, she says. Inder Lal takes a nap: she wakes him and feeds him English sandwiches, which he eats with interest and curiosity. Somewhat to his annoyance, she guesses *his* wish (to get on in his job); this is not difficult, since the subject occupies him obsessively. But *he* declares himself 'not a magician or other person with powers to read another's thoughts'. She makes the first moves, never minding that 'I could see – it was ludicrous! – how everything he had heard about Western women rushed about in his head' (p. 127).

Love and sexuality, in the romantic tradition, women's special paths to spiritual transcendence, are pleasant but of minor import-ance for the narrator. Mystery and meaning lie more with Maji and her spiritual practices – autonomously and subversively female. The healing powers of comedy colour this half of the novel, just as Maji's laughter lightens her intensity. Even the swamis in the ashram on the mountaintop are 'cheerful men' who 'laugh and joke in booming voices with the people in the bazaar' (p. 181).

More fundamentally, and more deeply embedded in this novel's structure, is the sense that, for the modern narrator, mystery and meaning lie not in romantic engagement, but in the engagement of the artist: traditionally, another male privilege, and another one that the narrator takes for herself. In her writings, her researches and her art are the real focus of her consciousness. Perhaps it is for this reason that she emerges unscathed from her encounter with India. She has withstood its dangers, despite the absence of 'Christ Almighty', and despite her unwillingness to armour herself with the vigilant resistance that the elderly missionary or Major Minnies recommended. Moreover, she ascends to the Himalayas with a child within her: in the realms of imagination and biology, her visit has borne fruit.

LITERARY ALLUSION: *A PASSAGE TO INDIA*

Reviewers of Jhabvala have almost uniformly mentioned her indebtedness to Forster, in this novel among others. Clearly, *Heat and Dust* has many links with *Passage to India*, published in 1924. Both novels explore the resonances of difference, barrier and attraction between a British lady and a Muslim Indian; both ladies take a critical stance toward Anglo-Indian colonialist attitudes. In both novels, innocent Europeans confront with increasing awareness and distress, the ancient and incomprehensible subcontinent and its human representatives. Their heroines share a good deal: Olivia in her frankness, her open-mindedness, her resistance to paternalistic and racist notions and her independence of spirit, recalls Adela Quested. Adela represents another manifestation of the 'presumptuous' heroine who thinks she knows better than her peers, and chooses naïvely. Her very name, 'Quested', suggests that she, like others of her type – Olivia included – is searching for the fulfilment of her high ideals.

Each lady comes to India because of a marriage, either actual or intended, to a colonial administrator; each finds repellent the unenlightened imperial attitudes of her compatriots; each ventures into Indian society, to the shock and disapproval of her peers; each becomes involved with a Muslim; each is viewed with incomprehension by Indians and British alike, and each is disgraced and finally repudiated by her man – in Adela's case, the fiancé, in Olivia's, the husband.

But their differences are telling. Olivia is far more attractive physically than Adela, and perhaps for this reason lacks the rather masochistic propensity for self-blame with which Forster endows his heroine. More fundamentally, Olivia's seduction really happens, while Adela's misadventure in the Marabar Caves may simply be the figment of an 'hysterical' imagination – even a perverse wish-fulfilment, Forster seems to suggest, since 'the lady is so uglier than the gentleman'.[26] Adela herself seems to accept the idea that 'I had a hallucination there, the sort of thing – though in an awful form – that makes some women think they've had an offer of marriage when none was made'.[27] Dr Aziz puts it more baldly: she must sign, he says, a paper saying 'Dear Dr. Aziz, I wish you had come into the cave; I am an awful old hag, and it is my last chance'.[28]

This element of Forster's plot is deeply problematical. I believe that it derives from an incompletely resolved relationship with women and with heterosexuality. Certainly, it represents a rather misogynistic aspect of male homosexuality, in which women are – perhaps unconsciously – subtly seduced, only to be rejected. After all, is it as common as Forster suggests for women to 'think they've had an offer of marriage where none was made'? Usually, such 'hallucinations' require the participation of the gentleman, who may then profess, in bewildered innocence, complete surprise. Ruth Jhabvala's novel *In Search of Love and Beauty* will sketch that very dynamic, in the portrait of relations between heterosexual women and homosexual men.

Since the publication of R. N. Furbank's biography, the reader may more directly relate Forster's life to his most well-known novel.[29] His involvement over many years with the Muslim Indian Syed Ross Masood, to whom he dedicated the novel and whom he tutored and remained close to for years, and his numerous erotic and emotional relationships with young men of Indian or North African nationality, suggest his own deep commitments to them. As he said, he *liked* Indians: 'I like being with Indians. It isn't broadmindedness but an ideosyncracy [sic]. Over the Anglo-Indians I have to stretch and bust myself blue. I loathe them and should have been more honest to say so' (letter to E. V. Thompson, 22 June 1924).[30] The images and psychology that inform Forster's

Maurice add to the sense that he liked Aziz; indeed, he was too fond of him to pair him, however briefly, with Adela, preferring to keep him emotionally for his own surrogate, Fielding. (His affection for Aziz may not have shown clearly enough for contemporary reviewers: 'Scarcely anyone has seen', he lamented, 'that I hoped Aziz would be charming' [letter to Lowes Dickinson, 26 June 1924].)[31]

From the perspective of modern feminism, Forster's work suffers from an unexamined masculinist bias, which leads him into unfortunate reductionism. As many feminist social critics have reiterated, rape is not a myth. As it is in 'Desecration', rape is often used by the socially disenfranchised to exact a crude and misplaced vengeance on the men who oppress them. Ruth Jhabvala, in 'Desecration' and in *Heat and Dust*, tells a tale that provides a corrective to Forster's view that rape is a myth. It is distressing to see Forster seeming to accept the joke – used to intimidate and humiliate women – about the old maid who checks nightly under her bed for the dashing rapist and is disappointed to find him absent.

'HARRY' AND E. M. FORSTER

The many allusions to *A Passage to India* suggest another set of associations: those to its author himself. One can hardly avoid associating 'Harry' with E. M. Forster. As is well known, Forster derived his first-hand knowledge of India from the eighteen months he spent there, of which almost a year (March 1921 to January 1922) was spent as Personal Secretary to the Maharaja of Dewas. The story is told in Forster's *The Hill of Devi*, a compilation of some of his letters of that year, with his own commentary, written in 1953.[32] Quite a few elements of Forster's story foreshadow Harry's.

Forster's description of Dewas matches Khatm: it was an unprepossessing little town set on a meagre and parched plain. Many of those descriptions were contained in letters to Forster's widowed mother, with whom he shared so much: the relationship matches Harry's with his mother, also 'on her own' and wanting him to come home. The Maharaja, as he emerges in Forster's delightful letters, bears not a little relation to the Nawab, as I shall show,

and those aspects that do not resemble 'H.H.' [His Highness] seem
to be based on Syed Ross Masood.

To begin with the descriptions of the Dewas palace, comparisons
with the palace at Khatm are unavoidable:

> I have discovered incidentally that 1000 pounds worth (figure
> accurate) of electric batteries lie in a room near at hand and will
> spoil unless fixed promptly. I can't start on the inside of
> the house – two pianos (one a grand), a harmonium, and a
> dulciphone; all new and unplayable, their notes sticking and
> their frames cracked by the dryness. I look into a room – dozens
> of warped towel horses are stabled there, or a new suite of
> drawing-room chairs with their insides gushing out. I open a
> cupboard near the bath and find it full of tea-pots . . . and so
> on and so forth. . . . It's no good trying to make something
> different out of it, for it is as profoundly Indian as an Indian
> temple.[33]

Compare the modern narrator's words in *Heat and Dust*:

> He took her into an underground chamber which seemed to be
> a kind of store room. And what stores! There was an immense
> amount of camera equipment which, though already rusting,
> did not seem ever to have been used; some of it was still in its
> original packing. The same had happened to some modern
> sanitary equipment and an assortment of games such as a pinball
> machine, a croquet set, a miniature shooting gallery, meccano
> sets, and equipment for a hockey team. All of these things
> appeared to have been ordered from Europe but had taken too
> long to arrive for interest in them to be sustained. There was
> not one piano but two: a grand and an upright.   (p. 86)

Forster describes the Maharaja: 'I only know that he is one of the
sweetest and saintliest men I have ever known.'[34] Harry describes
the Nawab: 'He gets terribly involved with his friends . . . because
he's so . . . *affectionate*' (p. 74); 'You can have no idea of his
generosity, Olivia. He wants his friends to have everything'
(p. 35). Yet, Forster writes to his mother, 'I never feel certain what
he likes, or even whether he likes me.'[35] And Harry observes:
'With him you can't tell. One moment you think: Yes he cares –
but the next moment you might as well be some . . . object' (p. 35).
As for Syed Ross Masood, Furbank paints him as

striking and vivid . . . large and magnificent-looking . . . volatile, expansive and masterful. . . . One moment on the crest of the wave, the next groaning in well-acted despair and loudly demanding comfort. . . . A blazing Muslim patriot, full of nostalgia for the splendours of the Mogul past. 'Ah, that I had lived 250 years ago', he would sigh, 'when the oriental despotisms were in their prime!'[36]

How reminiscent of the Nawab, from his preoccupation with his ancestor to his personal qualities.

Returning to the references to H.H., Forster recounts to his mother that H.H. is married but separated. The Maharani had returned to her home state, the powerful and wealthy Kolhapur. Dewas and Kolhapur had become implacable enemies, and spent a large amount of time and revenue in mutual spying.[37] In Ruth Jhabvala's novel, the Nawab's estranged wife Sandy is from Cabobpur (the word means 'place of kebabs!'): 'much bigger royals of course – he doesn't really count in those circles; not much of a title, and by their standards he isn't even rich' (p. 34). Forster's Maharaja and Harry's Nawab show courtesy by cables and letters back to the respective mothers. H.H. dispatches a cable to Forster's mother upon Forster's arrival at Dewas; the Nawab writes to Harry's mother assuring her of Harry's well-being.

In letters, not to his mother this time, but to his friend Lowes Dickinson, Forster mentioned 'naughtiness' in the palace. Though H.H. apparently did not share Forster's sexual preferences, he was aware of them, and helped arrange assignations with a number of palace guards and functionaries, including the palace barber. He *seemed* to take a tolerant, if amused and affectionately disapproving attitude toward Forster's homosexuality.[38]

However, this may be a naïve view. Richard Cronin, reading between the lines of Forster's letters in *The Hill of Devi* and another account by Forster, in Forster's autobiographical essay 'Kanaya', concludes that Forster's 'H.H.' had actually set him up in a variety of elaborately orchestrated situations designed to tempt Forster into embarrassing indiscretions, with the ultimate aim of humiliating the British.[39] He doubts that the palace barber (according to Forster's account in 'Kanaya') would be so indiscreet as to proposition a royal guest without express orders from the Maharajah himself. According to Cronin, 'throughout the six months that Forster spent in Dewas he was the victim of a very unpleasant game devised by an accomplished sadist'.[40]

'Kanaya' was first published in 1983, so Jhabvala cannot have intended any allusion to this aspect of Forster's Indian experience. But the Nawab's presentation of his attitude to Harry's homosexuality is reminiscent of H.H.'s, as Forster described it in *The Hill of Devi*. And there is a curious irony in the fact that the intentions of Forster's historical 'H.H.' are every bit as ambiguous, seventy years later, as those of Jhabvala's fictional Nawab.

Compared to Mr Rivers, 'a proper Englishman' (p. 44), Harry is improper, the Nawab jokes. The Nawab expatiates on the good education and 'excellent discipline' gained at the English public school, and adds that, of course, Harry thinks them ' – Savage', supplies Harry feelingly. 'What nonsense' (p. 44), the Nawab says. One thinks of Forster's judgement on his own public-school experience: 'School was the unhappiest time of my life, and the worst trick it ever played me was to pretend that it was the world in miniature.'[41]

In addition to these specific allusions to, or borrowings from, Forster's life, *Heat and Dust* repeats a thematic concern of Forster's that he expressed most fully in *A Passage to India*, but that he also referred to in *The Hill of Devi*: that is, English bafflement and disorientation in the face of India's ambiguous and incomprehensible signs. What is more, *Heat and Dust* actually uses the same metaphor for this as Forster uses in *The Hill of Devi*, and which he re-uses in *A Passage to India*.

Forster's wry account of the serendipitous anecdote is worth quoting in full:

Our train of villagers stopped and pointed to the opposite bank with cries of a snake. At last I saw it – a black thing reared up to the height of three feet and motionless. I said, 'It looks a small dead tree,' and was told, 'Oh no,' and exact species and habits of snake were indicated – not a cobra, but very fierce and revengeful, and if we shot it would pursue us several days later all the way to Dewas. We then took stones and threw them across the Sipra . . . in order to make the snake crawl away. Still, he didn't move and when a stone hit his base still didn't move. He *was* a small dead tree. All the villagers shrieked with laughter. The young Sirdar [Officer] told them I was much disappointed and displeased about the snake, and that they must find a real one. So they dispersed anxiously for a few moments over the country, after which all was forgotten.

I call the adventure 'typical' because it is even more difficult here than in England to get at the rights of a matter. Everything that happens is said to be one thing and proves to be another, and as it is further said in an unknown tongue I live in a haze.[42]

This crucial interpretive dilemma, how to know, how to draw the correct conclusion based on insufficient evidence is, after all, the problem of life itself – and hence, what novels are all about.

How to know is *the* issue of Forster's novel, and of Jhabvala's as well. It extends to the readers: both novels end with ambiguities left unresolved: the Marabar Caves incident, and what became of Olivia; whether her retreat up the mountain represents contemplative withdrawal or a kind of suicidal self-immolation (like that of the sati) is left to the reader to decide. Throughout both novels, the protagonists, Adela and Olivia, have trouble 'reading' correctly – though Aziz seems more innocent than the Nawab. The Nawab has clear ties to the dacoit outlaws. He takes his friends where he finds them, for Khatm *is* 'finished' politically. For the British, Major Minnies, for example, the Nawab is simply a villain. Describing Major Minnies' outrage at the Nawab, the narrator uses Forster's image, the snake, and her use of the image coincides tellingly with Forster's. She writes that Major Minnies 'was silent in order to collect himself. He was genuinely outraged. The others too were silent. A bird woke up in a tree and gave a shriek. Perhaps it had been dreaming of a snake, or perhaps there really *was* a snake' (p. 92). In the context of the problem of knowing, the parallels between Forster and Harry take on a significance beyond their intrinsic literary and biographical interest. The narrator, searching out Olivia's story through the old letters and journals, becomes a stand-in for Jhabvala herself, who, if the numerous connections to Forster's letters are more than coincidence, has done the same work.

Part Four

Back in the West

8
Difficult Adjustments: Three Stories

HOMOSEXUAL MEN, HETEROSEXUAL WOMEN

Ruth Jhabvala's latest Western-based fiction continues to develop the themes that have always concerned her as an artist. In the new setting they emerge differently, newly tailored to use the new material, as it were, yet recognisable products of the same artistic imagination. Again, she marks the clashes of generations; again, she examines her characters' paradoxical compulsions to love those who are indifferent; again, she portrays unscrupulous gurus and naïve (mostly female) disciples. I have already mentioned the new focus, perhaps reflecting the realities of the new setting, on the relationships of male homosexuals with each other and with the women who love them.

The European and American-based stories and novels do however seem bleaker in outlook, more pessimistic than the India-based fiction. The Westerners seem perhaps more alienated from one another, the author's ironies darker and unrelieved by the delight that suffuses the Indian-based tales. She herself seems at greater distance from her characters. If the author is God in relation to her characters, that is only fitting, since in the West one is at a further remove from God. 'Nothing had spoken' from the London skies, while the Indian skies seem to Judy in *A Backward Place* to reverberate with the presence of God.

There is comedy in these later tales, but it is often black. The search for authenticity, connectedness and transcendence persists in certain characters, but their paths are perhaps more circuitous and therefore more open to exploitation than the traditional and well-defined religious routes of the Indians. Often collapse and breakdown, even tragedy, occur because of a peculiarly Western devaluation of all that is named 'feminine': for example, Michael's terrible infatuation with the paramilitary 'Fourth World Movement' in *Three Continents*. Also peculiarly Western is the alienation of

143

women from each other, which a feminist reading of these stories and novels reveals. Even more than before, emotional and spiritual integration, wholeness, fulfilment are located out of sight, above the clouds and unseeable, as they were already in *Heat and Dust*.

The later, Western-based novels and stories are peopled by women isolated from community, by which I mean the communities of other women. Even if nature offers images of healing, relief and beauty, a symbolic all-nurturant mother, real life does not. Ruth Jhabvala's searching women, disappointed by men, find themselves without any consoling or important resources, which might be supplied by affirming or central relationships among women.

For the questing female protagonist Jhabvala sees only the absence of validating or nurturing relationships. *Not with other women*: relationships between women are exploitative and manipulative, usually in one direction, though sometimes mutually. Often the 'friends' are actually rivals for the same man. Generally one – wealthier – woman bullies the other, who good-naturedly, or foolishly, tolerates her arrogance. The mother–daughter bond is conspicuously weak – daughters, usually seen from the mother's viewpoint, are selfishly obsessed with their men. When mothers are seen from the daughter's viewpoint, they are usually absent. Natasha's (adoptive) mother Marietta is mostly away. And even Marietta's first act of nurturance toward Natasha – the adoption itself – is somewhat suspect (she wishes to adopt a 'one-hundred per cent guaranteed Jewish' (p. 13) child to reaffirm her lapsed Jewishness).

Grandmothers and granddaughters generally have a closer relationship than mothers and daughters, but grandmothers are powerless to protect young women from male predation. They may even fuel the social machinery locking granddaughters into destructive marriages, as in 'Commensurate Happiness'. In *Three Continents*, a step-grandmother (Sonya) tries to save the protagonist, but to no avail.

Not with heterosexual men: in this New-York-based fiction, a gulf that is wider than ever yawns between men and women, though the men characteristically fail to notice it, their obtuseness compounded by arrogance. The few heterosexual men in these latest works are not particularly attractive to the sensitive and artistic women who surround them, since the men's interests run exclusively to business, sport and 'dirty' jokes. These interests are shared even by Leo Kellermann, the guru-figure of *In Search of Love and Beauty*, who at least possesses a charismatic intelligence and psychological acumen, which render him attractive, if not morally sound. The one nominally heterosexual (actually bisexual) man, Crishi in *Three Continents*, is trouble, to say the least.

Not with homosexual men: though homosexual men inhabit and even *own* the urban cultural scene, their circles are closed to women in any authentic sense; they may dispense to some women a kind of love or friendship, but it is at a heavy price, usually financial (as in 'Grandmother' or 'A Summer by the Sea'). Jhabvala's recent focus on the relationships of homosexual men and heterosexual women probes a contemporary scene that places women at a new kind of distance from men, and that puts women at a new disadvantage.

Male homosexual characters are not new to Ruth Jhabvala's oeuvre: there was Harry, Olivia's friend in *Heat and Dust*; there was Raymond in *A New Dominion*; the stories 'Rose Petals' (*Like Birds, Like Fishes*), 'Grandmother', 'Commensurate Happiness' and 'Expiation' (the last three uncollected) present still others. The novel *In Search of Love and Beauty* expands and refines the exploration, so that we see further into the relationship of the male lovers. We also note its effects on the women who are close to it. Sister, mother, grandmother or 'patron', the woman in question may be dimly aware of the relationship; yet her reponse to it is peculiarly vague. Shrugging her shoulders, she accepts her loved one's homosexuality: but this often means accepting a kind of a second-class status for herself: *she* will never be good enough for him. Often she accepts a deep alienation in confidence: he will not talk openly about his emotional life. In some cases she refuses to acknowledge his homosexuality altogether, a manifestation of the familiar Jhabvala dynamic of interested misapprehension. (We 'read' the world to correspond with the way we wish the world to be.) While accepting his homosexuality, she often consigns herself to a kind of asexuality.

The male homosexuals in these works form part of a broad and varied culture, invisible to those who do not know how to read its signs, instantly recognisable to initiates. They are often successful and leisured, or perhaps only leisured: architects, lawyers, dealers in real estate, designers, as well as unemployed actors and dancers, part-time butlers or paid companions.

That they figure so prominently in these works is, I think, a commentary on the contemporary urban scene. The emergence of gay rights activism into politics, print and popular consciousness is both the result and the sign of an important social reality in the life of the late twentieth century, one which Jhabvala – without much company among current women authors – has chosen to highlight; in urban centres – such as Manhattan – male homosexuality seems almost more the rule than the exception. Whether this perception reflects actual numbers, or an increasing acceptability is not the issue here so much as the burgeoning importance and visibility of the 'lifestyle'.

One may read the increasing focus on male homosexuality as a kind of response to the disillusionment with heterosexual romance that is the cornerstone of Jhabvala's comedy. If demon-lovers mistreat the romantic heroine – as, of course, they do, by definition – perhaps she should look to men who might share her interests more, talk with her, understand her feelings: men who also love remote, awe-inspiring icons of power. She is quite naturally drawn to them, by virtue of shared interests and sensibilities, as Olivia is drawn to Harry.

Finally, one may see the focus on male homosexuality as a movement towards, and interest in, homosexuality *per se*, which would, of course, include female homosexuality. But lesbianism in Jhabvala's fiction is derided, ignored or viewed as revolting.

These novels and stories discount even the idea of love or support between women. Because they investigate female psychology and experience, and because they inquire into the world of male homosexuals, one might logically expect some acknowledgement of the female homosexual possibilty. This appears only in the latest novel at the time of writing, *Three Continents*. Before it, there are lesbian characters, but they are very minor, and their homosexuality is viewed as comic or pathological. In the terms of these novels and stories women have three *un*satisfactory options: they may love homosexual men (who ignore them) or heterosexual men (who despise them), or they may live without love altogether. In *In Search of Love and Beauty*, Natasha, Louise and Marietta represent the three possibilities.

Adrienne Rich has argued that there exists a powerful cultural imperative to ignore the lesbian alternative, which she sees not merely as a sexual preference, but as 'woman-identified experience', or, in its broadest definition, any other 'forms of primary intensity between and among women, including the sharing of a rich inner life, the bonding against male tyranny, the giving and receiving of practical and political support'.[1] Rich questions what is generally regarded as axiomatic: the assumption of female heterosexuality. Given the reality that for all human beings the original 'search for love and tenderness in both sexes . . . [led] toward women' (that is, the mother), Rich wonders 'why in fact women would ever redirect that search'.[2] Her conclusion is that there is an active societal impulse continually working to obscure, prohibit and deny love between women. For her the *absence* of lesbian or even woman-centred love in myth and fiction 'suggests that an enormous potential counterforce is having to be restrained'.[3]

These novels and stories, in which even female friendship is discounted, certainly illustrate the premises of Rich's thesis: that is, 'the virtual or total neglect of lesbian existence',[4] coupled with the idea that 'women are inevitably, even if rashly and tragically, drawn to men: even when that attraction is suicidal'.[5] So do other Jhabvala fictions I have discussed – 'Desecration' being the perfect illustration. And so, of course, do countless other works of literature, for 'compulsory heterosexuality' is the unexamined social norm.

The fiction of Ruth Jhabvala as a whole recreates a world illustrating Adrienne Rich's profoundly radical – that is, reaching to the root – insights. Again, to quote C. P. Snow on Ruth Jhabvala: 'life is thus and not otherwise'. By their attention to women's psychology, by their female perspectives, and by their inclusion of so many male homosexual characters, her novels and stories push us in the direction of at least *noticing* the absence of female friendships or love between women. At the core of the novel *In Search of Love and Beauty*, is a female 'friendship' – between Louise and Regi – about which the best that can be said is that with a friendship like that one needs no enemies. Bitchy Regi and tolerant Louise present a perverse image of friendship indeed, one that stands the concept on its head. There are many other examples.

For instance, from 'Myself in India', here is one passage that I hesitate to quote in this context because of its laudable, and I would even say courageous, admission of feelings that are not quite acceptable: speaking of her fictional Delhi hostess, the author dips her pen in acid:

> Our hostess . . . loves to exercise her emancipated mind, and whatever the subject of conversation . . . she has a well-formula-

ted opinion on it and knows how to express herself. How lucky for me if I could have such a person for a friend! What enjoyable, lively times we two could have together!

In fact, my teeth are set on edge if I have to listen to her for more than five minutes, yes, even though everything she says is so true and in line with the most advanced opinions of today.[6]

Her hostess, indeed, as India was her 'hostess' for some two decades! It is perhaps for remarks like these that she has been excoriated in the Indian press, which she says, liked her well enough until 'they found out that I wasn't Indian'.[7] In fact, she merely accords her 'hosts' their full humanity, which includes the possibility of their being as obnoxious as anyone else. And yet. In the light of the fiction's underlying assessment of women's relations with each other, I do quote this passage, in this context. The character – as usual, magically painted whole in a few deft strokes – could not offer friendship: poseurs never do. Perhaps, then, it is for this reason that she sets the author's teeth on edge.

But even more pointed is the Jhabvala protagonist's recoil from women who seem eager to engage in what Raymond, in *A New Dominion*, called 'undesirable revelation'. For example, Evie in that novel confides to Lee of her bliss with Swami, urging her too to live in the joy of submission. 'She was even holding my hand and pressing it ever so gently. I didn't like that much, though' (p. 158). The chapter breaks off here, in a clattering silence. The effect is one of physical revulsion, skilfully conveyed. Why, though, the overtone of awful, uninvited lesbianism? The juxtapositions here are significant. Evie's pathological realisation of an impulse inherent in all romantic lovers, and a shudder of revulsion from physical closeness with another woman.

Similarly, but more explicitly presented, is the narrator's revulsion in 'An Experience of India', in which Evie's counterpart, Jean, confides unasked in the narrator. Again, Jean praises 'the beauty of surrender', and whispers warmly into the narrator's neck, or touches her moistly and 'ever so gently'. 'It gave me an unpleasant sensation down my spine.'

Again, the recoil from physical closeness, utterly convincingly conveyed. Is this romantic propensity for 'surrender' what is most horrible about ourselves? In a world that devalues women, while overvaluing men, in a world constructed on women's alienation for themselves and from each other, we recoil most from the threat of intimacy with another who might be like us. The Jhabvala protagonist remains alone: more so than ever, since she now situates herself among male homosexuals from whom she is fundamentally set apart because of her femaleness. This apartness is particularly ironic since love between men, for all its *difference*, and for all that it consigns those who engage in it to a subculture apart, is not that different after all: that is, it often repeats the configurations of heterosexual romance. So in a way the novels and stories of this phase continue where the demon-lover stories leave off. But women take part mostly as observers. Refugees from homosexuality, they are still aliens in the world of gay men.

Appropriately, the next three stories I wish to discuss, which lead up to the novel *In Search of Love and Beauty*, are all set within the worlds of 'real' refugees, that is, refugees from state terror, still alien in their adopted lands.

'A BIRTHDAY IN LONDON'

'A Birthday in London' was Jhabvala's first published work to be set in the West. (An uncollected story, 'Light and Reason', 1963, was also set in England.) Appearing in *Like Birds, Like Fishes* (1963), it was published some twenty years before *In Search of Love and Beauty* (1983), yet it bears the seeds of the later novel. The story is little more than a poignant vignette on the theme of loss; the much later novel may be said to weave a complex design around the same fundamental idea.

'A Birthday in London' conveys the lives of the dispossessed with a Chekhovian economy, in which each detail is meaningful and revelatory. It bears interesting parallels to *In Search of Love and Beauty*: both works revolve around a mother and son whose relationship echoes the loss and alienation of all the refugees from the land that bore them. There are many other parallels, beginning with the birthday party referred to in the story's title, for birthdays also figure prominently in the novel.

In addition to their special and particular tragedies, the refugees share with everyone a more general vulnerability: that is, to time. Among many enemies to their dignity and sense of safety in the world, time is perhaps the subtlest. Its ravages go unnoticed most often, except for certain occasions, for example, birthday parties.

This modern-day ritual serves as the setting not only for this story and the novel that follows it, but also for the story 'Commensurate Happiness'. A birthday also represents the climax of the next novel, *Three Continents*. At birthday parties, time, relentless but ordinarily imperceptible, is formally acknowledged. Friends and family convene to mark the passage of a personal year. We are one year older, that much closer to our deaths; we celebrate having come through the year, and those who are there with us congratulate us, which is particularly meaningful for the refugees who have been torn from their kin. For everyone, but more so for them, beneath the celebration runs an undercurrent of regret, for the new marks of age, for the diminution of the future, for the inexorable decline – and for those whose absence is conspicuous.

There is something at once comical and touching about these birthday parties in middle or even advanced old age. Sonia, the main character in London, is a grandmother now, but she is still the 'birthday child' who makes a 'birthday wish' and receives a 'birthday letter' from her daughter Lilo in Israel (it arrives precisely on her birthday). There is 'birthday coffee' with apfel strudel, and naturally, birthday presents. It is an appealing moment. Yet the horrors of the past and the disappointments of the present loom large, contributing to the reader's poignant sense of the fragility of happiness or even consolation.

Does this party *compensate* for the losses they have endured? Well, it will have to. The idea of 'compensation' is thematic, more precisely the tragic absurdity of the concept. The refugees have lost worlds – fathers, mothers and sisters – the loss is only hinted at. What 'compensation' can there be? And when calculated in marks, pounds or dollars, how obscene is the suggestion that the balances are now cleared, and justice has been done. And yet, so it is. The money must be accepted, ugly as it is; the refugees are certainly in no position to turn it down. There is a further irony: Sonia Wolff, née Rothenstein, a widow with two grown children, receives ample 'compensation' because her deceased husband, 'Otto Wolff had been a very wealthy factory owner in Berlin'. Now 'Sonia was a rich woman again now, which was as it should be'. The others at the party, less favoured in the vanished, pre-Holocaust world, receive less 'compensation'. This is the best the world can offer: that the inequities that once prevailed shall be re-established.

Sonia Wolff recasts the favoured Jhabvala theme of loss and

disinheritance. Like so many of Jhabvala's other protagonists, Sonia, even if partially restored to her former prosperity, looks back on better, happier times: like Miss Tuhy ('Miss Sahib' in *An Experience of India*), like Louise (in *In Search of Love and Beauty*), like Olivia (*Heat and Dust*), like Dr Ernst ('An Indian Citizen', in *A Stronger Climate*), like the Countess of 'How I Became a Holy Mother', like the poignant Nilima of the story 'Like Birds, Like Fishes' (this title is used for the collection from which 'A Birthday in London' is taken).

The disinherited, those who amid present squalour or loneliness think bitterly or wistfully of the ease or comfort of their former circumstances: these melancholy subjects offer in themselves a kind of personification of Jhabvala's more general themes: loss and disillusionment. There is even a kind of mytho-religious reference in the image, since it recreates the human condition: we all, all of us, come into being 'trailing clouds of glory' – which are soon blown away. Miss Tuhy of the story 'Miss Sahib' has fallen very far, measuring out her meagre pension in a sleazy urban Indian setting. She had been a teacher, in love with India, with poetry, with feeling: and 'passionate' about the English Romantics.

The particular and modern tragedy of the German-Jewish refugees Jhabvala writes of – and, of course, one of whom she is – impinges on an event of such enormity that it shadows literally everything in modern experience. Nazism, the nightmare as reality, irretrievably altered the face of humanity: when this story was written, probably in the late fifties, the philosophical, literary and imaginative reponses to the trauma of German fascism, which have emerged and continue to emerge ever since, had only begun to take form. In this story, the name 'Auschwitz' is mentioned for the only time in Ruth Jhabvala's work to date – and characteristically woven in unobtrusively, in the usual subordinate clause. But, of course, the story is informed by that name and what it represents.

Ruth Jhabvala's work is practically devoid of direct reference to the Holocaust. She has spoken of this avoidance in her Neil Gunn Lecture, delivered in 1979 and reprinted in *Blackwood's Magazine*. 'Disinheritance' was its title.[8]

I don't feel like talking much about 1933 and after. Everyone knows what happened to German Jews first and to other European Jews after that. Our family was no exception. One by one all my aunts and uncles emigrated – to France, Holland, what was then Palestine, the United States. . . . My immediate family – that is, my Polish father, my mother, my brother and myself – were the last to emigrate, and also the only ones to go to England. This was 1939. I have slurred over the years 1933 to 1939, from when I was six to twelve. They should have been my most formative years, and maybe they were, I don't know. Together with the early happy German-Jewish bourgeois family years – 1927 to 1933 – they should be that profound well of memory and experience (childhood and ancestral) from which as a writer I should have drawn. I never have. I have never written about those years. To tell you the truth, until today I've never mentioned them. Never spoken about them to anyone. I don't know why not. I do know that they are the beginning of my disinheritance – the way they are for other writers of their inheritance.

This reticence is a typical response to the trauma of such loss, as many studies of political refugees and Holocaust survivors attest.[9] Refugees live *in* loss, to the extent that often even speaking of it is impossible.

The birthday party vignette, then, is particularly telling viewed as a literary portrayal of the dilemmas of survival in its specifically post-Holocaust sense – as well as the more generalised human context, in which we are all survivors. The fictionalised refugees of 'A Birthday in London' are matter-of-fact about it: '"There is something from my dear late Papa in him [a photograph of her baby grandson]," Sonia said, sighing for her father, a large, healthy, handsome man who had loved good living and had died at Auschwitz' (p. 127). So have the families and relations of all the others: Else, Mrs Gottlob and Karl Lumbik. Each is alone; each is a survivor; each has, now, twenty years after the Holocaust, recreated herself or himself as fully as possible – which is not very fully.

Else works as a seamstress for a Mrs Davis, an 'English Jewish lady' who condescends to her. It might be more accurate to say that Mrs Davis is too ignorant – from Else's point of view – to know what is due to Else Levy, 'daughter of Oberlehrer Levy of Schweinfurt'. Mrs Gottlob, once the owner of 'Gottlob's butcher shop, where you got the finest liver-sausage in the whole of Gelsenkirchen', now keeps a rather seedy boarding house, where Sonia and Otto stayed when they arrived in London. Karl Lumbik, a much-travelled Vienna gallant, is still paying court (to Sonia). He boasts, 'Budapest, Prague, Shanghai, Bombay, London, is that bad for one lifetime?' But enforced travels are quite different from the peregrinations of the man of the world he might have been. Some, he jokes, travel 'for kicks, thank you, and some travel because – yes, because they are kicked. Is this a bad pun, Mr Werner? I am being very English now, for I am making puns so that I can apologise for them.'

Though briefly glimpsed, the refugees have weight and individuality. Though her characters may be recognisable types, they are never only that, nor are they without their petty failings. Mrs Gottlob fawns on Sonia, now that Sonia is a wealthy woman again; but before Sonia's 'compensation', Mrs Gottlob was less kind. Mr Lumbik retains his German-Jewish anti-Semitism intact: ('Do you know about Moyshe Rotblatt from Pinsk who was taken to *Tristan und Isolde*?' – we do not hear the punch line, but the lead-in tells enough). And all the refugees feel superior to the English Jews, whom they find 'uncultured'.

Compressed into some sixteen pages are the four partygoers' strategies for survival, by turns comic and heroic. Like others of Jhabvala's heroes, they are victim-survivors of circumstances ranging from the nightmare of the Holocaust to the buffetings of ordinary life, no matter where. To take the largest view, Ruth Jhabvala's fiction is a celebration of human endurance, the small heroisms of those who feel and suffer, but go on. Major and minor characters alike display this quality of quiet resistance. For example, a minor character such as Eric, the failed actor/model of *In Search of Love and Beauty*, after being turned down by Mark, 'shrugged a little bit and smiled a little bit. Probably this was the gesture with which he met every little humiliation that life offered him' (p. 179). Dr Ernst of 'An Indian Citizen' is another version of Karl Lumbik, another elderly survivor of the Holocaust who carefully orchestrates his aimless days with small strategies for survival, such as an afternoon nap:

Of course, a nap in the afternoon was nothing to reproach oneself with – good heavens, at his age and in this climate! – but one also had to know when to cut it short. Otherwise there was a danger of sinking too deep and giving way to the desire to sleep for ever and not have to get up at all any more and walk around and meet people. He put away his handkerchief and patted and jerked and brushed at his crumpled clothes to get them dapper again.

Despair, even suicide, is always just around the corner, having to be kept at bay. Karl Lumbik of 'A Birthday in London' shares Dr Ernst's cheerful stoicism. But a dearth of it has brought about the death of Sonia's husband Otto, as she remembers: 'He never believed things could be well again one day. I would say to him "Otto, it is dark now but the sun will come again"; "no," he said, "it is all finished." He didn't want to live any more, you see.' Otto is a prefiguration of Bruno of the novel *In Search of Love and Beauty*, just as Sonia is a prefiguration of one of its main characters, Louise. Both Otto and Bruno are small and dark, emotionally vulnerable and deeply sensitive. Both Sonia and Louise are tall, beautiful, nurturant, but filled with regret for the lost 'beautiful times', as Sonia says. Each has a daughter who travels far away: Lilo to Israel, Marietta to India.

There are clear autobiographical references in these related pieces, which draw on Ruth Jhabvala's youth as a refugee. Like the refugees in London, she and her immediate family lost worlds: she recently counted over forty family members who perished in the Holocaust.[10] Like the families of Sonia and Louise, her mother's family in Cologne was comfortable and accomplished. Her maternal grandfather was cantor of Cologne's major synagogue.[11]

> There were aunts and uncles, all well-settled, all German patriots, all life-loving, full of energy, bourgeois virtues and pleasures, celebrating every kind of festival – all the Jewish holidays, of course, but what they really liked was New Year's Eve and, especially, the annual Cologne carnival and masked ball. We all had costumes made for that every year; one year I was a chimney-sweep, and another a Viennese pastry-cook. All this would be in the early 1930s – up to, but not including, 1933.[12]

I have already mentioned Marcus Prawer's suicide, a casualty of what his daughter called 'an epidemic' of suicides among Holocaust survivors in the London of the forties.[13]

Thus all the refugees know the temptations of suicide. Each has made his or her own compromise with it:

'There were many days I also didn't want to live any more,' Else said. . . . 'I would say to myself, Else, what are you doing here? Father, mother, sisters all gone, why are you still here, finish off now.' 'Who hasn't had such days?' Mr. Lumbik said. 'But then you go to the cafe, you play a game of chess, you hear a new joke, and everything is well again.'

But Otto had taken things too 'tragically' – as if it were possible to take too tragically the events he lived through. And yet, the story seems to say, it is: 'too' tragically being without the strategies for survival of those who go on, even if those strategies are denial, avoidance, stoicism and willed cheerfulness. Karl Lumbik reaffirms his resolve merely *to be*. When he asks himself what he has achieved in his life, the answer is that he has survived, he jokes, and 'this is already a success story'. In that offhand, joking remark he sums up the tragedy of the unprecedented genocidal war that wiped out the lives of millions, and with their lives all the things that they would have achieved.

At the birthday party, in 1959, two of the guests have good news: for one, Karl Lumbik has received his citizenship papers – no one can tell him again, 'Pack your bags, Lumbik! Time to move on', as he jokes: 'It is so restful, it is quite bad for my nerves.' Also, Else Levy has received her 'compensation', ten thousand marks – enough to take 'a nice holiday in Switzerland in a good hotel'.

Thus, the class differences that once prevailed have been re-stored. This is in contrast to the chaotic refugee years, when Sonia and Otto lived at Mrs Gottlob's rooming house, and had had to suffer her shouting at them up the stairs about 'lights that had been left burning and baths that had not been cleaned after use': all the petty indignities of poverty and unwished-for sharing. Otto would pale and Sonia would descend to placate the landlady and buffer Otto's greater sensitivity, which both clearly place first. But now Mrs Gottlob is all kindness, even obsequiousness, to Sonia. And her social inferiority is delicately suggested by the fact that she is addressed as 'Mrs Gottlob' in contrast to Sonia and Else.

The question of address comes up directly at the outset of the story, when Karl Lumbik tells Sonia to call him 'Karl'; by its end she gives in to this, his 'birthday wish'. The others notice; the change is cause for much merriment and joking. Still a gallant, Karl Lumbik feels he possesses a superior knowledge of women, especially Sonia's 'type', with which 'one had to proceed very gently and tactfully' – a view reflecting a gallant's condescension.

With the arrival of Werner, Sonia's son, the fragile glow and good feeling generated by the happy announcements will be extinguished. A handsome and animated youth, Werner treats his mother and her friends with a mixture of condescension and exasperation. He has forgotten the birthday, for which he duly apologises. But the talk of travel leads into another unexpected revelation, as Werner 'lazily' announces his intention of leaving: '"Off to Rome soon," and seeing his mother's face – "Oh come on darling, I told you I might be going."' He glosses over the surprise, but in Sonia's 'large anxious eyes' and clenched hand her shock and disappointment can be read.

This only annoys him, of course: '"Don't worry, darling," he said, trying to sound light and gay, but with an edge of exasperation all the same.' Sonia hastens to make amends, 'Of course I don't worry'. Now that there is 'enough money', he can enjoy himself doing 'a little film-work', 'a little art-photography', having his parties and girlfriends. Sonia knows that there is nothing wrong with a grown son's independence, yet she weeps: if the war had never happened, how different it would have been. Werner would have been 'Werner Wolff, Director of SIGBO, everybody would know and respect him'.

Werner's departure links up with all the other disappointments of her life, the general descent from privilege; at least she puts it in these terms, citing too her daughter's loss of advantage (which, presumably, a kibbutznik would not feel as loss):

> 'My poor Lilo – I have had such a lovely girlhood, such lovely dresses and always parties and dancing-classes and the Konservatorium in Berlin for my piano-playing. And she has had only hard work in the Kibbutz, hard work with her hands, and those horrible white blouses and shorts' – Her voice broke and she said 'My handkerchief is quite wet'. (p. 137)

In this small outburst Jhabvala brings to bear her uncanny ability to walk the fine edge of tragedy and comedy. The Kibbutz blouses may be 'horrible', but it is Werner's departure that makes Sonia cry. His presence delights her. The text makes clear her abundant good humour during the few moments that he is present, and before he makes his announcement. *In Search of Love and Beauty* repeats the relationship of Werner and Sonia, in Mark and Marietta. But many more of Ruth Jhabvala's stories and novels repeat it in its basic essence: the perils of loving and the indifference of the beloved.

The impatient departure of a loved one requires a major effort if it is to be borne gracefully. One may hardly admit it to oneself: yet there, at this level of human relations, the novelist's territory is located. Sonia's task echoes the refugees', in little: to withstand.

The refugees console each other, with reminders that they are lucky to be alive, with apfel strudel, and with flirtatious jokes. By the time Werner leaves for his date, they are laughing merrily: he 'smiled at their preoccupation: he was glad to see them having a good time' (p. 139).

This irony, the last line of the story, reveals the refugees' isolation. Certainly, their children cannot see their heroism in the face of loss. Nor is that surprising: 'We know who we are, but does my Werner know, and my Lilo?' Sonia cries. Youth in particular, with its slightly condescending affection and happy egotism, does not wish to understand; it sees only that the elders 'worry'. The currents of feeling among these five characters, glimpsed so briefly yet plumbed so deeply, the meanings of their smallest gestures being remarked and understood, make up a short text that not only illuminates the artistry of its author, but models the art of the short story as a genre, in which no word is superfluous, no detail insignificant. Like Chekhov's, whose they resemble in mood and feeling, Jhabvala's stories stand as the highest examples of their kind.

'COMMENSURATE HAPPINESS'

'Commensurate Happiness' is another, later, prefiguration of *In Search of Love and Beauty*, though certain characters also refer back to 'A Birthday in London'. It is a rather astonishing vignette pinpointing the making of a marriage, and in its implications it is, if not an outright indictment of marriage and family, at least a revelation of the very imperfect reality underlying the myth of domestic bliss.

The cast comprises a comfortable German-Jewish family living in New York. There is an aged and widowed grandmother,

Jeannette (who corresponds to Sonia Wolff in the story and Louise in the novel); her daughter Sandra (Lilo/Marietta) who 'had a lot of divorces and personal crises' and is thus essentially absent from the family; and the daughter's daughter Marie (Natasha), an isolated waif-like young girl. There is an overdressed female friend Wanda (Regi in the novel), who lives in an East Side apartment decorated in Bauhaus style – these elements come up again in the novel – and who has been the mistress of Jeannette's late husband (named Otto – like Sonia's husband in 'A Birthday in London').

Again there is a son, this time homosexual, unlike Werner, who had – at least his mother thought he had – 'a lot of girlfriends'. This son, Hughie, corresponds to Mark, a major character in the novel. Marie is in love with Hughie as Natasha is in love with Mark. Like Mark, Hughie takes frequent trips abroad with unknown companions, who turn out to be his male lovers – again, a reworking of the issue at the heart of 'A Birthday in London'. Hughie is sensitive and self-involved, given to unrequited love affairs with indifferent boys, and he accepts a certain comfort from Marie (as Mark does from Natasha) although once that is out of the way he is happy to dispense with her.

In the novel, Mark and Natasha are brother and sister – though only by adoption, not by blood. In this story the pair, Hughie and Marie, are cousins, a relationship that allows them to marry. Thus the plot: 'Jeanette wanted and expected Hughie and Marie to get married; Marie wanted and expected it too; and Hughie just expected it.' After years of fruitless waiting for the couple to become engaged, Wanda (the close family friend) hurries matters along. The moment comes at Wanda's birthday party, hosted by Jeannette. With supreme aplomb, Wanda toasts the engagement as if it were a *fait accompli*. Of course, it has never been mentioned. The young couple accept the ploy, and take the opportunity to 'announce' their engagement.

Like much of Ruth Jhabvala's fiction, this story is a commentary on marriage. There are two marriages in it to compare, Jeanette's and Marie's, and the reader is led to conclude that as they are similar at their inceptions, they will probably continue to resemble each other. Each marriage, desired by the bride but not by the groom, and engineered by the family, is an arrangement in which the woman, without realising it, is signed up for a lifetime of economic security at the price of emotional deprivation. Her youth and inexperience are partially to blame, but then again, the groom is clearly less than eager, a situation she could have seen had she been willing to look. Thus, women, by wishful thinking, collude in the oppressive arrangements.

Wanda indignantly justifies her high-handed intrusion thus: 'If young people don't know where they're going, the family has to take over.' She is correct: they had been waiting for her to intervene, and now Hughie will come through with a proposal – in his fashion – which poor Marie is only too happy to accept. Jeannette recalls her own engagement to Otto, which turns out to have followed a similar pattern. It too had been long in coming: 'She had adored him for four years and he had been kind to her.' It too had been prompted by the actions of interested others – aunts, in her case. However, 'It did not take Jeannette long to find out that the expectations she had had that night had been excessive. She did have happiness, but it was of a different order from what she had expected.' A flashback supplies an example of that last, drily ironic assertion. Jeannete's 'happiness' consists of an emotional abasement. It happens at another of Wanda's birthday parties, this one set a few years back, in the midst of Otto's last, fatal illness. As one of his last requests, he has asked Jeannette to host his mistress's birthday party in their home. She has complied with his wish, and he thanks her. 'In comparison with the great effort he was making just to press her hand – that seemed a very small thing to have done; and she had brought his hand up to her lips, to make him understand that it was she who was glad and grateful.' Although there is poignancy in this recollection, it is alarming that her fondest memory is that he was grateful that she tolerated his mistress! The marriage to which she urges her two grandchildren is to be drawn along similar lines, and she knows this. Still she does what she can to promote that commensurate happiness.

After Wanda's prompting, Jeannette questions Marie. Finding that Hughie has *still* not proposed, she takes up the argument, as if Hughie's recalcitrance is somehow Marie's fault.

'He does care for you. He loves you. As far as he can, he does. What more do you want?' she added – rather impatiently, for it seemed to her that Marie was being unreasonable in her expectations. She too would have to learn that one lived on earth and not in heaven.

When Hughie calls weakly from the next room, Jeannette pretends –

although she knows better – to take it as a sign that 'he can't be five minutes without you'. Marie too knows her cousin better: 'He wants the cologne' because he has drunk too much.

Though homosexual, Hughie is by no means egalitarian in his views of the sexes. 'He resented it – to be so commingled with a girl.' But he will grudgingly accept her nurturance. As she massages his temples, he whispers (they are being listened to), 'We could, you know. If you want to.' She demurs. He covers her mouth with his hand, a symbolic muting that echoes the dynamics of their relationship.

> As soon as Hughie took his hand away Marie whispered: 'We don't have to: just because *they* want to.'
> '*I* want to,' Hughie said – irritably, for he always disliked it when Marie didn't at once fall in with his wishes.

And so they are married, in an arrangement in which Hughie will carry on with his love affairs under the convenient cover of their marriage, and Marie will suffer silently, with everyone's consent, her own and her family's.

For Jeannette knows, even without wishing to, about her grandson's affectional and sexual preferences. After overhearing his side of a tearful conversation with 'Chuck', she stops demanding to know the identity of his friends, a point which had greatly concerned her until then. She even loses her temper with Wanda when Wanda expresses curiosity: 'She said it was none of my business, none of her business, none of anyone's business who are Hughie's friends. This she says to me!' So reports Wanda to Marie with her customary indignation.

Jhabvala's fiction certainly endorses authentic human relationships, male homosexual ones included, to be sure. The problem that her fiction highlights, however, is that women accept a position of marginality in relation to the male homosexuals in their lives, and do not avail themselves of the same privilege of intimate relations. In exchange for Hughie's company, Marie forfeits intimacy, centrality, sexuality – love. The privileges that Hughie takes for granted, Marie never dreams of for herself.

The social and domestic machinery grinds on, and women's willed suppression of the knowledge of their own disadvantage in a male-centred society keeps it running – to women's own self-mutilation. Indeed, the 'happiness' that Jeannette has claimed, and that Marie will claim in her turn, *is* commensurate with that state of diminished expectation and resigned acceptance that is offered to the disinherited. And it is above all women who are the disinherited: from our history, from our strength and from our sense of self-worth. By showing the machinery in action, this story forces us to confront what Marie, Jeannette and Hughie might well deny.

'GRANDMOTHER' AND OTHER OLD WOMEN

This vignette, published in the *New Yorker* in 1980, is still uncollected. Like 'Commensurate Happiness', it is clearly preparatory for the novel *In Search of Love and Beauty*; it is set in New York, and explores the relationship between the eponymous grandmother and two young gay men. Its subject overlaps somewhat with the Merchant–Ivory–Jhabvala film *Roseland* (1977), which was set in and around the New York City dance hall frequented by elderly ladies of means and impecunious young gay men.

Minnie is one of many old women in Jhabvala's work; old age, particularly female old age, offers rich possibilities for ironic revelation of character. Behind the stereotypes and expectations limiting old women, live individual human beings who would, if we listened, prove them false: Jhabvala brings us the voices of not a few.

The old women in Jhabvala's Indian fiction to some extent escape the particular disparagement that is the lot of old age in the West, as Indian society traditionally values the last phase of life as a special period of freedom from the responsibilities of the householder and parent. Spiritual practice may now become a full-time pursuit; one learns from Jhabvala's pages that many, with full social approval, voluntarily adopt a life of itinerant begging, travelling from shrine to shrine. A number of Jhabvala's old women do achieve a spiritual strength that is associated with their devotions. 'The Old Lady' (*Like Birds, Like Fishes*) is a character study of one such: her daily meditations fill her with such joy and satisfaction that she grows a stranger to her family – a sorry collection of irascible, dissatisfied and very worldly individuals. Maji's band of 'merry widows', in *Heat and Dust*, spend their days cavorting with one another in an all-female clan that the narrator appears to view with a kind of rueful outsiderhood. Maji herself, the adept midwife and sage, personifies a powerful female old age.

In *A New Dominion*, Banubai certainly possesses power, though there is the suggestion that her power is not all to the good. Like many another Jhabvala guru, she is too adept a manipulator not to be seriously flawed. So skilled is she at turning circumstance to her advantage that she camouflages her liaison of the moment with her advancing years: Gopi and she are chaste mother and son – it would only be ill-mannered and dirty-minded to think otherwise, as Gopi angrily accuses Raymond of doing.

Diametrically opposed to Banubai we might place another elderly lady of Jhabvala's, the Minister's wife of the beautiful vignette 'Rose Petals' (*An Experience of India*). This character-study reveals its narrator, a dreamer. Otherwise unnamed, the Minister's wife passes her days in a kind of reposeful aimlessness, in the company of her husband's cousin Biju, homosexual and emotionally finely tuned. 'Life is only a game' for them, in painful contrast to the Minister and Mina, the grown daughter. Mina and the Minister are all earnestness, duty and busyness, as they rather self-importantly bustle from one to another committee and speech. They embody Ruth Jhabvala's deep ambivalence about, if not outright distrust of, engagement in a world fuelled by greed and corruption. The disengagement that is often characteristic of old age, then, is congenial to this writer's moral vision, which so often locates self-interest and pride officiously masquerading as good works.

Even in the stormy realm of sexual love, old women may achieve happiness in Jhabvala's fiction. The story 'The Man with the Dog' (*A Stronger Climate*) alludes in its title to Chekhov's 'The Lady with the Little Dog'; its narrator, an Indian woman, cheerfully adores her 'old man', the Dutchman Boekelman, whom old age has now trapped in Delhi (Boekelman is one of the three elderly Europeans who, in the stories, make up the 'Sufferers' section of the collection). The elderly narrator is Boekelman's landlady, and she is also his mistress. Her grown children strenuously disapprove of the liaison, but she is one of the happiest of the tormented lovers in Jhabvala's oeuvre. She makes the connection between the erotic and the divine herself: 'Perhaps B. is a substitute for God whom I should be loving, the way the little brass image of Vishnu in my prayer-room is a substitute for that great god himself', she muses.

Boekelman's mistress no longer pays too much attention to her appearance. Nor, for that matter, does she mind her lover's missing teeth, his bald spot, and so on. Old age strips away the appurtenances of busyness, and social position, and even the physical self which helps us to maintain our dignity. The old lady and Boekelman, fighting, feigning indifference, threatening to leave each other, finally confront each other in all their frailty.

False self-importance may fall away in old age. A category of that is national pride, the absurd patriotism that so concerns 'Shammi', the old lady's officer son. Granted, Boekelman and his friends give Shammi plenty of cause: 'B.' rages peevishly against the 'damn rotten backward country' into which fate has washed him and his refugee friends (who, for their part, are also forever complaining about India). Shammi, the lieutenant-colonel who 'passionately' loves his army career, is very angry, and his mother, apologetic. She knows that Shammi 'loves talking . . . about his regiment and about tank warfare and 11.1 bore rifles and other such things, and I love listening to him. I don't really understand what he is saying, but I love his eager voice and the way he looks when he talks – just as he looked when he was a small boy and told me about his cricket.' The old woman knows how much that is thought to be serious and adult is only a more dangerous version of children's games – very much like the Minister's wife who mused that 'life is only a game'.

In contrast to their daughters and granddaughters, these old women possess a greater measure of freedom: freed now from the public scrutiny that confined ladies such as Sofia or Olivia; freed from duties to husband and children; freed, mostly, from the demands of the Romantic, according to which they re-create themselves as objects of beauty.

But one remembers Shakuntala's singing teacher's joke: 'You should burn her, that's the only thing old women are good for, burning.' These freedoms come at a heavy price, for to be a free woman is to be marginal, sacrificeable, stigmatised.

Shakuntala's teacher's remark is not without its Western equivalent. If the old are superfluous in the consumer society, old women are doubly superfluous; evidence of this appears in their poverty, but not there alone. Sentimentalised but actually held in contempt, old women are only now beginning to be acknowledged as a special underclass.[14] At worst dehumanised as ugly old witches, at best trivialised as little old ladies, women as crones are far from positions of dignity or respect which one would like to think might accompany old age. Ruth Jhabvala's probing analysis indirectly reveals these sad conditions. Her old ladies live with them. But they also manage, sometimes, to turn them to advantage, for not to be seen is to possess a certain valuable freedom. As they are for Jhabvala's unassuming writer-heroines, marginality and the invisibility that it bestows are in a sense privileged states.

A crucial factor, of course, is money. The fates of Leelavati, in *Heat and Dust*, or even, to take a non-Indian example, Miss Tuhy ('Miss Sahib', *A Stronger Climate: The Sufferers*) show that.

The 1980 story 'Grandmother' presents one free old lady with the power to use her freedom, for Minnie's husband has left her plenty of money: thereby hangs the tale.

Like her Polish-Jewish grandmother, whom she has come to resemble, Minnie is 'happy, and it showed'. It shows so much that at times she has to disguise it, particularly in the company of her daughter Sandra, tall and blonde (a romantic heroine), who is much given to suffering over the neglect of her husband, Tim. Minnie, on the other hand, enjoys a companionable friendship with 'the boys', Ralph and Mickey, aspiring actors in their twenties who live together in a studio near Minnie's Upper East Side hotel. Minnie pays their rent. The narrative draws the reader into a representative scene between Minnie and the boys: Ralph plays the guitar and sings; the three of them discuss the boys' auditions; they chat about astrology. Sandra appears, weeping and railing about her troubled marriage. To Minnie's horror she even suggests moving in with her. Conveniently, she becomes pregnant and is reconciled with Tim.

Tim is also the name of Marietta's husband in *In Search of Love and Beauty*. The cool, rather distant relationship of Minnie and Sandra prefigures that of Louise and Marietta in that, like Marietta, Sandra has little interest in her mother. The young view the old as flat, two-dimensional backdrops for their own lives, assumed to possess centrality and importance. So it was with Werner and his mother. Until old age causes us to resemble our own grandparents, the old are minor characters. To be fair, Sandra has little interest in anyone, for she is preoccupied with the suffering engendered by her failing marriage; but she takes no comfort from her mother, nor, for that matter, is much offered. Minnie's advice to Sandra is rational but superfluous: 'But why do you go there!' For her part, Minnie cannot understand Sandra's frantic attachment to Tim: she 'had never been that way with Sam. When he was away, she was glad, and when he returned it was like being put back into irons'. The women have little to say to one another.

Indeed, they are at odds, while Sandra and Tim *are* united at least in their rather amused disapproval of the relationship of Minnie, Mickey and Ralph. The relationship represents a considerable financial drain, from their point of view: Minnie spends a good deal of money on Mickey and Ralph – money that would probably be theirs one day. When Sandra becomes pregnant, she and Tim hope that Minnie will become 'a proper grandmother'. She shows no sign of doing so.

The characters' names suggest that they inhabit a Disney cartoon. One hears the Klezmer music that the Disney studios appropriated. For Minnie, with her 'bright Polish-Jewish eyes that sparkled and danced' and 'skinny' Mickey, life is a game – as it was for the Minister's wife and her 'Biju'. Such creatures, while they may be subversive, are harmless. They do not outrage respectability, though they may elicit patronising laughter. Tim, normative heterosexual male, treats Ralph and Mickey 'as if they were his equals, except that the way he looked at them, his frosty blue eyes glinting with amusement, was not the way one looks at equals'. However, Tim shares one thing with Ralph and Mickey: namely, his visits to Minnie usually coincide with requests for money. But Mickey and Ralph have the grace to stay for a while, whereas Tim takes the money and runs. Yet it must be said that his departure is a relief: his attempts at small talk are oppressive monologues concerning sport, or worse, dirty jokes.

So in relation to Tim, Ralph and Mickey are an improvement. They have real charm; they treat Minnie with warmth and familiarity. Minnie loves 'her two boys'; they are the sons she never had. Ralph, though actually Muslim by birth, is 'the beautiful Jewish boy of her dreams' – a clue to Minnie's shaky grasp of reality. She enjoys their conversation about astrology and ghosts; she enjoys reassuring them about their talent and consoling them about their failed auditions; she likes to calm their domestic quarrels. She is comforted by the sight of 'lithe Ralph or skinny Mickey' stretched out on her brocade sofas; she enjoys ordering from room service for them ('one or the other of the boys was always hungry and had to call for something').

It is, in many ways, a pleasant picture. But on what, really, is this friendship based? Clearly, one must applaud Minnie's triumph over her respectable and selfish daughter and son-in-law; one must appreciate her indifference to their disapproval, her freedom to be as close as she wishes to Ralph and Mickey. But surely one must also attend to the fact that Minnie is the source of Ralph and Mickey's income, and that they would not be there if not for that. How valid, how sustaining, can a purchased friendship be? And there is no doubt that this is a purchased friendship.

Jhabvala's portrayal of this friendship of an old woman and two homosexual men is ambivalent, as is her portrayal of women's relationships with homosexual men throughout her oeuvre. By and large, it is a positive portrait: she appears to see gay men as primary sources of nurturance for her women protagonists, who have such impoverished emotional relationships with other women or with heterosexual men. But the portrayal also demonstrates the limitations of such a friendship for her woman protagonist: she will never have centrality for him, and he will never willingly reveal himself to her. The fiction is full of evasive young men and their doting mothers or sisters (Raymond, Mark, Werner, Hughie and in Jhabvala's tenth novel, Michael). Harry and Olivia's friendship in *Heat and Dust* demonstrates the pitfalls of women's reliance upon friendships with homosexual men: when pushed, Harry betrays Olivia and allies himself with the Nawab.[15]

Gay men, concerned mostly with each other, do not truly *see* the women who form friendships with them, in Jhabvala's fiction. They view them at arm's length, as images of femininity, or peripherally, as dispensers of service or advantage. For example, Mickey loves to see Minnie in her rocking chair 'just like I've seen ladies sitting on their porch with little children, reading them stories.' (Ralph comments acidly that Mickey has seen that only in the movies.) At the end of *In Search of Love and Beauty*, Eric, Regi's young homosexual escort, realises that Louise's fall will be fatal. He has worked in enough dance-halls to know that when aged ladies fall, it is often to their deaths. Yet he shrugs her death off. He has no reponse. Perhaps this is appropriate: he is employed by Regi.

Women are devalued by homosexual men in general just as they are by heterosexual men. Hughie allows Marie to comfort him but is ashamed to 'be so commingled with a girl'. Mark will not talk openly to Natasha. The basis of the relationship in 'Grandmother' remains Minnie's money. Without it there would be no friendship, no songs, no room service. We congratulate Minnie for having, in old age, the independence and means to do as she pleases, but we must be disturbed by the fact that her money is paramount in this friendship. In the same way, we must applaud Sofia's choice to exercise sexual freedom; but we must be disturbed by the outcome of that choice. We applaud Shakuntala's decision to be an artist, not only a housewife: but we have reason to believe that her teacher will not treat her well. The same scenario appears even more sharply etched in 'A Summer by the Sea'.

Emotional options for Ruth Jhabvala's women are hedged with severe limitations; yet they persist in the quest for feeling, searching to know and be known. In the next novel she will focus again on the tragi-comic search for love and beauty.

9

In Search of Love and Beauty

THE GOTHIC WAY AND THE GREEK WAY: THREE GENERATIONS OF SEARCHERS

Every protagonist in Jhabvala's fiction has been 'in search of love and beauty'. Her Western women in India particularly are so committed to this search that they willingly leave home, country and family, all that they know, to embark on it, feeling that their drab lives lack even possibilities for search or discovery. This novel, whose slightly ironic title contains the essential Jhabvala theme, examines the effects of this search on a group of German and Austrian refugees in New York, and two generations of their descendents.

Like Jhabvala's other novels, this one examines the effects of interpersonal power, particularly its erotic aspect. Whether in male-dominated 'spiritual' groups or between lovers, the power relations between human beings are isolated and held up to the light in the subtlest of portrayals. When the lovers are both male, as often in this novel, the dynamic can be seen in a new way, but, to be sure, it exists still: power simply resides with the more 'male' of the two. From Natasha, who loves Mark, to Mark, who loves Kent, the line of masculinity and power ascends. But the novel also counterposes, as does *Heat and Dust*, a nurturant, transcendent force in nature, which may sustain unhappy lovers through the dangerous grip of erotic love. And, as before in *Heat and Dust*, this nurturing presence is implicitly female. Its imagery, as we shall see, reaffirms the existence of a sphere of nurturance and love between women, unattainable, unthinkable, experienced as repellent in reality, but present in symbolic form throughout women's lives.

One may surmise that Ruth Jhabvala's marriage of almost forty years to the successful architect Cyrus Jhabvala has contributed to the importance given in her work to architecture and interior design as revelations of character. Never has this been more true than in *In Search of Love and Beauty*, in which architecture performs a major thematic function. Two Hudson River Valley mansions, with their inhabitants, are counterposed: one 'Greek revival', one 'Gothic' – both are styles that evoke a rich set of literary associations.

A gay man buys, restores and inhabits the Greek revival; a charismatic, compulsively womanising guru takes over the Gothic, with his followers. These two mansions, 'on their eminences', and the traffic between them, form much of the novel's setting, and since they are explicitly compared, we are encouraged to regard them as poles in its hermeneutics. The two architectural styles image two contrasting modes of being: the Apollonian 'Golden Mean' versus the dynamic striving of late medieval Christianity; in turn, these modes of being may be associated with two erotic directions, as it were: the homosexual ('Greek') withdrawal from the male–female struggle, and the heterosexual ('Gothic') acceptance of the clash. Having made such a formulation, however, one must immediately withdraw its absoluteness: for what might *look like* classical order and moderation in the world of male homosexuality is on closer examination no less chaotic, no less desperate, no less absurd than the familiar disorder of the heterosexual impasse.

NEW YORK AS A SETTING

Perhaps because the novel is set in New York, and not in India, it lacks both the sense of adventure that travel provides for other of Jhabvala's Western protagonists, and the warmth of some of the Indian characters; it presents a set of cool alternatives indeed. Nevertheless, a Chekhovian regret permeates and softens the bitterness of this tale of disappointed lovers, while the droll observations of the ironist contribute to its redeeming comedy.

In Search of Love and Beauty is an audacious departure for a writer who had built a career on the interpretation of India to the West. It indicates that her real concern is, and always was, not primarily with cultural difference but with character. Reviewers have rightly observed that Jhabvala's Delhi is as universal as Faulkner's Yokna-patawpha County.[1] Yet, in a way, the New York setting represents a return to the author's 'roots', or the closest she can come to them, given the tragedies of twentieth-century history.

Isaac Bashevis Singer, like Ruth Jhabvala, another displaced central-European Jew, commented that Upper Broadway in New York is the nearest approximation that he knows of to prewar

Warsaw.[2] The Ruth Prawer who, with her family, fled Germany at the age of eleven was, in any case, never firmly rooted, as I have already mentioned: her father himself was a Polish-Jewish refugee from the forced conscription of the First World War, and her mother's father a still earlier refugee from Poland.[3] The three stories I have just discussed explore the lives of refugees in the West, but this was the first longer and more ambitious work to be set in the West; though not in Europe: that still 'smells of blood'.[4]

Like Singer, Jhabvala has compared New York's Upper West Side to pre-Hitler central Europe. Something about the ambience, even the foods available at the local deli, she says, recall to her, in the manner of Proust's madeleine, long-forgotten tastes and the childhood memories that surround them.[5] After a voluntary exile of some twenty years, her return to residence in the West, in the late seventies, must have been enormously affecting. She has written of such a return in 'The Englishwoman' (*How I Became a Holy Mother*).

If that story has an autobiographical thread – and it is difficult to imagine that it does not – the move back to the West was imperative. One of Jhabvala's reviewers, writing in *Midstream: A Monthly Jewish Review*, in 1974, commented rather prematurely, as it turns out, that 'we are left with the disturbing glimpse of Mrs. Jhabvala living as a near recluse in Delhi, reclining in her air-conditioned room with all the blinds down . . . dismayed by India, no longer at home in Europe, she envisages ultimate defeat'.[6] Happily, time has disproved that glimpse.

It is fitting that Jhabvala found her way to New York, city of European refugees. She has said that her move to New York 'magically opened the door into [her] personal and ancestral past'.[7] For there, on New York's Upper West Side, were 'the people who should have remained in my life – people I went to school with in Cologne, with exactly the same background as my own'.[8] And these are the people who appear in this first novel to be set in the West.

It may be the personal link with the past that accounts for the anti-chronological organisation of this novel, which juxtaposes events that take place over a span of sixty years. This new fluidity contrasts with the classical novelistic unfolding of narration in her early works, like the Austenian *Amrita* or *The Nature of Passion*. Even *A New Dominion*, from the seventies, with its increasing narrative fragmentation, or *Heat and Dust*, which dips back and forth in time, with contemporary present and remote past repeating each other, have a more classically ordered structure. In *In Search of Love and Beauty*, time is compressed and often reversed.

This is a filmic technique and may be attributable to the collaboration with Merchant and Ivory. By 1983 Ruth Jhabvala had written more than a dozen screenplays, and seems to have intended this novel for adaptation to the screen.[9] In a recent profile she is quoted to the effect that the 'fluid movement, back and forth in time' of her recent novels is particularly due to watching the editing of film.[10]

'Flashback' is a cinematic technique in that the transition in time is effected instantaneously, without the mediation of narrative explanation. *In Search of Love and Beauty* incorporates flashback rather than the more literary 'reminiscence' in the sense that one is plunged, without regard for chronology and with a minimum of explanation, into moments throughout the course of three generations. 'Here is Louise in her sixties', the narrator may report (p. 3). Or, in a pointed reference to the screen, she may supply the reader with bare dialogue – 'this is the way their conversation might go' (p. 11).

Reviewing the novel in the *New York Times*, Michiko Kakutani described the scenes as 'brief, cinematic "takes"' and commented justly that 'though this structure tends to heighten the distance Mrs. Jhabvala maintains from her characters – thereby resulting in a certain coolness at times – it seems a fitting narrative strategy for this story of emotional waifs and strays'.[11]

A further distancing derives from the fact that the novel contains more characters than Jhabvala's previous works (more than twenty-five are introduced by name). It follows some of them through three generations, which represents another innovation for her, and makes this novel a variant on a particular (woman's) genre, the popular 'dynastic' novel. Thus, to examine the novel's imagery and reveal its aesthetics, let us first reconstruct its lengthy plot.

Louise and Regi are girlhood friends in a 'suburb of the town of D—— in Germany'. The initial letter is at once a stylistic allusion to the fiction of nineteenth-century Europe, in which tradition Jhabvala is firmly rooted, and a reference to the remoteness of the European past, which is a theme of this tale of exiles. 'D——' suggests Dresden, whose beautiful opera-house – which figures in the story – was bombed to the ground along with virtually everything else in the city.[12]

At eighteen, Louise, beautiful, cultivated and Protestant, is courted by Bruno Sonnenblick, a sensitive and poetic Jew of thirty-six. His name, signifying 'dark sunny expression', alludes to the paradoxes of suffering idealism. That idealism is revealed most plainly in his love letters to Louise, one of which the narrator quotes: Bruno did not believe in heaven, he tells Louise, but now he believes in 'heaven on earth. Thanks to you, my goddess, immortal thanks' (p. 32).

Aphrodite, Greek goddess of love and beauty, and later 'the Ceres of his household' (p. 43) appears to this first seeker after the immortal in the persona of his beloved Louise. Though she will betray him, he will continue to adore her.

Eleven years later, after their move to New York in the thirties – the dreadful reason for which is not explictly mentioned – Regi and Louise are still friends; more modern and more moneyed, Regi lives on Park Avenue, not the less fashionable Upper West Side. It is she who introduces Louise to 'the Adonis' – Leo Kellermann. While Louise and Bruno's daughter Marianne is still a baby, Leo moves in with them in their large, dark, Upper West Side apartment. Both consider it a privilege to help this charismatic, already accomplished, young man.

As early as the first line in the novel, its premise is reported: 'Everyone always knew that Leo Kellermann had something, was someone, special.' He has published in *Querschnitt* and worked with Max Reinhardt.[13] He has 'met Freud' before the era of Reich (p. 2). His 'movement', which will be of the theatre 'though reaching far beyond it', will 'train initiates' for revolutionary developments on the social, psychological and – 'why not?' – biological plane (p. 33).

This character contains satiric elements of the popular psychologist Fritz Perls, founder of the Esalen Institute in California, and the Russian mystic Gurdjieff (the subject of Pietr Demianovich Ouspensky's similarly named but completely humourless account, *In Search of the Miraculous*, 1927);[14] not to mention any number of equally charismatic and more or less unscrupulous 'healers'. One remembers that the writer Katherine Mansfield was a follower of Gurdjieff, and that she met her untimely death, of tuberculosis, at his 'Centre for the Harmonious Development of Man' at Fountainebleau. Gurdjieff, like the Swami of *A New Dominion*, did not believe in Western medicine, at least in the case of Katherine

Mansfield.[15] And, like Margaret in *A New Dominion*, she died believing that her illness was essentially spiritual.

Leo's personal power is remarkable. He maintains a life-long emotional hold ('a ball and chain') on Louise, and to some extent on her friend Regi as well. Both women, though older and more moneyed than Leo, vie for the privilege of supporting him, and put themselves, with 'no hesitation' into his hands (p. 40). Like many other young women who give Leo their 'personalities, or inner beings, or souls (except that he disliked that word)' (p. 40), they feel a sense of necessity since they have 'proliferated' into such 'complicated personalities' that they can no longer 'manage themselves' and must 'hand themselves over to someone else, someone stronger' (p.41).

At their regular rendezvous at the café 'Old Vienna', Louise and Regi discuss Leo and his work – and reveal, or do not reveal, to each other, according to their personalities, the extent of their involvement with him. (Each sleeps with him; Regi never tells Louise, but Louise tells Regi.)

Marianne renames herself Marietta.[16] She grows to hate her mother's lover, who flirts with her too, even in her childhood. Leo's manner causes her later in her life to exempt herself from the entire arena of sexual love, except for Ahmed, her Indian lover. Bruno always takes her on outings when Leo and Louise are together (he is well aware of their affair), but the adults are not always successful in maintaining discretion: as a young girl Marietta witnesses a scene of Dionysian lovemaking between the pair. She says nothing about it, though she wonders mightily at its meaning, and of the meaning of her mother's exclamation, 'I'm coming!' (p. 226).

Louise and Leo have a stormy relationship, as befits two Olympians. Soon after the love scene that Marietta observes, Leo humiliates Louise at a dinner party at which are assembled the many students and disciples of his experimental theatre group, and Louise breaks with him – though only for a time. Public humiliation is one of Leo's standard teaching techniques.

Marietta becomes a beauty and a dancer. Early on, she marries Tim, a WASP from a wealthy and once-powerful family. But this family is fragmented: Tim is an alcoholic, one of his sisters is mentally ill, the other a lesbian – again, lesbianism as pathological – and the father is a suicide. Marietta becomes pregnant with Mark, simultaneously deciding to leave Tim, who for years after

unsuccessfully tries to win her back. Uninterested in eros, Marietta
is a successful entrepreneur and clothing designer. Her relationship
with her adored son, she says, suffices for her, though Mark
jealously guards his emotional distance.

Wishing to repudiate the Protestant identity of her mother's
family and Tim's, and preferring her father's Jewishness, Marietta
adopts a war orphan, the 'one-hundred percent guaranteed Jewish'
Natasha. Natasha is a solitary, serious and introverted child,
inordinately sensitive to the sufferings of others. She is happiest
at home with Louise and Mark. Even as a child, she functions as
sympathetic confidante to Louise, who is again in the throes of
her slave-like attachment to an unreliable Leo (he disappears to
California for long periods of time; he calls at odd moments,
reversing the charges). For her part, Natasha loves Mark passionately and hopelessly. He allows her to comfort him as he suffers
over various boys in his class; he frequently falls in love. Unlike
Marietta, Natasha knows about his homosexuality: she knows that
being Mark's consoler is the closest she can get to him.

After Tim's death, probably also a suicide, Marietta meets Ahmed,
an older Indian musician, and through her affair with him discovers
India. Leo also likes Ahmed's company, and now incorporates into
his teachings tantrism, the yogic practice employing sexuality as a
means to spiritual enlightenment. At Louise's sixtieth birthday
party, Leo and Marietta have a sexual encounter, in which Marietta,
though she still 'hates' Leo, at last experiences sexual desire and
orgasm – which have hitherto eluded her. 'Yes, yes, I'm coming!'
she too calls, this time partially in response to the impatient
summons from Mark, for the candles on the birthday cake are lit
and Louise is waiting to blow them out! While Regi is in bed with
a migraine, and Marietta and Leo are betraying her together,
Louise 'gives thanks in her heart' for her dearest ones around her:
droll though it may be, the comedy has a bitter taste when the
daughter can so betray the mother.

Marietta travels yearly to India, over a six-year period, for her
successful business now imports Indian fabrics and handicrafts.
She meets Sujata, an ageing but still amorous woman singer: Sujata
is in love with Ravi, a charming young man and friend of her
teenaged son. Sujata voices the novels crucial question:

'If it was so wrong to have these feelings, then why were they
sent? Why did they come to a human being – as suddenly,

unexpectedly, irresistibly as those notes of perfection, those high moments of highest art that her grandmother had taught her to lie in wait for? If it was wrong, if it was shameful, then why was it there? And why was it so glorious?' (p. 101)

During her final trip to India, Marietta takes her sixteen-year-old son Mark along, and he enjoys an innocent and sensual dalliance with Ravi. Though Marietta actually sees them in bed together, she does not realise or even suspect that her son is homosexual. However, when she is bitten by a kite, she enters a phase of disillusionment with India, and she never returns. The incident has revealed a cruel aspect of Hindu pollution taboos.

Like his mother and his maternal grandfather, Mark has a good business sense. As a dealer in real estate, Mark negotiates the sale to Leo of the old Gothic mansion on the Hudson: there Leo establishes his 'Academy for Potential Development', a sort of Western ashram catering for the 'psychospiritual needs', as defined by him, of dissatisfied and well-bred young persons, mostly female.

Natasha, by now in her early twenties and unemployable, being able to do nothing except write, is given a secretarial job there, though Mark secretly pays her salary. Unimpressed by Leo, as he is uninterested in her, she appreciates the Academy, where she is left alone except, again, to listen – this time to the impassioned soul-searchings of Leo's students and disciples.

Only now do we reach the novel's present time, the time of Leo's Gothic 'Academy' and Mark's neo-classical 'Van Kuypen' house. Mark's present lover is the rather indifferent Kent, and Mark's rival a much older and richer man named Anthony. Events reach a climax on the day of Regi's eighty-fourth birthday party. Marietta, Louise and Eric, Regi's young male companion – paid, of course, and homosexual, of course – have decided to celebrate at the Academy.

All is in a state of confusion. Anthony has chosen this day to make his *grand geste*, arriving at the Van Kuypen house to win Kent away from Mark. But his action is premature, for Kent, while quite willing to goad Mark to jealousy, has no intention of actually leaving him for Anthony. Anthony briefly indulges an impulse to stab Mark with a carving knife, but stops at putting a small hole in his sweater. Mark is indignant: 'it was a favourite sweater.'

To make matters worse, for the first time in his seventy years, Leo has fallen in love, with the young and beautiful Stephanie, a 'student' at the Academy. *Her* lover is Jeff, a handsome young man (who also sleeps with both Natasha and Mark). When Jeff decides to move on, and Stephanie to accompany him, Leo becomes distraught. Driving to Mark's house, he picks up Natasha: she thinks he is heading for Regi's birthday party, but he is actually searching for Stephanie, intending to overtake her and Jeff on the first leg of their journey westward. His car has no headlights, a snowstorm has begun, he is known for his reckless driving. Blinded by tears, he drives Natasha off into the almost complete obscurity of the snowstorm. There we leave them.

Back at the Academy, Marietta, Eric, Louise and Regi arrive from New York. The two old ladies walk in the frozen gardens; Regi, annoyed, gives Louise a push. The fall is fatal for Louise, an aged lady with brittle bones. As she dies, she calls again, 'I'm coming!'; again Marietta wonders, 'Where's she coming? Where's she going?'

CRITICAL RESPONSE

Unlike Jhabvala's previous work, *In Search of Love and Beauty* was not very well received. Both John Updike in the *New Yorker* and Robert Towers in the *New York Times Book Review* were annoyed by the author's detachment from her characters.[17] Towers saw her as a kind of schoolma'am, one of a school of British novelists 'usually, but not invariably, female', who 'deal firmly with any amount of nonsense from their characters . . . instantly see through their little games, laugh at their pretensions and call them to order when they step out of line'. He goes on to compare Jhabvala unfavourably to Jane Austen, who did not, as she does, 'revel . . . in [her characters'] discomfiture and degradation'. He deplores the 'grotesque horror' that he finds in this comedy, 'embellished with grinning skulls'.

One has to admit that there is a chill about this novel. The very abundance of characters militates against closeness to any one of them. And the most sympathetic and fully presented characters here, grandmother, mother and daughter – Louise, Marietta and Natasha – are notable for their lack of involvement with others (including, to some extent, each other) except for the unresponsive objects of their loves – Leo and Mark. The novel negates and discounts friendship; and sexual love is certainly problematical.

Yet, this tale of searchers and exiles whose travel was not voluntary is comedy, and I do not find it unrelievedly dark. What is more, it is rich with meaning and, like all literature, a source of hope. Like all literature, it yields more when one follows its suggestions – in this case, by considering its mythological allusions.

THE PANTHEON OF *IN SEARCH OF LOVE AND BEAUTY*

To small children, adults truly possess the powers of gods. Even more so, perhaps, when we as adults look back through layers of time, do our parents take on a numinous, mythical dimension. Remembered, they are our personal, individualised gods, present throughout our lives to be loved and wrestled with. And so it is entirely fitting that the Olympian metaphor be brought into Jhabvala's ninth novel, the first one to be set within her own cultural heritage. Among these characters, 'the people I should have known', the reader senses partial portraits of Jhabvala's own parents. As I have mentioned, Bruno and Louise resemble Otto and Sonia Wolff of 'A Birthday in London', and both couples may be loosely based on Jhabvala's own parents. Support for this guess comes from the fact that Jhabvala uses the name Sonya again, in her tenth novel, *Three Continents*, in which Sonya is a motherly figure who attempts (unsuccessfully) to protect the heroine from her own dangerous passions. In any case, the characters of *In Search of Love and Beauty* are frequently linked with Greco-Roman mythology. 'Love and Beauty' themselves constitute the province of Aphrodite, and the phrase, I think, connotes the goddess. Particularly central to the story is the Demeter–Persephone myth, as I hope to show.

The references are shifting and associative. For example, Leo is not one god, but many: he is an 'Adonis' and 'an Apollo' on the first page of the novel; he is 'the reigning deity' (p. 37), 'a Dionysian figure' (p. 15); bathing, he is 'pink, plump and naked as a pagan god' (p. 102), and a sponge in his hands is Neptune's 'trident' (p. 102).

Leo is variously Bacchus and Adonis, Louise is Demeter and Aphrodite, while Natasha is Persephone. The male and female gods of the earth in the Greek pantheon were Dionysus and

Demeter – clearly Louise and Leo, whose troubled but ongoing love affair underpins this story.

The ending of the novel is especially significant. The simultaneous deaths of Leo, Natasha and Louise, as in some Greek or Greco-Elizabethan tragedy, emphasise the fatal resolution of the search for love and beauty. Leo abducts Natasha into a maelstrom of darkness and cold, and Louise, who has been compared with Ceres, dies simultaneously. The mysterious 'Point', which all the searching characters try to discover, remains a mystery; in our time-bound world, we cannot express it directly.

Birthday parties, the novel's leitmotif, image the inexorable passage of time, as they did in the three short stories discussed in chapter 9. Birthday parties are annual rites, recurring in this novel which spans the adult lifetime of two women: from young girlhood to old age, 'the whole of life' (p. 218) apart from the kind of timeless unconsciousness of childhood. These several birthday parties in the novel might be compared to the Eleusinian mysteries, which celebrated the return of Persephone and the meeting of Demeter and Bacchus.

Fire and ice, darkness and light are poles in the novel's symbology. Leo is 'hot' – impulsive, expansive, dangerous and sexual. His Dionysian (irrational) heat is contrasted to Mark's Apollonian (reasonable) coolness. In Greek mythology, there were two mediators between Dionysus and Apollo: Hermes and Pan. The novel recasts them both in Jeff, who literally travels between Leo's and Mark's neighbouring headquarters more often than any other character: he is employed by both. Like Hermes, Jeff is bisexual; like Pan, he is explicity associated with nature and the earth.

The author, who strews these mythological allusions in our path, encourages interpretation, that is, she leads the reader to make analogies, to engage in the literary process of seeing relationships. She even has her own characters repeat the process: at one point Leo, in a rare sympathetic act, tells a story to the toddler Natasha, 'about two princesses, a tiger, and a horse, in the course of which three generations grew up and several kingdoms were won and lost' (p. 16). Like this novel, Leo's little story asks, 'And just because they were angry with each other and fifty years passed during which they were not on speaking terms, do you think they could stop loving each other?' (p. 16). Leo (the lion) is clearly the tiger and Bruno perhaps the noble horse, but the two princesses can be none other than Louise and Regi. In view of what I see as the novel's underlying, hidden theme, the loss of the mother and of love between women, and its symbolic reaffirmation in the Demeter/Persephone allusions, this little story of Leo's is full of significance. Though at first glance, and in the context of the bedtime story scene, the two who could not stop loving each other would seem to be Louise and Leo, in fact, though 'they were not on speaking terms', the two could only be the two princesses. At least the identity of the two who were angry with each other for fifty years is intriguingly ambiguous.

Leo/Dionysus is once explicitly compared to 'some superannuated circus animal' (p. 85); his eyes are 'wise and ancient as an elephant's' (p. 82). Dionysus was associated with wild beasts, as well as with intoxication, which releases the bestial in human beings; and the name 'Leo Kellermann' wittily conflates both qualities, for Leo in astrology is the lion, the 'hottest' sign, ruled by the sun; while *Keller* is the German for 'wine-cellar' – an image that incorporates the ideas of underworld *and* of intoxication.

Throughout, Louise is nurturant womanhood: Demeter, goddess of earth and harvest. Louise is warm, expressive: she appreciates, exclaims, enjoys, delights. But she is strong, too: she is large and capable. She always wears the royal purple – burgundy, plum. Her name, like Leo's, derives from 'lion'. Moments before her death, she is declaiming enthusiastically about the landscape: her German-accented 'just nice for skating!' (p. 224) is characteristic. It is she who has organised the little party; she who has bought the pastries and the birthday cake. 'Brr – aren't you glad you've got your mink?' she jokes to Regi, after pointing out the icicles that have formed on the nipples of a stone nymph in the frozen fountain (foreshadowing the deaths to come).

Louise and Leo are like two 'giants'. She is 'Ceres'. She is like 'some rooted old tree'. The imagery is sylvan and pastoral, recalling both pre-Christian myth and Elizabethan lyric. Louise and Leo, in their zestful lovemaking, are, respectively, 'hunted and hunter' (p. 108) as Marietta spies them. The pair 'romped around as if they were out in the open' (p. 108) until Leo captures Louise, a 'stag at bay' (p. 109). The encounter takes place in Louise's apartment, under the chandelier 'hanging down in clusters of grapes'. And at last they arise and walk together back to the bedroom, 'like loving friends now, their arms around each other' (p. 109). Not only are they explictly compared to Ceres and Dionysus; they are also referred to as Venus and Adonis, the other reigning male–female Olympian pair.

Undoubtedly, the novel's language and imagery associates Natasha primarily with Persephone. Orphan of the Holocaust, she is literally associated with the Kingdom of Death in modern terms. Even as a baby, she weeps like 'an old woman . . . full of hopeless grief' (p. 48). She is Louise's granddaughter, of course, and as such, automatically associated with Demeter's daughter Persephone. Her eyes are 'so dark and deep they seemed to reach down into caverns way beneath the earth' (p. 16). She is compared to a seagull, 'swooping between sea and sky as if trying to decide to which element [it] belonged' (p. 112). She is always physically *cold*, though warmhearted. Shirley, one of the students at the Academy, exclaims over her cold hands: 'If this is how you are in summer, what are you like in the winter?' (p. 137). 'The same', Natasha smiles, and inwardly compares herself to Louise, so warm-blooded that she would 'fling off her dress and stand there in her petticoat with naked shoulders fanning herself' (p. 137). Finally, as Natasha drives off unwittingly with Leo to her probable doom, at the close of the novel, 'it seemed to [her] that the pale twilight, the fading earth were swallowing them up, sucking them in, as into water or clouds' (p. 226).

Regi is a kind of snow-queen, another version of the Queen of the Underworld whom Adonis loved, and who shared his affections with Aphrodite – as Regi does with Louise. All coldness and light, she is imaged by her Bauhaus-style apartment on Park Avenue, with its tubular steel and glass furniture, which, of course, contrasts with Louise's cave-like, dark and comfortable Upper West Side apartment, full of large Bavarian antiques. Regi herself is repeatedly compared to ice. Her breasts are 'little icebergs', in a stylish expressionist painting of her in the nude, which hangs in her Park Avenue apartment. Leo 'called her iceberg and shivered – "Brr" – when he came near her' (p. 86); but he praises Louise for being 'warm, *like a bed with a woman in it*. [My emphasis.] What a relief after Regi' (p. 73). Such praise, while seductive, of course reveals Leo's penchant for playing one woman off against another – and his view of Louise as a material object, a bed with a woman *in it*!

The Hellenic theme reverberates throughout, as Jhabvala's careful and witty use of details reveals it. For example, when Marietta bursts into the apartment with news that she will marry Tim, Bruno – who in his idealism persists in calling her Marianne – has been reading, partly to take his mind off what might be happening in the bedroom, where Leo and Louise are together. His text is Goethe's *Hermann und Dorothea*. That he is reading at all during Leo's and Louise's assignation is a telling enough detail. But the fact that his book is identified is a clue to its importance.

Hermann und Dorothea is an epic of domestic life. Written in 1796, it was enormously popular throughout the nineteenth century – perhaps it is a reference to Bruno's courtly old-fashioned ways.[18] Moreover, *Hermann und Dorothea* is considered Goethe's most Hellenised work, a conscious disavowal of the Gothicised romanticism of *Werther*.[19] Goethe considered himself to be 'the last of the Homeridae'.[20] Like *In Search of Love and Beauty* itself, Goethe's epic concerns refugees, an engagement, and parents' relations with their children. It celebrates the beauties of the Rhine valley – very much like the Hudson valley. The Hermann of the title is a reserved, modest young man who falls in love with heroic, beautiful and large Dorothea. In this the pair are reminiscent of modest Bruno and heroic Louise. Although it seems unlikely that this detail is an intentional parallel, the action of Goethe's poem takes place at an inn called 'The Golden Lion', and Leo – the lion's – blondness is repeatedly referred to in the novel!

The theme of Goethe's poem is the impossible tension between the ideal and the real: this is Jhabvala's theme too. The French revolution is shown, in the poem, to embody the failure of the dream: the 'dangers in every attempt to create the city of God here and now' [Goethe's words in translation].[21] Leo's Academy is certainly such an attempt; so, in a very different way, and on a very different scale, was Hitler's Germany, the first home of the refugees.

The lifelong association of these two women predates any other relationship in the novel, and forms a dark backdrop to the story of Louise and her descendants. 'Ah, those two poor old women – when I think of what they were' (p. 209) cries Leo in the final pages of the novel; and indeed, this exclamation is almost a summary of the novel. Its time marks their passage through the years, from the bloom of girlhood into the decrepitude and senility of their extreme old age. The birthday parties that punctuate the novel and serve as dramatic settings for major events are always Louise's or Regi's.

If Louise is nurturant earth-mother and goddess, Regi throughout has represented another face of femininity – the bitch. Catty and self-aggrandising, she glitters with the accoutrements of fashion gone haywire. Her bright red hair, the spindly legs which she places coquettishly, unaware, later in the novel's time, that they are grotesque, the young male companions whom she pays to accompany her: all contribute to the final pathos of the child she ultimately becomes.

Regi is that anomaly, a 'successful' woman; one who plays her feminine role to the hilt, gleaning from it the maximum it can yield in social and economic power. She has three wealthy husbands, from whom she collects alimony, which enables her, as she ages, to remain comfortable, to 'look after myself well' (p. 46), and to have always some young man around 'whom she paid as little as she could get away with' (p. 47). She has the invulnerability that such self-absorption brings. *She* does not search for love and beauty. But the mask of 'femininity' has been so firmly cemented that the human being underneath is no longer visible. All that shows through her mask is naked self-interest at its crudest.

So when, in the novel's final scene, Louise clings to her on the ice, she delivers a characteristic response: 'Let me go, you stupid goose', she says 'crossly, in German' (p. 224), and Louise falls, to her death, as it turns out. So ends their friendship. Regi's nastiness and selfishness, relieved only by her senile disintegration, in which she becomes a child and Louise her parent, makes it difficult through the novel to believe in Louise's continued attachment to her. (To her credit, Regi does possess a certain refreshing venom – she does not like Leo. But she dislikes him for the wrong reasons: he is too 'intellectual'!)

Louise and Regi have the only friendship in this novel, and it is notable for its complete lack of reciprocity, in the manner of other female friendships satirised in earlier pieces by the author: English Clarissa and Hungarian Etta in *A Backward Place*, or the two Englishwomen Elizabeth and Margaret in the story 'Two More Under the Indian Sun' (*How I Became a Holy Mother*).[22] In both the earlier novel and the story just referred to, one woman is good-natured, warm and impulsive, the other an egotistical bully. Louise and Regi repeat the dynamic, throughout the seventy-year course of their involvement; at the last, Louise weeps when the ancient Regi soils herself. Time, while it has not altered their relationship, has reduced the queen to the stature of a small child (the narrative makes this point explicitly), at which point she finally achieves pathos, feeling.

The bleak view of female friendship contrasts somewhat with the Indian novels, where Indian women may appear who do extend to the protagonists a friendship worthy of the name. In *A New Dominion*, Asha's friendship with Lee, and in *Heat and Dust*, Maji's with the modern narrator, have a healing warmth; both women offer a human connection to the Western wandering women, which is the closest they come to communion with another.

In this novel, there is one Indian woman, Sujata who 'lived for love'. Her name derives from the Sanskrit for 'nobly-born', and she is – of a long line of singers. She comes into the novel not to provide friendship, but to voice her shameful delight in her young lover, and also to wonder what really *is* shameful about it; but her appearance in the novel is brief and peripheral. We do learn that she dies in an accident with a motorcycle rickshaw, with a driver 'who drove like a crazy man' (p. 152). Her death, then, foreshadows that of Natasha, who presumably dies in a similar manner, but her friendship with Marietta is briefly sketched and of minor importance.

With the possibility of female friendship obstructed by jealousy, and even the fundamental inadequacy of the female Other, women are consigned to search for love and beauty in the personae of men – who, like Leo, hate them.

Early in the narrative, we witness an exchange between Leo and Mark, who visit with each other in a very 'feminine' and overdecorated boudoir belonging to one of Leo's 'rich lady admirers'. Mark congratulates Leo on his good fortune in securing this *pied-à-terre* for himself (rent-free, of course). But to Leo the place 'smells of the five P's' – an obscure reference to a dirty joke which the reader is left to imagine. 'You and I are the same', he tells Mark: 'We don't like women.' Mark corrects him – doesn't Leo like them too much? – to which Leo replies that though he needs them, he can't stand them, they make him 'positively, physically sick' (p. 9).

The conversation occurs just after the first oblique reference to Mark's homosexuality, and, of course, explicitly refers to it. Mark has been ushered into Leo's presence by a butler whom he recognises, though he does not know from where. But when the young man 'discreetly' reminds Mark, both smile in 'remembrance' (p. 18). This interchange compels us to read between the lines: Mark and the young butler have been together sexually (and yet barely recognise one another, so casual is the sexual milieu!). However, characters within the novel refuse to read between the lines. Marietta does not acknowledge Mark's homosexuality until quite late in the novel, and even then, she never does so explicitly. Louise, Marietta and Natasha will always be dissatisfied: they do not take the clues that they are given. Leo and Mark, whom they love, return less of their affections – each in his own way, of course. They are either homosexual and uninterested in women – like Mark; or heterosexual and still uninterested in women – like Leo, by his own description.

'THE POINT'

In an earlier, more romantic and less funny story, called 'The Old Lady' (*Like Birds, Like Fishes*) Jhabvala shows love, particularly unhappy love, to be a sign of readiness for spiritual awakening. The widow and grandmother of the title has attained consistent ecstatic and transcendent joy through meditation. Her grown children, who live with her, are blind to her strength and to its religious source. But there is one character whom she knows she might reach: her daughter's estranged husband, who still wishes to avoid the divorce that the daughter is trying to negotiate. (Again, the mother–daughter betrayal – though this is another issue.) Suffering has softened him, and he is almost *there*, almost at what this novel will call the Point, the point of spiritual openness to the transcendent bliss that the old lady experiences in her meditation.

> Krishna got up at once and said 'Let me' [accompany his wife]. His eyes and voice begged quite without shame. But Leila turned away from him. . . . Krishna sat down again, looking unhappy.
> Perhaps she could show Krishna. She looked at him tenderly. . . . The old lady put out one finger and laid it on Krishna's wrist. What she had to communicate could not be said in words. But she felt him to be ready for it: he was unhappy and tender and lost. She could feel him seeking for something, straining for something, without himself knowing it. Slowly she stroked his wrist with her finger. Come with me, she wanted to say.

Krishna is the aspect and image of God as beloved. The

milkmaids' amorous play with him images the soul's love of God and is a great theme of Vedic mythology. That this character is so named underlines the story's suggestion: the unity of erotic and spiritual longing. This is evident in an Indian context, where devotional music merges religious and erotic longing, as Jhabvala reminds her readers in her essay 'Myself in India': 'The soul crying out for God is always shown as the beloved yearning for the lover in an easily recognisable way ("I wait for Him. Do you hear His step? He has come!").'

This much earlier story may elucidate *In Search of Love and Beauty*, however different the novel is in mode and feeling. Unlikely as it may seem, the novel is a comic rendering of that great tragic theme, the analogousness of erotic and spiritual love. Regi's triumphant self-interest is a measure of her failure to love, even to embark on the doomed search for love and beauty – while that search is an earmark of moral worth. Heterosexual men generally share her empty triumph, in this novel, for they, unlike the other women and the homosexual men, do not search, do not love and do not suffer. *Their* eyes are not 'dimmed by tears', but neither do they see what the others, with their vulnerability to charismatic and phallic power, can make out: that is, the 'Point'.

Besides Leo, the heterosexual men in the novel are minor characters. There is Tim, Marietta's alcoholic husband, who walks in and out of the novel and her life in a stupor of alienation. There is Ahmed, who views Marietta as a 'pet kitten': at least his is a relatively benign alienation. There is Jeff, whose real passion is tinkering: who tells Natasha 'for Chrissake, relax!' as he supplies her with her first sexual experience. There is Mr Cross, 'successful male, husband, father, Elk' (p. 133), who is, Mark thinks, 'out of it'. And finally, there is Bruno, Louise's long-suffering Jewish husband, the only fully sympathetic exemplar of his sex in the novel. But he only idealises his younger wife to the point of parody – rather in the manner of the Raja Sahib in 'Desecration' or Douglas in *Heat and Dust*. For her part, Louise is guiltily bored by him; human desire being what it is, on those rare occasions when a fully sympathetic man *is* present, women spurn him for being too available.

All the heterosexual men except for Bruno are out of the snares of this desire which is, if one follows Mark's train of thought in the Old Vienna café, really the 'Point' of it all. This 'poignant, refined' desire is what Leo 'in his later teaching' had called the Point (p. 133).

The Point that Leo names and that he on one occasion tells Natasha that she has found (p. 159), is the point at which soul and body converge: 'orgasm of body and soul', Leo says. But mystic Natasha (the orphan who is 'born', according to her name) is unaware of any distinction between the two. So is Ahmed, who cannot understand what Leo, with his worrying Western fragmentisation, might mean. 'Surely the one is there to express the other', Ahmed would have said, if he had thought about it, in answer to Leo's question 'Is your music of the senses or of the spirit?' (p. 88).

Leo's definition of the Point, a verbal concept he himself has invented, may not be the correct one in the novel's world, however. Mark defines it differently, as we see above. For him it is merely desire, that desire which can be read on the faces 'of the most sensitive, the most intelligent, the finest in nature' (p. 133). Major Minnies uses the same set of superlatives when he describes the kind of people who are most vulnerable to India, in *Heat and Dust*. India as he means it is a set of ideas and associations – beauty, myth, the transcendent, the ideal. The same people who are vulnerable to India will be vulnerable to desire.

Finding the Point is ostensibly the point of the activities in Leo's Gothic Academy. Certainly, the large, dark mansion reminds us not only of Gothic architecture but of the Gothic in literature, as earlier Jhabvala novels, notably *A New Dominion*, alluded to it in content. But so much of Jhabvala's novelistic material is the investigation of romance and desire, that she alludes often to the Gothic, that is, that branch of fiction/imagination, written by and for women, which takes sexual love as the supreme Point and adventure.

Mark's light-filled, 'classical' Van Kuypen house, on the other hand, represents the Greek way, not the Gothic. Yet looking more closely at what goes on inside it, one sees that the calm and moderation its architecture suggests is only superficial. There too, characters are searching for the Point. But the male homosexuals and the women in this novel are impelled by a chaotic, paradoxical and irrational set of desires; and all are drawn toward the (phallic) Point.

There do exist in the novel characters whose erotic connections lack apocalyptic urgency: for example, Mark takes 'possession' of

Jeff casually, as part of 'the pleasant summer nights' so full of movement and passionate insects (pp. 126–7); and Natasha and Jeff make love like two children: 'It's like we're both ten years old' (p. 162), he tells her (though in the context of his previously quoted remark to her, I do not think this can be read without irony. Whether *she* feels so childlike is not stated). But though Jeff manages to 'love' without suffering, it hardly matters who or what he makes love to. In Stephanie's temporary absence, he approaches Natasha, since 'there were the two of them alone in the night and he would have considered it unnatural not to get together' (p. 161). The remark is both a wry commentary on pre-AIDS American sexual mores, and a reference to the indiscriminate sexuality of Jeff's archetype, Pan.

TWO HOUSES

Passion without suffering cannot exist in this novel – indeed, etymologically the idea would be a contradiction in terms (the Latin word *passio* means 'I suffer'). The joyous, uncomplicated eros associated with the Greeks, and to some extent with male homosexuality, is held up to the light, and found to be a sham. The Van Kuypen house is really a house of intrigue. Natasha calls it 'the burned house': a wing of it had once been deliberately destroyed in an insurance-related fire. *Kuipen* is a modern Dutch word meaning 'intrigue'. Behind and beneath the classical lines of the Van Kuypen house, which Mark has so lovingly restored, play the same tragi-comic principles that motivate the heterosexuals in their Gothic Academy nearby. Only, if anything, they are now further complicated by the necessity for *intrigue*, secrecy and pretence.

Just prior to the finale between Mark and Kent, Marietta and Mark have their own confrontation, during which they *almost* manage to discuss his homosexuality. Marietta has avoided the significance of the many clues she gets to her son's identity, until now, in the final pages of the novel, when she at last makes conscious her refusal to know about or acknowledge his homosexuality. 'Is he going to tell me now?' she thinks in panic, as he wonders in panic, 'Is she going to ask me now?' 'But it was she who didn't want it.' She leans against him and weeps while he stands 'quite still' and allows her to. When she tells him she loves him 'so terribly' he answers, sensibly, 'Well of course, naturally. I expect you to' (p. 204). This is as far as he goes. Neither wishes to speak about it: Marietta does not wish to know. Mark does not wish to be known.

There are a number of ironies in the finale at the Van Kuypen house in which Anthony makes his final play for Kent, and threatens his rival Mark with a carving knife. His intended crime disintegrates into no more than a *faux pas*: urbane professionals in love do not so easily loose their aggressions; his sober transition from the initial impulse (he wants to murder Mark) to its bathetic resolution (he tears Mark's cashmere sweater) is comic in itself. But more than this, the scene contains telling characterisations of all its participants. Kent remains silent through the struggle (for him) between Mark and Anthony: clever manipulator, he says only as much as he must. His calculated lack of affect is a tactic of interpersonal control: his measured indifference represents a subtle power that hooks both Mark and Anthony.

Significant imagery is used to describe Kent, whose name means 'known'. In the context of Marietta's and Mark's elaborate strategems not to know or be known, this is significant: he *is* power and sexuality – fatally attractive. He is like 'a giant in his keep' (p. 196), he is 'towering, fierce and gigantic' (p. 214) as he hovers over Anthony, during their last scene together; Mark finds it 'too exciting to have Kent towering over him in this way, scowling' (p. 57) during one of their squabbles. His head is 'like a Roman Emperor's' (p. 51), and, of course, the pairing of the names 'Mark' and 'Anthony' further alludes to that idea.

Marietta thinks of Kent as 'a large stone statue – and [she] felt that if she were to hit him, it would be like hitting against stone' (p. 190). Kent is 'a rock against which others had to break themselves' (p. 193). Indeed, he is one of those that have power to hurt and will do none; one of those who, moving others, are themselves as *stone*. When Stephanie and Jeff leave for Arizona, it is to work at a friend's 'stone-crushing plant' (p. 168), a detail that wittily picks up the stone imagery: Stephanie has crushed the stone that was Leo, and Jeff has finally, indirectly, moved Kent (for Kent is jealous of Jeff's relationship with Mark).

Desire has a structure, and, homosexual or heterosexual, it is the same: 'perverse' in the sense that it thrives on a certain amount of neglect or indifference. Exactly how much is difficult to say, although Kent intuitively knows. As Mark observes of Anthony and Kent when he watches them at the Old Vienna, 'the more abstracted [Kent] became, the more intensely determined was his companion to hold him' (p. 132).

As Kent listens impassively, Mark recognises in his manner what had been, for him, a major part of his charm: that abstracted manner suggesting that Kent was 'somewhere else, somewhere more beautiful and pure'. But Mark knows, too, that Kent is 'very much here in the Old Vienna', and enjoying its luxury; and that 'though appearing to ignore them, he was perfectly attuned' to the gestures and expressions of the companions so eager to 'hold him' and his attention. Kent knows how to respond or 'if he so chose, not respond to them' (p. 130).

One of the puzzles of this tale is Marietta's attraction to Kent, perhaps in identification with Mark, as she surmises. 'She dared not look at Kent. The strange thing was that the sensation his presence evoked in her was not for herself but for Mark' (p. 190). Unaccustomed sensations shake her, as Kent's presence overwhelms her, a presence that 'loomed, . . . was as huge as he was' (p. 189). It is the thought of Kent and Mark's relationship – 'what they did together' that 'penetrated' her more than any of her own, hitherto unsatisfying, love affairs (p. 190). Could his homosexuality in itself represent an alternative to the heterosexuality that she knows, and that leaves her cold? Marietta's physical attraction to Kent is an intriguing detail. His super-phallic masculinity, which 'penetrated', 'loomed' and 'was huge' is reserved for other men. But perhaps his homosexuality contains the idea of alternatives to her own unsatisfying relationships with men who, as we have seen them in this novel, have been pompous and dull. This unexplored world of same-sex relationships would include love between women.

Clearly too, Kent and Mark's erotic bond reminds Marietta of her own intense love for Mark as a child. Again, Ruth Jhabvala's close observation of human relationships throws light on nuances of feeling that are generally ignored: the latent eroticism of the mother–son relationship, for example. Kent shows Marietta some of his portrait studies of Mark, in which Mark lies 'stark naked' on a brass bed. Marietta is struck at once by the expression in Mark's face, the same one she used to see when as a very little boy he had lain on his bed after his bath waiting for her to dress him – his eyes full of 'flirtatious love' (p. 191).

'Heartbreakingly familiar' and yet out of bounds, these images of Mark, and his intimacy with Kent, are icons of a vital and joyful erotic connection that is denied to most of the women in this novel, with the occasional and partial exception of Louise. Marietta and Natasha, both in love with Mark, stand outside and alone.

Kent is oblivious to Marietta's interest in him. Women, if they enter the Van Kuypen house, will not find 'love and beauty' available to them. They may function as willing and sympathetic friends, but they will never have centrality; they will probably be evaded and put off with half-truths. At the deepest level, they are not wanted there.

What, then, of enlightened heterosexuality, as it may be practised in the opposing structure on the Hudson? Enlightened, one might suppose, because the Academy exists to liberate, to be revolutionary. All, male and female, are enjoined to know themselves and to live up to their fullest potential. For example, Stephanie, who 'ardently' studies Leo's teachings and performs his exercises, and feels herself thus becoming a more integrated person, or, as the Academy has it, 'a more *become* person' (p. 123) (like many another such movement, this one has its own vocabulary).

The delicious satire soon reveals the abysmally secondary status that women are afforded at the Academy. It would not be too extreme to say that they exist as objects for Leo's pleasure. For example, 'with their long hair in the ankle-length flounced skirts they had stitched for themselves' (p. 136), they are aware that Leo can't 'abide' girls who cut their hair or wear trousers; that Leo wants to be turned on by real women – not 'women who weren't women' – 'and what were they there for, he joked, except to turn him on' (p. 136). Leo preaches that 'impulses' must be satisfied. He illustrates his points on his disciplines – in this case a boy, but most of his disciples are young women. When Leo satisfies his impulses by twisting Robin's nose, he does not even know why he might wish to twist Robin's nose – only that he does wish to. And Robin is pleased to accommodate the satisfaction of these impulses, and with his 'flaming nose', to have been chosen to occupy the special position of example (p. 138).

Such acquiescence, however, is not really the point. As Leo says,

'It's no fun unless the fish resists' (p. 21). In his masculine, 'heroic' view of experience, all is 'conquest'. Leo's Academy is, no less than the Van Kuypen house, a male world, though women live here. In both houses, a pragmatic instrumentality reigns, a masculine tool-centred approach of which Natasha's altrusim is the opposite. Leo even preaches instrumentality: we must, we *should*, use each other.

Women who are not young or beautiful do not interest Leo: he cannot use them. They understand and accept his lack of interest, expecting nothing else. See, for example, a scene between Natasha (not beautiful) and Shirley (not young), while a party which neither attends is in progress in the grounds. Shirley is a middle-aged divorcée whose husband has remarried 'to a much younger girl'. Generally speaking, she blames her mother, who 'like all mothers . . . had damaged Shirley and had been the first person she had to cut loose from' (p. 136). Once a devotee of psychoanalysis, with Dr Koenig, she has switched allegiances to Leo. Together Natasha and Shirley watch Leo 'acting out his drive toward satisfaction by chasing Stephanie' (p. 138) through the grass. 'At least he has fun', Shirley comments. Though she is younger than Leo, she herself doesn't have much: when she goes at last 'to join in the fun that was going on outside', she walks through the grass looking for a partner; she finds only Janet, 'another middle-aged woman, on the same mission'. And so they dance together, though 'it didn't matter, for each had her eyes shut and was doing a dance of her own' (p. 139). With the meekness of the disenfranchised, Shirley and Janet accept their diminished status, and each other, without opening their eyes. The Academy, scene of Leo's revels with a long succession of beautiful young girls, of which Stephanie will be the last, is not the place where their eyes will be opened.

The Academy is a cheap exploitation of the valid human 'search for love and beauty'. Just as its fake Gothic architecture, its spires and arches, is itself an ersatz version of medieval spirituality, its denizens play out a fake, cheap version of the 'psychospiritual' search in the mass-produced 'human potential movement'.

Leo's narcissism and selfishness outdoes Regi's. What makes his subjects richer subjects for satire, perhaps, is their earnest conviction that they are the first to tread untrodden ground, that they are psychological revolutionaries of a sort. The satire comes quite close to reality. For example, Fritz Perls's 'Gestalt Prayer', popularised in the seventies on posters and greeting cards, read

I am not in this world in order to live up to your expectations;
you are not in this world in order to live up to mine. You do
your thing, I do mine. If we meet, it's beautiful; if not, it can't
be helped.[23]

In this satire, it becomes Leo's 'stirring' song:

> *Don't fence me in. Don't pin me down.*
> *I'll flutter my wings, you flutter yours. Let's see*
> *who'll make it first, up to the sky.*
> *That's where I'm heading for: look out, brother,*
> *I'm flying high!*
>
> (p. 153)

Both the subtle sexism ('brother', says Leo, though most of his
followers are female) and the patent competitiveness ('let's see
who'll make it first') of Leo's brand of spiritual development are
evident, though his naïve disciples miss them. And the narrator's
acid comment, which ironically by-passes what the reader has been
led to mark, only underlines the disparity between real and bogus
transcendence: 'It could be quite stirring when they were all
together and expressing their longing for freedom and expansion
in this united cry' (p. 153).

NATASHA'S ANSWER

Though Leo may be wrong about what the Point *is*, he and his
disciples are on to something. There *is* an imperative to look for
the Point – the Point of it all, the meaning of our lives. In this
novel, the Point is the convergence of eros and death. When
Marietta and Louise cry 'I'm coming!' at three moments in the
novel, twice the reference is sexual, and comic. But the third time
the words are uttered by Louise as she dies, and they clearly
equate, by the repetition, eros and spiritual transcendence, that is,
the soul's departure from the body at death. Natasha alone of the
three female protagonists, grandmother, mother and daughter,
never cries 'I'm coming!' But she has, as Leo says, 'found her
Point'.

Like the others, Natasha is racked by unrequited love. But she has a resource that no one else in the novel has: she is able to draw strength – love and beauty – from the natural world. Her meditations connect her to a transcendent source of peace that serves as a counter-force to the frenetic and futile *ronde* of unrequited lovers.

It is important that Natasha is a writer, even if only potentially. Her character personifies Jhabvala's unstated values, in this and other novels: her active passivity, her receptivity to feelings – her own and those of others; her compassion (to a fault); her autonomy. Her waif-like appearance belies her inner strength.

In the sphere of human relations, Natasha vibrates with fellow feeling, but usually bungles things. Too sensitive to function at a real job (during her ill-fated stint at the home for retarded children – she is attacked and overpowered by one of her charges), she accepts the pretence of employment at Leo's Academy. But she recoils from his (phallic) humbug to the inarticulate and nurturing natural world, a female-centred connection echoed by the novel's Demeter/Persephone theme.

Natasha takes no part in the Academy workshops, nor does she attend 'Leo's famous Saturday night lectures' or the party afterwards – preferring her own company up in the attic. There her thoughts and feelings are 'not lonely but on the contrary deeply and strangely fulfilling' (p. 134). As in previous works – for example, *Heat and Dust*, or the story 'In the Mountains' – the movement upward, toward the isolation of the heights, represents greater awareness. Again, the sky, even a 'fragment of sky' represents an enfolding, nurturing calm which seems to embrace the one who looks at it: 'It was as if she were enfolded by it' (p. 139).

Natasha differs from the denizens of the Academy in that she looks to her own resources. Quiet and contemplation show her 'love and beauty'. In contrast to the disciples' fervent soul-searching, she is the only one among them who does not 'sigh and confess at night', who instead lies down 'with a light and happy heart as if she had done a great day's work' (p. 20).

As a child, Natasha weeps at the sight of a derelict. As an adult she wears Indian clothes merely to provide employment for a destitute family on the other side of the world. And, alone in the novel, she is always willing to help another, even at the expense of her own pleasure. In one significant scene, she leaves an exalted state of creation – she is writing poetry – to be with Louise. It is one of the few moments in the novel to illustrate warmth or disinterested fellow-feeling.

At a beach in the Hamptons, near New York, where Louise, Natasha and Regi are holidaying together, Natasha sees Louise run nimbly down to the edge of the waves in a gathering storm. Fearing the worst, Natasha rushes to her. (The scene recalls the suicide scene in Woody Allen's film *Interiors*, also taking place in the Hamptons.)[24] But actually Louise is in an ecstasy of excitement, for Leo has just telephoned after a prolonged absence. True, he has a request – to use her apartment as a base for some fifty of his experimental theatre disciples – but in spite of herself, Louise is overjoyed, even offering to come in to take care of the practical details (she is refused). When Natasha reaches Louise, the older woman throws her arms round her granddaughter's neck and allows her silently to support her: 'Natasha was used to this.' Yet the act it is not without difficulty for Louise is 'heavy' (p. 114).

As Louise reports that she has heard from Leo, the rain begins to fall on them 'like round, warm tears', and Natasha tries to propel Louise indoors. Too excited to be sensible, this passionate grandmother embraces her granddaughter in the warm, healing rain, and the pair conduct a dialogue on the issue of love. Earth goddesses counsel together about Dionysus, their male counterpart: or is Leo more like Hades, Lord of the Underworld? The ambiguity in the novel's associations is, I think, deliberate. This is the crucial question. It is debated in the ensuing dialogue: just how bad *is* Leo? Natasha thinks not so bad, when understood correctly; but the plot undercuts her assessment. He probably causes Natasha's death, though the event is only implied and will happen offstage.

Louise is passionately attracted to Leo, and yet wishes, or claims to wish, she were not. The issue is how to deal with Leo, or, more precisely, how to deal with one's own vulnerability to charismatic power. Realising that she is allowing herself to be used, Louise still wants to rejoice in his return, temporary though she knows it to be. On the horns of a dilemma that is fundamentally a moral question, she struggles with her 'masochism'.

Should one love, if 'love' is an absurd and predictable structure linking passionate lover and indifferent beloved? Or should one renounce, remove onself from the ebb and flow of illusory desire? To nurture oneself – to treat one's self ethically – perhaps one should remove oneself from the flux of unsatisfiable desire, which automatically brings suffering. Yet that desire brings joy too, although evanescent, and to repudiate it altogether might leave one even more desolate. Sujata earlier has asked the question.

What is a lover to do? Regi says that Louise must, if she has any self-respect, tell Leo unequivocally good-bye. If Regi says it, though, it is highly suspect. Natasha disagrees – Natasha who *has* relinquished even the hope of her beloved's regard, for Mark will never love her as anything other than a sister. When Louise presents her case – she *must* give him up – Natasha argues: '"It's his nature, Natasha. I've had enough." "But Grandma, if it's his nature –"' (p. 115). The sentence is broken off. The implication is, *love anyway*. The conversation continues in the storm: nature's healing rain hints at nature's potential for destruction. In the same way, that 'it's his nature' is no guarantee of Leo's benignity.

Louise is ready to follow Regi's advice: she regrets not having told Leo off on the phone: 'that's it, good-bye' (p. 116). Natasha counters, 'But Grandma, you like it when he's there. He makes you laugh.' No, she doesn't laugh, she *screams*, says Louise – and 'the storm did it for her' (p. 116). The scream is not to be discounted: it is real. But Natasha reminds her again that Leo makes her laugh too. 'You run up and down and do things for him. You like it.'

Louise is taken aback. She did not expect Natasha to take Leo's part, and here Natasha reiterates what is at the heart of the novel's comedy: that if Louise would satisfy her 'impulses' as Leo satisfies his, she would give in to her desire – which happens to be for Leo. 'I said *you* like it. I'm thinking of you' (p. 116). Again, the implication: *love anyway* – but know that you are playing with fire, with a force that like the lightning, and like the lion, has a clear potential for destruction.

Natasha catches flu as a result of this episode, a detail which nicely re-establishes the comic mode. But again, it also functions to underline Natasha's compassion, for she has put Louise's need to talk above her own desire to get out of the rain, and this is a response that contrasts sharply with Regi's. Before running out into the storm, Louise had knocked on Regi's door. Regi 'was very indignant with her: she said she had never heard of such a thing, to come in and disturb a person who was lying down for her afternoon siesta' (p. 113); and of course their counsel differs in the same way: Natasha's takes Louise's feelings into account, Regi's does not. Or perhaps it does, perversely: Regi too is attracted to Leo, and so her advice is tainted with self-interest. Natasha is now permitted the only direct criticism she utters in the novel: 'I wouldn't want to learn anything from Regi' (p. 116).

The feeling is mutual: Regi dislikes Natasha too. She refers to her as a creature not quite human, an excessively disparaging remark even for her. Even less, perhaps, than one's own flesh and blood, an adopted child cannot be 'guaranteed'. When one adopts one does not know where 'it' comes from, Regi points out, capping her argument with the rhetorical question, 'You wouldn't buy a horse that way, would you?' (pp. 118–19).

Regi misses the Point: Natasha finds it. Louise, Mark and Marietta dance around it. The novel argues for an acceptance of the *totentanz* of eros, which drives its characters. 'Le petit Mort' of sexual release is one way of experiencing the Point of it all, the Point that Louise finds in her literal dying. None the less, Jhabvala's novels in general, and this one in particular, underline an (unavoidable) destructive potential of eros – and, particularly, of women's double jeopardy in relation to men: at a disadvantage from the outset because of social conditioning in which everybody values males more than females, a woman who loves is even more likely to suffer.

Since the erotic impulse emanates from a spiritual longing for connection, wholeness and transcendence, we ignore it at our peril. But since in our delusion we direct it toward those who demonstrate by their personal power, indifference or dominance, a super-human strength – the Kents and the Leos of this world – we engage in it at our peril as well. 'Desecration' and *Heat and Dust*, among other of Jhabvala's works, tell the story of eros's descent into pornography and violence, its metamorphosis into obsession and fragmentation of the self. *In Search of Love and Beauty* repeats that theme, but in a lighter and more comic vein, so that love's failure is qualified. It is only a partial failure, and the search will continue for those characters who survive – trapped though they may be in a round-robin of unsatisfied and unsatisfiable desire. Leo does manage to show up every year at Louise's birthday celebration; Mark does manage to hold on to his 'best beloved boy'. But the birthdays that keep recurring in this dynastic epic point to the most inexorable and the cruellest lord of all: Chronos, Father of Demeter. To him all are vulnerable: the invulnerable Regi most of all.

Natasha is aware of the impermanence and fundamental illusoriness of the world of experience. For her it is mitigated not only by love – even if unreturned – but also by her meditative practice, which is linked by the narrative to her unrequited love.

In the autumn landscape near the Van Kuypen house, as a 'chill wind' blows through the dead leaves on the ground and those on the trees sigh and drop 'like tears', Natasha falls into a melancholy longing for 'permanence' – or for something like it, for permanence is not quite the right word, she thinks (the spiritual home that the skies – of which Jhabvala often speaks – have always represented?). Mark's entrance dispels the melancholy feeling of 'shiftlessness and impermanence' which, as long as he is there, does not return (pp. 168–9). The loved one, again, as an emmissary of the divine.

As a war orphan, Natasha might well long for a vanished past. But this longing is common to everyone, not only the victims of war, since we have all experienced at one time, like the abducted Persephone, the bliss of connectedness to the mother. Natasha in her withdrawal is privy to that bliss. The passage now continues with a description of Natasha's meditative inner landscapes:

> She felt reluctant to move, as if in moving she might be displacing, disturbing something. There was a peculiar sensation of being attentive and waiting and yet at the same time having already received what she was waiting for. The feeling in her heart was the same she experienced in Mark's presence: a fullness – as of a very full cup – which came to the point of being a physical sensation. That was why she was afraid of moving: as if she really did hold such a cup in danger of overflowing and spilling some drops of its precious contents.   (p. 169)

So, Natasha's example seems to say, the only way out of the human tragi-comedy of interested misapprehension and misplaced affection is the withdrawal of the artist or the religious. Like the title character of 'The Old Lady', Natasha finds a transcendent joy in contemplation, the state of active passivity described in the passage just quoted. Like the narrator of *Heat and Dust*, Natasha as a fledgling writer uses that spiritual awareness in the service of literature, the quest to make sense of experience through narrative images. Both take on the mantle of divinity themselves: through the passive course of direct apprehension through 'waiting' for spiritual knowledge, or through the active course of relaying that knowledge to the world through the mediation of art. Both courses take courage and persistence: Natasha 'stubbornly . . . did not cover her ears but made herself be present to hear and know' (p. 214). What she finds out, listening to Louise, to Leo, to Mark and to Anthony, is that everyone who loves, suffers. Natasha, an artist, represents a direct contrast to the suicide, Sofia, who attempts, if unsuccessfully, to 'cover her ears' twice in the course of her story. Art makes it possible to live meaningfully in the face of the knowledge that 'There just wasn't enough love to go round and never would be – not here, not now – with everyone needing such an awful lot of it' (p. 225).

Louise shares somewhat in Natasha's ability to withdraw to a nurturing solitude: just before Louise's death at the end of the novel, we enter with her into a reverie in which she relives the happy events of her girlhood in sensuous detail, her colourful memories contrasting with the whiteness and hardness of the frozen landscape through which she is actually passing, in the car with Regi, Marietta, and Eric.

As they head northward and into a frozen countryside they see water now 'turned to ice' and Eric turns around to point out to Regi and Louise a stream frozen into icicles midway in its fall. Thus does nature's own imagery so clearly repeat, once the artist underlines it, the human condition, in which death and time suspend the fluid movement of life. Louise and Regi are asleep, says Eric – and Louise, though hearing him and wishing to deny it, does not. 'Was she really asleep?' she wonders (p. 216).

From the mysterious state between sleep and waking, she relives the crucial moment in which Bruno proposed to her, years ago in 'D——', seeing herself as an actor even then. For she never felt for Bruno the passion that Leo would inspire in her.

> She wanted to get back to her drink – she loved it so – but desisted, for she realized this was a very solemn moment; so she made a solemn face and he talked – oh, so poetically! She was deeply stirred and thrilled and thought to herself it is forever, for life, for the whole of life.   (p. 217)

Louise's Woolfian inner monologue, nostalgic, elegiac, and again delivered with Jhabvala's characteristic light touch of irony, prepares us for her imminent death, a moment in which she is filled with 'a sensation surpassing all others, a pain so sharp that it became transporting' (p. 226).

Bernini's famous sculpture of St Teresa is an apt image of this novel's leitmotif, the Point. Literally pierced by the point of an arrow – of divine rapture? Worldly suffering? Religious martyrdom? Sexual ecstasy? – St Teresa is represented in a state of exaltation that may be variously interpreted. The power of this image has sparked psychoanalytic commentary in our time; this novel seems to supply another meditation on it.

In her death-throes, Louise cries out softly, 'I'm coming!' The revelation of the final hour remains a mystery: as incomprehensible to us as adult sexuality is to a child ('And Marietta wondered now as she had wondered then – *What's she mean? Where's she coming? Where's she going?*'). In the time-bound world of experience – our world of the here and now, as opposed to Natasha's 'not here, not now' (p. 225), the contemplative communion of which Natasha alone in the novel is capable may provide a refuge from the pangs of ever-present, unsatisfied and unsatisfiable desire for love and beauty.

And if not that, the tragi-comic *ronde* of obsessive lovers and indifferent beloveds, the dance of desire itself, is another kind of divine gift to human beings. Desire for 'love and beauty' is itself a state of beatification, so that in *desiring* them one receives them. As Natasha in her meditation at once waits, and receives that which she is waiting for, the lovers in this novel are granted love and beauty *by the state of desiring*, a state that troubles and even shames them. Perhaps that is the answer to Sujata's rhetorical question: 'If it was wrong, if it was shameful, then why was it there? And why was it so glorious?'

10

The International 'Trick': *Three Continents*

After the publication of *In Search of Love and Beauty*, Ruth Jhabvala's career may be said to have arrived at a new plateau. The year 1986 saw the release of the Merchant–Ivory–Jhabvala film based on Forster's *A Room with a View*, which received three Academy Awards and was widely viewed by mass audiences. With that, Jhabvala as screenwriter emerged into celebrity status. That same year, John Murray in England and William Morrow in the United States brought out a new collection of her stories–all of them reprints–calling it *Out of India* (perhaps in response to the filmed version of Isak Dinesen's *Out of Africa*, also being viewed by millions). Jhabvala began to receive coverage in the popular and literary press that outdid anything that had come before for her; and 1987 saw still more publicity, especially with the appearance of her tenth novel, *Three Continents* (London: John Murray; New York: William Morrow).

As everyone knows, fame appears to be a mixed blessing, requiring accommodation and resistance both, but clearly it has arrived for Jhabvala, Merchant and Ivory. Within a few weeks of each other, feature articles appeared in the US mass readership magazine, *People*, reporting first on Jhabvala's career, and then on that of Merchant and Ivory.[1] The filmmakers too had catapulted to celebrity with *A Room with a View*. Their next film, released almost simultaneously with *Three Continents*, was a remake of Forster's *Maurice*. That choice of material, along with public knowledge of their twenty-five-year relationship – they live together, in an apartment immediately below Jhabvala's on New York's Upper East Side – opened the door to direct inquiries about their personal lives. While James Ivory's reply, in *People*, was carefully noncommittal, the film certainly makes a courageous statement. And the interview quoted Merchant's remark, 'it would be wrong to turn our backs from the homosexual community'.[2] In the same interview, he referred to Jhabvala's decision not to write the screenplay for *Maurice*: 'She felt it was a flawed book.'

Meanwhile, features about Jhabvala stressed, as always, her reticence and reclusiveness: 'The Teeming Imagination of Novelist Ruth Prawer Jhabvala is Her Window on a World She Avoids', *People* headlined, next to a double-page close-up of the author reclining on a couch, holding a long-stemmed rose whose thorns, in blurred outline, stand out against her recumbent form. The prop, traditionally expressing romanticism, is not out of place: one wonders whose idea it was. It speaks of Jhabvala's identity as a chronicler of passion.

With the author's emergence into celebrity has come a fictional equivalent: the use of characters who are themselves in the public eye, people like Leo, or the Rawul. The issue of publicity *per se* becomes a theme, as in the recent story 'Farid and Farida' (1984), and in the novel, *Three Continents*. Celebrity is suspect in itself, because usually based on all the wrong things. A character's moral worth is generally in inverse proportion to the public esteem in which s/he is held; and if celebrity is actively courted, one may safely assume even larger helpings of humbug. In *Three Continents*, the main activity of the 'Movement' is public relations: this underlines its emptiness. One may read in the most recent fiction Jhabvala's struggle to integrate her newly arrived at celebrity into an almost Talmudic system of values, in which glitter represents vanity, while what is truly of value passes unnoticed; for the moral centre of Jhabvala's fiction has always resided in the most modest and unassuming characters.

SOME PREPARATORY STORIES: 'FARID AND FARIDA', 'A VERY SPECIAL FATE', 'PARASITES', 'ON BAIL', 'A SUMMER BY THE SEA'

A number of stories, most as yet uncollected, seem relevant to introduce Jhabvala's most recent novel: for each rehearses characters and themes that will be incorporated into the longer, more ambitious work. The 1984 tale 'Farid and Farida' concerns the problem of worldly success and fame, achievements highly suspect, and proof, in the story, only of the ability to swindle. Farida's new success as a guru contrasts with the unworldly romanticism of

Farid, her estranged husband, who observes, and rejects, her celebrity.

'A Very Special Fate' (1976) recounts the anonymous and impoverished old age of yet another guru's faithful follower, a now-elderly English woman holed up in a remote Indian village. She will reappear in the novel, cast in a minor role, that of the still-faithful follower of a once-internationally famous guru who is now in the last illness of his old age.

'Parasites' (1978), like the two stories just mentioned, was published in the *New Yorker*. This tale displays Jhabvala's growing interest in, and sympathy for, those who earlier came in for her severest criticism, manipulators and hustlers who carefully insinuate themselves into the affections of the wealthy. In a curious way the New York-based story sets us up to notice that Paul (the homosexual 'companion') and Annette (the elderly 'best friend') are hustling the unsuspecting, dying old lady (Stella) for her millions. But it denies us the easy judgements. We come at least partially to agree with Annette that Stella and her unassuming, rather literary niece, Dora, are the real parasites. They have the luxury of moral integrity: they have never had, like Paul or Annette, to struggle for an uneasy economic foothold by cunning and lies.

'On Bail', twice collected, in *How I Became a Holy Mother* and *Out of India*, also prepares for *Three Continents*: its introspective Indian narrator–protagonist is akin to Harriet Wishwell of *Three Continents*. This young woman (unnamed), has been her unconventional, intellectual father's hope for the future: how he revelled in her high exam scores, encouraged her to crop her hair and smoke cigarettes! But she falls fatally in love with the handsome, fast-talking Rajee instead. As the story glimpses the characters, the narrator has had to do some fast talking herself, to get bail money for Rajee from his wealthy mistress. The narrator doesn't seem to mind: in the arithmetic of eros, as Jhabvala shows again, the rival only makes the beloved more valuable. This economically viable triangle foreshadows the ones in *Three Continents*, as we shall see.

Jhabvala's compassionate interest in hustlers and con men, and the women who love them, can also be seen in the wrenching jail sequences of her screenplay for *Quartet* (1981). In the Jean Rhys novel, the protagonist herself is a scrounger, and her 'art dealer' husband incarcerated for fraud.

Most apposite to the novel, I think, is the story 'A Summer by the Sea', which also appeared in the *New Yorker* in 1978. It is set in

Nantucket (perhaps 'the Island' which appears in the later novel?), and narrated by another introspective, dispassionate young woman, a recasting of Natasha and a preliminary version of Harriet Wishwell, again. Like others of Jhabvala's unreliable narrators, Susie creates some narrative problems; but the story, it seems to me, is short enough to contain her limitations, whereas the novel suffers from them.

Susie is the wife of 'Boy', a gay man, perhaps so named to signal a certain abstract, almost allegorical quality in the story. Boy is delightful in large part because he is *not* a man. He is sensitive and emotional, an aesthete without the financial power to indulge his fine tastes – that is, until Susie, heir to her father's millions, comes into his life. Susie is quite happy to spend her legacy on him; so the summer finds an odd assortment gathered at the beach cottage: there is Susie, Susie's widowed mother, Boy, Boy's latest flame, the hustler Hamid, and assorted other gay men friends.

Susie and her mother represent polar opposites. Mother, called 'the golden oldie' by Hamid – behind her back, of course – is an ikon of tastelessness among these arbiters of taste. She teeters on high heels on the beach and goes in for lavender bikinis, despite the prominent scar on her abdomen (hysterectomy?): she sees herself as passionate and tempestuous and is sublimely oblivious to the ridicule (of herself) that enlivens the group in her absence. She is animated now by her flirtation with the charismatic, super-erotic Hamid. He tolerates, even encourages her, since the flirtation has the virtue of inflaming Boy's already warm interest in him.

Susie, on the other hand, is content to sit on the sidelines and 'hear their voices', this party of men who chit-chat contentedly as they idle away the sunny days together, only minimally irritated by the intrusive presence of the two women – whose inherited fortune has made it all possible. Handsome and bronzed, their skin glistening with drops of water 'like pearls', they are also urbane and intellectual. One of them reads Baudelaire's *Intimate Journals*, a hint at their unorthodox and lively sexuality.

Despite their homosexuality, the men still occupy a superior rung in the social hierarchy. Both women are hopelessly in love, Susie with Boy, Mother with Hamid. But where Susie keeps a prudent silence, Mother is foolish enough to air her complaints. Bored and resentful, she charges that Boy has married Susie for her money; and if she stops complaining when Hamid shows a timely interest in her, she thus becomes even more ludicrous in everyone's eyes.

It is somewhat difficult to credit Susie's assertion that she loves Mother 'for the way she is'. Indeed, the story reads as a painful study of female self-fragmentation, the split experienced by women between self-as-person and self-as-woman. If Mother is a 'part of' Susie, as Susie maintains, she is a repellent part. For 'the friends' are not far off in their assessment of Mother: she *is* ridiculous, boring, overdressed and undignified. Worse, she is a slob: when one of the 'friends' ventures into her room (he is looking for Hamid) his expression registers distaste. Susie explains: 'I don't notice it myself, but I guess the feminine smell around her *is* rather strong, with all those perfumes and creams she uses and the little underthings she has discarded lying scattered around the room.' Those 'little underthings' will reappear in *Three Continents* in the Rani's room – she too is a slob. They also recall the scene that details Leo's disgust with femaleness in *In Search of Love and Beauty* (the 'five P's').

Mother is a nightmare vision of 'femininity' taken to its most narcissistic extreme. Mother, like Regi, has bought every image that American advertising has come up with: her very face is hidden by a mask of make-up; only when it is bathed by tears can it actually be seen, looking like 'a grandmother's'. One can hardly wonder that Susie turns away.

But again, as in 'Commensurate Happiness', or 'Grandmother', to what does she turn? The choices that Susie has made have certainly cast her in a place of solitude and frustration. Her querulous complaint, thrown out like a challenge to the reader at the end of the little tale, fails to convince: 'I'm getting tired of people deciding for me what I can stand and what I can't. How do they know? Maybe I like things the way they are.'

For all her protest that she likes her situation, it is Susie who has rendered it for us in all its bleakness: the two lonely women, at odds with each other, and their exploitation by Boy and his friends, to whom they represent only a necessary evil. Everyone, including Susie herself, knows that Boy would never have married her without her money. At least Susie's relations with 'the friends' lack the painful self-delusion of her Mother's; at least Susie is not ridiculous. But her solutions to the problem of being a woman are highly imperfect at best.

In *Three Continents*, Hamid will be metamorphosed into Crishi, and Boy into the narrator's twin brother, Michael; although the narrator steps out of the role of mere observer, one would hesitate to say that she fares better than her predecessor.

THREE CONTINENTS

As its title makes clear, *Three Continents* covers a lot of ground. It is bursting with characters and incidents, full to the point of discomfort with people and things, all brilliantly described. It seems to have cost its author no little effort: 'I feel drained for the first time in more than thirty years', she said to an interviewer. 'I don't know if it is age or what, but it certainly wiped me out.'[3] One hesitates to use the author's candid admission against her – but one must allow that there is a laboured quality to the novel. It lacks the delicacy, the apparent effortlessness of the earliest novels, in which Jhabvala had no reputation to uphold, no audience to please, and no already-used situations and phrases to fall back on.

That there are parallels and similarities, patterns that emerge in a writer's work is, I think, one of the joys of literature, which is, after all, a way of entering into a time, a place and a consciousness that is different from our own. Having read widely in an author's work, we readers can step back and mark the reappearances of like characters and configurations, and so, in a way, come to share the consciousness behind them. But when the familiar passes a certain point one begins to speak not of pattern but of formula, not of relation but of repetition: and to a certain extent I think *Three Continents* suffers from this overuse of old material. Even the central twinning of the heroine seems a predictable use of the alter ego: Jhabvala's female protagonists are almost always paired with a homosexual man, starting with Olivia/Harry: there was Lee/Raymond, Natasha/Mark and now Harriet/Michael. As always, the male half of the dyad is given a relative dignity, is purposeful where she drifts; is conscious where she is in a state of anomie. Throughout *Three Continents*, one recognises details that have been mentioned before. Consider the ending: 'Was it from up here that the Rawul had looked at and absorbed the sky until it entered his eyes and made his mind soar?' It sounds so much like the ending of *Heat and Dust*: 'Perhaps [the sky] is also what Olivia saw: the view – or vision – that filled her eyes all those years and suffused her soul.' There are many such details, uncomfortably repetitive.

Another factor contributing to the laboured quality of the novel is the overabundance of characters and scenes; as one reviewer commented, one never has a chance to grasp the emotional significance of any.[4] The very ambitiousness of the novel, its epic quality, works against it.

Three Continents has received rather poor notices, breaking the tradition of critical acclaim that Jhabvala has enjoyed. The *New York Times* was sarcastic: 'Four hundred pages of this sexually starving young dummy allowing herself to be exploited by a cad is a lot.'[5] The *New York Review of Books* found it 'disappointing'.[6] *The Times Literary Supplement* reviewer thought the novel's intention 'overwhelmed' by its detail.[7] Almost all the reviewers have located the novel's central flaw in the choice of 'exasperating' Harriet Wishwell as narrator.[8] Certainly, the choice has led to a number of artistic and narrative problems; yet, as I read the novel, this choice is also one of its most interesting aspects. Harriet, a recasting of Lee (of *A New Dominion*) or Natasha, or the Susie just mentioned, is clearly representative of the authorial voice in a way that, say, the Indian man who narrates 'Expiation', a story to which we shall be returning, is not. By staying with Harriet so insistently, Jhabvala has chosen the most difficult course, has undertaken what Yeats called 'the fascination of what's difficult'. The novel is part, by no means without merit, of an ongoing process of integration. 'You have to try all the time to conquer new territories', the novelist told an interviewer, speaking of *Three Continents*.[9]

Harriet puts into relief that which has not yet been resolved in Jhabvala's art. In her character reside precisely the vexing contradictions that have been problematical all along. Harriet's election to the crucial role of heroine–protagonist–(unreliable) narrator renders inescapable those unresolved dilemmas, philosophical and artistic, that run throughout the whole of Jhabvala's work. If the novel is flawed, it is flawed in interesting and provocative ways.

Three Continents is Jhabvala's darkest story yet, as she herself allowed: 'Most of my novels do end on a deep note of pessimism. Shadows seem to be closing in.'[10] Parents and children all but devoid of feeling for one another, inheritances lost, stolen or squandered, the triumph of greed and cunning: it is not a pleasant tale. The plot is constructed on a favourite Jhabvala theme: the almost entropic decline of generations. Earlier generations steadfastly work to build up fortunes that later ones take for granted and finally squander. This is a variant of the broader theme of disinheritance, also a staple of Jhabvala's art: here self-disinheritance, as it were.

Michael and Harriet Wishwell, both eighteen years old when first we meet them, are the last fruits of a long line of energetic, hardworking individuals, idealistic and committed to the common weal. The falling-off has started, perhaps, with Grandfather Wishwell, who has tended to abdicate responsibility, characteristically standing 'a little to one side, as though it were nothing to do with him' (p. 93). And his son, Manton, anticipating the generation of the sixties, has lived out a kind of Playboy philosophy. Lindsay, the twins' mother, is also heir to a fortune, the Macrory estate: she is now a lesbian, having taken up with Jean after her divorce from Manton.

Harriet and Michael, in contrast to their ineffectual, ambivalent, rather muddled parents, are aloof loners, full of conviction: Harriet's, that only she and Michael could ever understand or be worthy of each other; Michael's, that all is *neti*, 'not it', false, phoney, not up to standard. At eighteen, Harriet and Michael are tired of their wealth and their privilege, tired of the International Schools that they have attended between sojourns at the various embassies to which their Grandfather has been posted: tired of the rounds of getting and spending – mostly spending – in which their forebears have engaged. Thus Michael, who is gay, has already spent several years wandering on the Kathmandu–Goa trail, that path worn by a steady stream of disaffected, drug-using, hitch-hiking American and Northern European youth. In Delhi, Michael has met up with Crishi, whose charismatic presence for once energises the lethargic hippies. When Crishi reappears in London, cleaned up and gentrified, he has become part of a 'human potential' scam, the 'Fourth World Movement'. When he discovers that Michael is staying at the Embassy, a fast friendship develops – but fast only in the sense of 'fast foods'. Crishi becomes Michael's lover and Michael becomes a Movement devotee. Since Harriet does whatever Michael tells her to do, the rest of the story is only a matter of finding out how the inevitable is accomplished, that is, how the Wishwell millions get into the clutches of Crishi, the Rawul and the Rani.

These funds are ostensibly required for the Movement's vague political programme, which aims to bring about lasting peace and plenty in the world, through meditation, lectures and the force of personality. Halfway through the novel, the Movement will become, with Jhabvala's fondness for name-changes, 'Transcendent Internationalism'. And the new name signals a new emphasis, as we shall see.

With their pale and earnest followers, the triumvirate consists of these: the Rawul, fiftyish, plump and affable, also the last of an ancient family, originally descended, if you please, from the moon, 'through a series of semi-divine incarnations' (p. 78). Behind him, and pulling strings, stands the Rani, who halfway through the novel also changes her name, becoming only Renée. The noble title turns out to be a conveniently misleading nickname – that is, when the real Rani, the Rawul's legal wife, appears with her three teenaged daughters. This Rani–Renée is a voluptuous and powerful creature of mixed lineage, the product of a French–German mother and an Afghan father, an unfortunate melding of all that is worst in each tradition.

Crishi, who is known as her 'adopted son' (read lover), is also racially mixed, his mother part English, part Assamese, his father unknown. The mysterious origins only contribute to his appeal: his super-charismatic genial charm soon has both Harriet and Michael in thrall. Crishi is practised at seduction: to him generally has fallen the task of 'chatting up' those likely to prove useful (p. 35).

Now come these three, Michael's specially invited guests, with their retinue of followers, into Lindsay's family's Victorian estate, known as 'Propinquity' and located on the third continent, in a lush and desirable section of Connecticut or the Hudson Valley. Propinquity being the parent of boredom, however – we do not appreciate that which is too available – we may expect the estate to be devalued in the family's eyes, and it is. Lindsay impulsively announces her decision to offer up Propinquity, which would, everyone can see, make a nice setting for the group's headquarters. But midway through the novel, Lindsay regains her senses and reneges on the offer, influenced largely by Jean, one of the novel's few sane voices. It is worth noting that the Macrory fortunes are saved, at least temporarily, through the intervention of Lindsay's lesbian partner. Symbolically, the twins' disinheritance is less than complete only because of this despised relationship. The telling detail, it seems to me, is a reference to Jhabvala's unspoken subtheme, always denied and even satirised in the manifest content of the work. As I have argued, women's forbidden resources for each other, which might represent an antidote to the poisonous and rapacious heterosexuality portrayed, rests just below the surface of these novels and stories.

At any rate, Michael and Harriet, less-well-protected than Lindsay, are to be entrapped far deeper into the Movement. The traps are delicately laid. Crishi and Michael, already lovers, now include Harriet on their nightly nude swims. Michael and Harriet inform Grandfather Wishwell of their plan to donate the Wishwell money to the Movement. When, soon after that, the old man dies, leaving everything to his grandchildren and bypassing his son – who, ironically, is finally settling down – his motivation is clear: an overriding wish to mortify Manton, who 'disgusts' him. Here at least, in their contempt for Manton, Grandfather and Michael are united. And in his good-natured forbearance, Manton emerges as one of the few more likeable characters in the novel. If Harriet/Michael are a darker version of Natasha/Mark in *In Search of Love and Beauty*, Manton is a correspondingly lighter version of Leo.

But neither Manton nor Lindsay deems it within a parent's sphere to intervene as the inevitable marriage plans take shape. Clearly, for the economy of the Movement, Crishi must marry Harriet, and in short order it is arranged, though not before Crishi has turned his sexual attentions to Harriet, effortlessly awakening in her a 'devouring Hunger' and a 'fury of desire' (p. 162) about which we are told little – though, relative to the author's previous work, she goes rather far. The defloration (his penis a 'potent weapon') takes place at the 'Linton house', undoubtedly a literary salute to Emily Brontë's germinal romance of sexual obsession, also set against the decline of a once-potent family. As in *Wuthering Heights*, the 'Linton house' has an aura of hauntedness about it: for one thing because Mr Linton has, it is rumoured, murdered his young and beautiful wife in its ornate, now empty swimming pool; for another, the mansion is in the process of slowly being swallowed up by the ocean. The abandoned pool, which becomes Harriet and Michael's trysting place, is also symbolically rich (about which more later). As Crishi 'Quickly and ruthlessly' enters her, Harriet barely has time to think 'not here' – *neti*, she might well have translated; for this relationship will not, as we might guess, be It.

And so the marriage is accomplished, and the action now moves on to the second continent, as the characters settle down to wait for Harriet and Michael to reach twenty-one and gain control of the Wishwell fortunes. If one thinks of the three continents in their historical order as sites of old-world civilisation, then the movement of the novel is backward into history. With each move eastward, a layer of knavery is revealed, so that in London, a little more of the ugly truth is shown. Crishi now divides his attentions among Harriet, Michael and Renée, occasionally sharing a bed with the two women – Harriet going along doubtfully but obediently.

In London appears the Bari Rani ('Great Queen'), with her three teenaged daughters in tow. A rather refreshingly domestic matron, she is smugly occupied with her husband's career – as the Movement now begins to seem – and the proper supervision of the daughters and their boyfriends. If she vaguely attempts to open Harriet's eyes, she does not try *too* hard, since she and her daughters stand to profit handsomely from the Wishwell estate. It turns out that even this attempt is calculated, for the Bari Rani is even cleverer – and more deadly – than the Rani herself.

In London the reader meets another set of followers of another world leader, the more traditional Babaji. Age has reduced this once-famous figure to a querulous old man whose two remaining devotees, still in love with him and still in a manner beatified by their love, pass their days serving him in every conceivable way: Maya Devi (goddess of illusion) and Nina Devi are two cheery Englishwomen whose sisters we have met so often before in Jhabvala's work. These characters are thrown into close proximity with the Movement's high command, since all occupy together the same London quarters. (The Rawul etc. plan to purchase it just as soon as Harriet and Michael come of age.) This gives Jhabvala a chance to inquire closely into the Babaji's habits. At one point the old man, bedridden and in his dotage, demands that nubile and attractive Harriet stay to masturbate him; it is clear that this is a service that the two older, less desirable, Devis have been performing regularly. This subset of characters, the Babaji and his jolly followers, continue the stripping away of the humbug surrounding the movement, in a manner that makes it look even worse by comparison: nothing but a criminal ring.

In London too the reader becomes aware that behind the pieties of the Movement is an international art-smuggling ring, with the practised and ruthless Crishi at its hub. Thus, a London gallery specialising in Indian miniatures is introduced, complete with supercilious young women receptionists. The proprietors are Rupert and Nicholas: Rupert is the fall guy, there to take the rap and serve the jail sentence when necessary. Rupert turns out to be married to the Rani for the same reasons that Harriet is married to Crishi. Again, it is sex that serves as harness and reins, for he is in thrall to Renée, for whom he is only a means to an end. Even their child, Robi, is actually Crishi's, though it falls to Rupert – and then to Harriet – to care for him. Harriet notes Rupert's intense emotions (his Adam's apple rising and falling under his Old Etonian necktie whenever Renée makes an entrance): she realises that Rupert is a willing victim of the same shock that passes through her and Michael ('as of an electric wire'), whenever Crishi appears to them.

The gallery, we understand, is the last stop in the legitimised sacking of the Indian subcontinent by opportunists of every nationality, a phenomenon Jhabvala has referred to before, for example in *Heat and Dust* – where she also gives the opposing argument, that is, that a corrupt government bureaucracy in India has left little alternative to those to whom the treasures have come down. In *Heat and Dust*, it will be remembered, the narrator pays a visit to the Nawab's heirs, Karim and Kitty, in London. One of their 'set' relates that her family had tried to turn their palace into a hotel, but had been stymied by officialdom, leaving them 'no alternative but to get all their stuff out' (p. 99). Though their avowals of concern for India's heritage are a bit too earnest, the reader credits the explanation. So the disinheriting of Harriet and Michael takes place in the broadest international context, the disinheriting of the heirs to the civilisation that produced those palaces and miniatures. Significantly, Crishi manages to be the agent of both swindles. Yet, of all the many characters in the novel, it is probably he who best knows poverty.

This novel touches on a subject of which Jhabvala has said she cannot escape awareness, though 'God knows I've tried'.[11] It emerges that Crishi comes from the ranks of the disinherited, disenfranchised multitudes living out their lives in abject poverty. At the heart of the action of *Three Continents* is what one might call the great disinheritance, the poverty that Jhabvala could not avoid seeing during her years in India: 'You can't live there and eat and be comfortable when you see how others have to live.'[12] As the action of the novel wends its way eastward, this theme emerges more clearly. The seduction of Michael and Harriet takes place within a context that looms larger and larger; and the economic, historical and social realities emerge through the journey eastward.

The middle section of the novel, the part set in London, is given the ironic title 'The Family', for so Harriet calls the shifting collection of tricksters, drifters and muddlers who gather around Crishi. To underline the irony, back in the New World her biological family, Manton and Lindsay, are re-evaluating, in a very 1980s sort of way, the importance of family and tradition. But too late for Harriet and Michael.[1] Manton is now coupled with young Barbara, Lindsay with Jean, and new families are being formed. Though intercontinental invitations are issued, the twins boycott Manton and Barbara's wedding, as they boycott the christening of the baby boy who is its issue. They anticipate instead the move eastward, to the very source of the Movement, that is, the Rawul's kingdom of Dhoka (the Hindi word meaning 'to trick').

Now that the dénouement, the twins' twenty-first birthday, is fast approaching, the Movement personnel move to Delhi, where they install themselves in a luxury hotel – to Harriet's chagrin: *she* is anxious to reach Dhoka. Michael, however, is beginning to have a pang of doubt. The ugly truth, to be fully revealed in Dhoka, is slightly more visible in Delhi. Crishi's actual origins can at least be guessed at. Though his birthplace is given as 'Brussels' on his passport, he speaks not only Hindi, it turns out, but the dialect of Dhoka – as indeed he should, this arch-trickster, this 'trick' in gay male parlance. (A 'trick' is a partner in casual sex.)

In Delhi, one meets a group of characters called the 'Bhais' (in Hindi: 'brothers'), supposedly the Rawul's Indian followers, actually penniless and unemployed youths, recruited from Dhoka. There they had been hanging around the bazaars, and were usually in trouble with the police. A rowdy, sinister group, they are installed in a house on the other side of the river – still comfortably removed – where they crowd in together with their many weapons, openly displayed. As if these images were not sexual enough, one soon sees them dancing the eunuch's dance, the same one that started all the trouble in *Heat and Dust*, with Crishi joining in amid loud laughter. Michael, witnessing the rough parody of what, after all, has drawn him most magnetically to Crishi, is 'furious'. He virtuously demands to know why Crishi is not at home preparing for a Movement meeting the following day. Such stupidity is, the reader feels, amply rewarded when Crishi lashes out at him: 'I don't care one fuck for your meeting. Not this much: not one fuck.'

Now, in Delhi, and finally in Dhoka, 'the cage door swings shut upon the deluded, hapless and besotted Harriet', as one reviewer put it,[13] and the only too obvious truth – that the Movement is a scam – finally dawns on Michael, as he first forces himself to utter the word 'idealistic' (p. 289) and then allows that 'sometimes you just have to admit you've made a mistake' (p. 334). But, as always, seeing too clearly is a risky business. Once the Rawul, the Rani and Crishi discern that Michael is having a change of heart, and that he may even be planning to withdraw his share of the inheritance at the last minute, the Bhais are quickly given the order (by the Bari Rani, of all people, that ostensibly domestic matron) to dispatch Michael. As for Harriet, on her arrival at the ruins of the Rawul's 'palace' in Dhoka, Crishi tells her the tale that Michael has committed suicide – a transparent lie that even she cannot believe. Yet she obligingly pens a 'suicide note' for him.

This passage, on the last few pages of the novel, is worth a close look. For once, though only now, with Michael forever gone, murdered by the Bhais, the reader is allowed a glimpse of Harriet's version of the inner life of this shadowy figure who is her brother. Michael has been physically absent from most of the novel: when he appears it is only to mouth cult slogans, and one sees him gradually losing himself in the ever-clearer fascism of the Rawul's proto-empire.

In Michael's suicide note, Harriet ventures to explicate the psychology of these *neti*-sayers: the disappointed idealism that has, with a terrible irony, led the twins to embrace the tricksters and scoundrels who are 'Transcendent Internationalism'. Though in Delhi Michael is finally wooed away from the Rawul and company, by the clever ministrations of Grandfather's wife Sonya, he has been in pretty deep – too deep to get away alive. Transcendent Internationalism more and more comes to resemble National Socialism in miniature, as the renaming subtly suggests; the parallels are there: the military drills and parades, the irrational conviction, the inane righteousness, the unswerving fealty to the leader, the lobotomised stare. In London, Harriet has borne witness to Michael's fall from humanity in the name of the Movement, as he repeatedly kicks a defenceless and bleeding man (Nicholas) whose obedience to Movement directives has been less than complete. To one extent or another this cruel absolutism has marked all the essentially fascistic cults that Jhabvala has again and again been drawn to investigate for us: the Swamiji, the assorted gurus, and even the relatively benign 'Academy for Potential Development'.

For me, Jhabvala's brilliance rests in the terrible clarity with which she has located the human vulnerability to the comforts of fascism. We are prey, she demonstrates, because of the very idealism that may also give rise to what is best in us. Here is Harriet's heartfelt explanation of her and Michael's psychology – with which readers may certainly identify:

> I said that if once you have these expectations – that is, of Beauty, Truth, and Justice – then you feel cheated by everything that falls short of them; and everything here – that is, here in this world – does fall short of them. It is all neti, neti.

To the tantalising Hellenistic ideals of Love and Beauty, Jhabvala has added the difficult Hebraic pursuit: social Justice is, after all, the ostensible goal of the Rawul's ludicrous 'Movement', travesty though it may be. Harriet continues:

> I wrote with ease – I mean, it came easily to me because I knew it was what Michael felt; but at the same time I was writing I was crying because it wasn't what I – I, Harriet – believed at all; how could I, and especially with Crishi sitting there beside me.

Harriet's unconvincing disclaimer is a good example of the kind of bizarre irony that results when she overlays her pointed observations, her incisive descriptions and her obvious intelligence with the extreme stupidity required to justify her relationship with Crishi. Even without this last little joke, the passage states the theme that rings throughout Jhabvala's oeuvre: the essentially tragic vulnerability of those who dream – which is all of us who are, for better or for worse, in search of love, beauty, and now justice.

William Butler Yeats remarked that debate with others is politics, while debate with the self is poetry. The epigram works well when applied to Ruth Jhabvala's fiction, a debate with the self on the nature of passion. Nowhere is this more apparent than in *Three Continents*, which in many respects is a distillation of what has come before, a further examination of the experience of romance. This time the boundaries are pushed back so that the object, Crishi, is viewed at his worst – a hustler *par excellence*, a self-serving master of deception. Supremely confident, he, not the Rawul, rules the

Movement, by force of personality. As a friend he is without interest, that is, as an equal, an intellectual or spiritual companion. Harriet observes at one point that 'nothing was further from Chrishi's interests than any kind of flowering natural thing' (p. 330). And this is to be expected, for he is Otherness at its farthest remove, at least from the novel's protagonist, that serious, frowning young woman with her idiosyncratic and arrogant modesty. Crishi loves fast cars, rock concerts and night spots.

To understand what it is about Crishi that Harriet finds so immensely appealing is the problem of the novel, and its weakest point. For me, the novel's flaw is to be found in a certain abdication of authorial responsibility. It is as if the debate with the self became so polarised – to put it crudely, Crishi is irresistible, Crishi is a swine – that the author saw no recourse but to smooth everything over with a bland and cryptic frosting of irony. But she fails, therefore, to convince us either of Harriet's passion, or, on the other hand, of her stupidity.

I have spoken earlier of a kind of misplaced irony that the author turns on those characters representing the authorial self, Natasha, for example, or, much earlier, Sarla Devi, the ascetic and would-be political activist of the early novel, *Get Ready for Battle*. Harriet's lack of self-awareness – indeed, her complete lack of awareness where Crishi is concerned – is difficult to credit. One has to keep reminding oneself of the extenuating circumstance that she is between eighteen and twenty when the events of the story occur – though the narrative is constructed, she tells us, much later. By telling the story through Harriet's eyes Jhabvala has taken on two major problems in narrative structure: first, she must negotiate the clumsiness inherent in the first-person narration of a long and crowded novel. This leads to such devices as (when about to launch into a quoted monologue running a page and a half): 'This is more or less what he said, and it was so unusual for him to speak to us at such length, and so intimately, that I can still remember it almost word for word after these many years' (p. 82).

Even worse, Jhabvala must manage the difficulties inherent in the choice of an unreliable narrator. Just how unreliable is Harriet? The answer, which varies according to page, hinges on authorial ambivalence about Crishi, as well as a kind of unwillingness to admit to it. That is, Jhabvala shows us Harriet madly in love with a character whom Harriet herself presents as a swine; Harriet keeps telling us about, or rather referring to, Crishi's sexual appeal; but she also tells us that she doesn't like sex *per se*: she picks up a stranger in London (another third-worlder) and sleeps with him out of politeness, deriving no pleasure from the rather nightmarish encounter. So it is difficult to credit Harriet's and Crishi's endless hours of lovemaking. One wishes, as usual, for more revelation. If we are cheerfully told of the marathon lovemaking sessions that bind poor Harriet to her captor, we wish for a glimpse of the feelings that presumably flow so abundantly. The 'sick' sex she suffers from – exactly what is it? To this reader at least, the mysteries of sexuality fade here into mystification, being invoked to account for Harriet's enormous stupidity, but never shown. (In an analogous omission, one wishes to hear a bit more of the Rawul's programme, the inspiring ideology that has presumably enticed others, as well as Harriet and Michael, to give abundantly of themselves and their worldly goods: again, one has to take Harriet's word for it.)

VICTIMS OF GLOBAL DISINHERITANCE

It is only at the end of the novel that Crishi's curious appeal falls into place, I think. The truth is that Crishi is not only a bounder and a cad, who has inexplicably charmed Harriet into complete submission: he is also himself a victim. Oddly enough, he finally emerges as an innocent, a boy with a boy's enthusiasms and endearing silliness. Crishi is of the downtrodden, anonymous hordes of poor upon whose backs – 'as on the back of an animal', says Jhabvala in 'Myself in India' – live the Indian middle classes. Crishi comes from the beaches of Bombay, the bazaars of Dhoka, from the poorest urban strata. With this realisation, which comes in the final pages of the novel, Crishi takes his place beside other struggling Indians loved by Jhabvala's comparatively privileged protagonists, all the unsuitable men from Judy's husband Bal in *A Backward Place*, to Har Gopal of 'Passion' or Shakuntala's singing teacher of 'The Housewife', or Raju, Elizabeth's husband in 'Two More Under the Indian Sun' or Rajee, the criminally inclined husband of 'On Bail'.

Like all the smart women who have made such foolish choices, Harriet would rather be with her lover than anyone else: he makes her laugh. Crishi is marvellous fun to be with: Harriet, who often seems so grim and humourless, revels in her desire, which transforms her.

Perhaps Harriet's devotion might be more credible if we could call it not just sexual attraction, but love. This possibility lurks below the surface: Crishi is, after all, named for and directly compared to Krishna, who hid himself from those lovesick milkmaids, 'only showing enough of himself to keep them in line'.

If Crishi is only a village tough, one of the downtrodden of the earth, Jhabvala stands on his side, and through her, so does Harriet. Once that is grasped, Harriet's inexplicable passion for Crishi takes on weight and believeability, and the novel becomes much more than just 'a novel about an innocent rich girl in the clutches of an unscrupulous fortune hunter', as Walter Goodman charged.[14] Harriet's passion is subversive, and she is a sister to Olivia, or to Betsy – the graduate student so in love with the altogether unsuitable Har Gopal – or even to Sofia with her Superintendent of Police. These passionate women, mistakenly or not, assert, through their stubborn insistence on loving an unsuitable man who is far beneath them socially, their rejection of the social norms and hierarchies that they abhor. And they do abhor them, even if they are only dimly aware of the essentially political roots of their passion. Throughout her narrative, and in passing, subtly, and with humour, Harriet, for one, reveals herself as a sharply observant commentator on social hierarchy and its small, ever-present, injuries.

Harriet's grasp of social dynamics becomes a problem in itself, since she is the 'unreliable narrator'. The conceit of the unreliable narrator is something of a literary *tour de force*, and the author risks a certain heavy-handedness at all times. In page after page of evolving story, we entrust ourselves to Harriet, and she shows herself worthy of that trust, through lively description, exact choice of detail and intelligent selection of material. Harriet has a wonderful eye for the revealing detail, and a dry and pointed wit; these clash most disconcertingly with the ninny she is also supposed to be. The disparities end by irritating and annoying the reader, who feels, I think, the authorial hand at intervals making Harriet stupider than she could possibly be. Harriet says of another writer in the book, the journalist Anna who appears briefly in London, 'she was not a writer for nothing' (p. 137), and the same may be said of Harriet herself, who is able to note, of Crishi, that 'as usual when he was or pretended to be worked up, his London

accent became more pronounced' (p. 151). She muses about Manton's new wife: 'As for Barbara – the one person who really disliked
Crishi – she so adored the idea of a wedding that the actual
protagonists didn't matter; or was it that for her, once a person
was a bridegroom, he became automatically good?' (p. 144). She
observes a confrontation at Propinquity:

> Lindsay, cool and crisp in pale-green linen, and with her good-
> girl expression, was so shocked by this sudden attack that she
> was speechless. We all were, and the Rani actually said, 'I'm
> speechless.' She said this in general, to air her indignation in a
> dignified way, before addressing Jean in particular: 'Don't you
> think it's rather inconsiderate to make a scene when we have a
> guest in the house?'

Besides being an astute observer and generally a fine stylist –
except at those spots where Jhabvala wishes to draw our attention
to her stupidity – Harriet has a sound moral sense as well, at least
whenever Crishi is absent. She distrusts publicity. She cares, with
genuine involvement, for the child Robi, who is neglected by
everyone. She feels her kinship and compassion for Rupert. Yet
every so often she exhibits a glaring error of judgement, all having
to do with her unquestioning adoration first of Michael, then of
Crishi.

All along, Harriet sees too clearly to be so blind. A kind of
coyness pervades the novel, as Harriet must convey information
without knowing it herself, or, more to the point, without admitting
that she knows it herself. A good example of the kinds of narrative
strategies into which Jhabvala is forced by this confusion (just how
stupid is Harriet supposed to be?) occurs at the climax of the novel,
in which Michael is murdered, offstage. As Harriet, distraught,
rushes about searching for her brother, who has last been seen
alone with the menacing Bhais, she receives some dozen clues (on
one page) that Michael has met with foul play. The hotel staff who
usually greet her today 'kept their eyes strenuously on their
task'; the 'quite-fluent English of one failed him and he couldn't
understand a word I said' (p. 356). Others 'hadn't been on duty'
and are 'exceedingly busy'. All seem to know something and
regard her with a too-innocent stare. At the same time, she notices
a group of kites 'swooping down continually to a particular spot
on the lawn', and pecking away at *something*. She investigates and

finds 'just a mess of what I presumed to be chicken bones'. She notices still more kites hovering about the spot in which Michael has last been seen. Again, people on the job are too busy to talk.

Clearly, that mess of chicken bones *is* Michael. Harriet, who is, after all, selecting her material, has to know it. The elaborate strategem must be employed to accommodate Harriet's not realising that her beloved Crishi has just engineered the murder of her beloved Michael, and that she herself is even more deeply enmeshed in his trap.

But throughout, Harriet's irony is deft and well-placed, anything but naïve. It combines strangely with the wide-eyed innocence that overcomes her whenever Crishi (and before him, Michael) comes on the scene. The odd clashes in tone and style prompt one to wonder just who is being fooled. The terrible ending, with Harriet trapped, alone with the Bhais and Crishi, a million miles from anywhere (in Dhoka, 'the place of the trick') – was it really so terrible? If she is telling the story 'many years' later, at least she has survived. And we hear of no change of heart about Crishi.

Another kind of coyness, then, underlies the telling of this odd memoir: it is animated by a piquancy not unlike sexual excitement, especially in its last third. One reviewer noted that in the Indian section, the novel 'quickens to a climax of horrifying, almost hilarious suspense'. As the heroine-narrator moves inexorably to Dhoka, with its dark scenario, its suggestion even of gang-rape, one hears the breathy accents of fantasy. And with this scene the whole tale takes on the aspect of a benign sexual daydream, spun for the pleasure of its listeners, in the tested tradition of the 'bodice-ripper'. In fact, Harriet's wide-eyed ingenuousness is typical of the quintessential pornographic heroine, whose innocence exists, as I have said before in this study, only to be violated. The cast of characters, involving the swashbuckling, antisocial desperado, scarred by the struggles of his murky past (Crishi, like the S.P., is mysteriously scarred) who is redeemed – even if only temporarily – by the heroine's love, populates, in various guises, entire libraries of romances. The redemptive romance of criminal and lady offers a fleeting vision of economic and social distinctions breached and healed by the power of eros – on one level.

On another level, the dynamic is less lofty: it may be only an aphrodisiac for jaded middle-class appetites. So says Quentin Crisp, in a review of, of all things, the Merchant–Ivory version of *Maurice*. Mr Crisp ventures that homosexuals, lacking the built-in differences that heterosexuals must bridge, need to invent differences to create sexual polarities, hence the importance of class distinctions. 'Where I see class distinctions inflaming desire', he writes, 'Mr. Forster saw love conquering prejudice. His problem was that, at any rate in literature, he was not content with a bit of rough trade, but longed for eternal love. It is here that the story abandons all probability.'[15]

Mr Crisp's theory sounds plausible, but we know that heterosexuals are not immune to the same sexual iconography of class. In my view, there is no opposition between the two views, which one might call idealistic and venal: the turn-on may come in part from the deliberate flaunting of a class system that is intuitively perceived as immoral.

Whatever the provenance of this scenario of cross-class and cross-race relations, which surely encompasses a multitude of various motives and psychological impulses, it figures prominently in both Jhabvala's novel and Forster's. Although Jhabvala declined to write the screenplay for Merchant–Ivory's *Maurice*, ironically, her tenth novel relates to the film anyway.

Maurice's working-class lover Alec is a good example of the mythical phallic knower, whom Jhabvala's heroines also tend to fantasise. A classic illustration of the fantasy might be the first encounter between the gentlemanly Maurice and Alec the handyman. After one brief, polite conversation with Alec, Maurice, that night, leans out his window and calls, 'come!' And Alec appears:

> The head and the shoulders of a man rose up, paused, a gun was leant against the window sill very carefully, and someone he scarcely knew moved towards him and knelt beside him and whispered, 'Sir, was you calling out for me? . . . Sir, I know. . . . I know', and touched him.[16]

Forster quite consciously insisted on a 'happy ending' for his novel, for ideological reasons. 'I shouldn't have bothered to write otherwise. I was determined that in fiction anyway two men should fall in love and remain in it for the ever and ever that fiction allows', he wrote in 1960.[17]

Forster's rather improbable scenario of lasting 'sharing' between the upper-class hero and his working-class lover presents an interesting contrast to Jhabvala's very ambiguous non-resolution.

Three Continents, sadly, seems less improbable, based as it is on extortion and revenge, not only on love. Yet Crishi, with his scars and his poverty-stricken origins is, like Forster's caretaker, 'rough trade'. To borrow another expression, again, from the vocabulary of male homosexuality, Crishi is a trick who stays on.

The authorial ambivalence about Crishi, which runs through the novel, is a literary manifestation of the same debate that is currently dividing feminist thought: where do we draw the line on our fantasies? As *In Search of Love and Beauty* asks, do we allow ourselves to fall under the spell of the Leos, the Kents, and their like? And which is worse – loving them, or not loving them?

'EXPIATION': OTHER VICTIMS

The brittle distancing that mars this novel is offset by one of Jhabvala's recent stories, still uncollected: 'Expiation' makes an interesting companion-piece to the novel.[18] Set in India, it has to do with the sociopolitical inequities and their tragic consequences for individuals. It is the story of a newly rich family devastated by the sins of one of its sons, a dissatisfied dreamer who falls under the influence of an even more pathological type, from a milieu of abject poverty.

In her earliest novels, *To Whom She Will* and *The Nature of Passion*, Jhabvala painted for her readers, with a lyric ruefulness, clans and communities of Indians living non-Westernised, traditional lives; we glimpsed them feasting and wedding and making music; though they were not her main focus, she showed us enough of them to accord them a place, and a place of harmony, in the worlds she drew. In accordance with the sunny mood of these two comedies, her non-Westernised Indians may have been materially worse off than the middle-class families of the protagonists but they lived satisfying, communal lives governed by still-vital traditions. In the lives of these traditional clanspeople there was time to play, to repose, to practise the traditional arts which still took places of importance: one remembers, for example, the lyricism of the Punjabi wedding ceremony with which *To Whom She Will* closes.

In 'Expiation' (uncollected, 1982) the poor are also there. Again, they are glimpsed briefly, in a few phrases only. But they are a very different poor. Wretched, urban poverty, grinding and pitiless, creates the sociopath Sachu, who in turn poisons the lives of the family, and exacts the expiation referred to in the title. In the novel, the sociopathic Crishi's roots appear to be almost as miserable.

'Expiation' is one of Jhabvala's most expressionistic stories. The sombre account is related by 'the eldest brother', a rather prosaic and literal-minded shopkeeper who none the less manages to convey the depth of his feelings, all through indirection. Recalling events from a vantage-point after his brother's execution, the narrator emerges with a wrenching vulnerability. He still calls his younger brother, Ram Lal (one of the names of God) by his baby name, Bablu. If Bablu has become a thief and a murderer, in the brother's memory he is still Bablu, with 'eyes serious and pure like a child's'. If he has plotted, behind those innocent eyes, to steal the savings of the narrator and his wife, that narrator, the eldest brother, seems to bear him no ill-will. After the boy absconds with the money, having just missed killing the narrator's wife for it, the narrator worries: 'I thought of the bundles of money he had taken with him and of how unsafe it was for anyone, let alone a young boy, to travel with so much cash.' So the story reminds us that each of the young men who fill the world's prisons was, not long ago, a child. By entering the consciousness of one of the forgotten victims – the family of the murderer, who remember him as the dreamy, withdrawn child that he was – Jhabvala forcibly dislodges our comfortably held assumptions of innocence, guilt and justice. Even for a crime as heinous as this one – Bablu and his friend have murdered another child, a rich boy with roller skates – one is led by this story actually to *do* as the lofty motto carved over the prison gates directs: to 'hate the sin but not the sinner'.

After stealing the narrator's savings, Bablu eventually returns home, this time with 'the other one', Sachu, who will be his partner in crime, and whose eyes are 'blank like glass'. His enigmatic expressionlessness hides a terrifying amorality, for he turns out to be a murderer many times over, barbaric in his simplicity: he will kill for any trinket that catches his eye. Sachu is a nickname, a diminutive based on the Sanskrit word *sat*, 'being, that which is, the divine'. As a representative of the faceless mass of the poor, upon whose misery live all the prosperous middle and upper classes (of which Bablu's family have just become members), Sachu is well, and symbolically, named. Though one might rather not see them, they are, with a terrible irony, 'that which is', especially in India.

Sachu, like Crishi, is an escapee from the prison into which he was born. A product of the most wretched poverty, he has developed a crude ideology of despair: crime alone provides the way out of the poverty that swallowed up the life of, say, his father, who had pulled a handcart to support nine children – of whom those surviving to adulthood are also now pulling handcarts. Weighed against the slavery of such a life, a few years of plenty followed by the gallows seemed the better choice. There is not much that can be said to that, except perhaps to remember the other eight children, still shackled, as it were, to their handcarts: the poorest versions of those urban poor who go about their ordinary lives struggling to support their families – whom Betsy of 'Passion' apotheosised in Har Gopal.

Bablu and Sachu, inspired by a popular film, kidnap a child for ransom. They rape and murder him; they are caught, tried, convicted and hanged. The victim is the only son of the chief of police, a child of the educated gentry, people with 'wheat' complexions, who seem like 'higher beings' even to the wealthy tradespeople of the town. The abduction presented no problem: the boy was open and friendly, eager to show off his new roller skates, the like of which no one in the town had ever seen. Bablu and Sachu, with their victim, hide out in the empty ruins of an ancient bathing tank. The boy is chained: there is 'sodomy'. Once they have murdered him and run away to a neighbouring village, Bablu and Sachu are easily found: people notice the roller skates. But each one claims sole responsibility for the murder. As in some logical conundrum, at least one must be lying: one guesses Bablu, to protect Sachu.

The elder brother's narrative is studded with details that reveal the sociopolitics of this kidnap attempt. One fills in the broadest economic background through his rather self-satisfied descriptions of his family's relative wealth. By virtue of a boom in the cotton trade, brought about by black marketeering, which in turn was brought about by government mismanagement, he has managed to parlay his grandfather's debt-ridden stall in the bazaar into a large and successful cloth factory. He is now the proud owner of a 'white Ambassador car' and a spacious suburban house. But their wealth has surged ahead of their habits: the family actually do their living in a small back room furnished with cots and cooking vessels, while the large front room in which guests are received contains blue velvet sofas and china cabinets full of dolls. There Bablu and Sachu had installed themselves.

To these newly rich tradespeople, with their deeply held sense of family and face, the public shame of Bablu's execution has been particularly painful: the eldest brother mentions the photographers, the whispering spectators at the trial. To escape, another brother has emigrated to Canada, but the eldest brother and his family stay on, beginning, now, for the first time, to *use* their front room. Expiation has been made, the family has given up its sacrifice.

Despite the eldest brother's sad literalmindedness – he had thought Sachu a good friend for his little brother who spent so much time 'thinking' – the reader *sees* Bablu through his spare description. Bablu has always been a loner and a dreamer, fastidious and unhappy in the family's earlier circumstances – sharing a bathroom with eight other families, for example. (Is this undue fastidiousness? How would *we* fare?). His devotion to fine clothes and sweet-smelling hair dressings lend him a kind of Bovaryesque anguish; and the film magazines to which he is addicted signal both his dissatisfaction and his passivity. As Jhabvala creates him through the eldest brother's eyes, one credits his attraction to the craftier, more desperate and more dominant, Sachu.

The overriding motif is the tragic futility of the eldest brother's devotion to Bablu. His irrational guilt, too, is convincingly rendered.

My prayer to be relieved of their crime has been answered, so that it is no longer there before my eyes day and night. Now it is as if it were locked away in a heavy steel trunk; this weight may be taken from me at the last hour, but until then I carry it inside myself, where only God and I know of its constant presence.

Perhaps the authenticity and the feeling that emanate from this short tale, in some contrast to the novel, has to do with this odd admission by the narrator. The locked 'steel trunk' of his guilt and pain is peculiarly charged, it seems to me, coming from the pen of Ruth Jhabvala, who over and over answers reporters' questions about the sorrows of her early life by saying that she has 'wiped them out', that she 'never draws on them' in her work.[19] Clearly, the fiction belies these reserved disclaimers, as it almost invariably, particularly in the later work, creates a mood of hidden and

unspoken intensity and pain. In this story, the direct reference to
the inadmissible guilt and suffering seems in keeping with the
softened emotional tone. Perhaps the expiation of the boy's crime
has been, for the brother, the very telling of this sad tale. Again,
Indian characters more readily serve as a conduit for this kind of
charged theme, lacking the brittleness of the Westerners; and a
man, rather than a woman, narrator keeps it at a remove. In *Three
Continents*, on the other hand, the spotlight, as it were, is given to
a Western woman: and this very identity necessitates a different
kind of authorial approach: more circuitous, more ironic and more
distanced.

One narrative detail, in particular, rings with significance in light
of the author's other work: that is, the abandoned bathing tank in
which the 'sodomy' and murder take place. One recalls that Harriet
and Crishi first make love in an abandoned swimming pool on
'the Island' in *Three Continents*. In that same ornate swimming
pool, the millionaire Linton of an earlier generation had murdered
his wife. The reappearance of this image provides a startling clue
to the symbolic level underlying the fiction. Remembering, too,
the desert shrine in the parched landscape, at which Olivia's
abduction took place in *Heat and Dust*, or the abandoned fort of
'Desecration', which was the site of Sofia's sexual awakening with
the Superintendent of Police, one is struck by the commonality
among all these dreamlike images. All describe once-functioning
places now fallen into ruin, now the scene of destructive and
obsessive sexual encounters.

It is almost as if the writer were fashioning images of the
dynamics of sexuality in the fragmented modern psyche, the
psyche maimed by the horrors of the twentieth-century state, by
the isolation of rootlessness, by the absence of community. The
empty swimming pools and bathing tanks particularly suggest,
psychoanalytically, the female enclosed space now drained of that
which would have made it whole. If we read this missing water as
the nurturant and healing emotional dimension – *love* – which
should be there and is not, these empty pools and bathing tanks
in which murder and violation take place acquire a new and
revelatory significance.

'Expiation', like the similarly named 'Desecration', possesses
almost a fabular quality. The eldest brother's family watches
helplessly as Bablu is lost, in his own way a victim. The eldest
brother dares not meet the eyes of the father of the murdered child

with the roller skates. But both victims, the boy and Bablu, have been sacrificed to expiate the original social tragedy: the hunger of the masses whom we would rather not see – 'we' being the Police Chief in the unnamed town where the murder occurs, the eldest brother with his spacious home, and certainly us, Jhabvala's readers.

In 'Expiation', one glimpses the Jhabvala who spoke with a deceiving easiness about the untenable conflicts of living well in India, in the face of such privation: 'Can one lose sight of that fact? God knows, I've tried.' What is openly visible in the third world is, of course, comfortably removed in the West – but it is there none the less: that which is, a fundamental basis of our moral universe. In 'Expiation', Jhabvala connects directly with her passionate feeling for the victims of any kind of oppression: the outrage at injustice that simmers, veiled by irony, throughout her work. Justice was, after all, one of the aims of the corrupt 'Fourth World Movement'.

The result here is a moving story, devoid of the irony and cool reserve with which Jhabvala customarily regards her wealthier and more powerful protagonists. As a companion-piece to *Three Continents* I think it puts in perspective the odd ambivalence with which Crishi is treated. It even indicates a way in which Harriet Wishwell's rage to be rid of the fortunes to which she is heir is in some measure a laudable desire, emanating from a profound and simple sense of the immortality of accumulated wealth in a world in which millions hunger.

This concern for justice, as well as truth and beauty, this muted outrage, this sharp eye for the topsy-turvy morality of this world: these are characteristic of the work as a whole. Ruth Jhabvala is a survivor of the worst inhumanity yet perpetrated in man's history of inhumanity. She was snatched from the jaws of death at the last moment. Her childhood was lived in the shadow of terror. Just recently, in an interview, she admitted that 'going to school wasn't pleasant. . . . Other children would scream after us and throw stones'.[20] We know that this description is only the tip of the iceberg. One can imagine only with the greatest difficulty coming of age in the nightmare of Nazi Germany. The terrors of such a childhood must inform a writer's vision, in whatever way, and such is the complexity of experience that there are infinite numbers of ways for this to happen.

For all its irony and dryness, Ruth Jhabvala's work is animated by a passion for the ideals of truth and justice, a passion that harks back to the Hebrew prophets. At the same time, she writes as a woman, with a concern for the aesthetic and the romantic that is associated with femininity. This breadth of vision makes Jhabvala's work particularly rich. To a postmodernist interest in sexual politics, she brings the ancient literary tradition to which she is in some sense an heir.

Perhaps Jhabvala's Jewishness is the source of her deep interest in the issues of heritage, disinheritance and so on, for the heritage of five thousand years of history cannot be taken lightly. Similarly, and again in the context of Jewishness, the pressing and tragic consciousness of responsibility with which survivors are generally burdened may also be related to Jhabvala's attraction to the themes of heritage and disinheritance.

Equally important, as we have seen, is Jhabvala's interest in the feminist debate on love and sexuality. In her tenth novel, these large strands of material are interwoven. The ambitious work, far from being the simplistic or formulaic piece that some critics have deemed it, is a meditation, at times playful, at times anguished, on the themes that have always concerned her. If it conveys ambivalence, if its narrator-heroine is by turns wise and stupid, and the object of her affections by turns a comedian, a scoundrel and a victim, that does not detract from the novel's interest. It is part of a process of literary investigation that takes up where the previous work left off. One looks forward to Ruth Jhabvala's next contribution to the debate that is literature.

Notes

When citing Ruth Jhabvala's novels, I have given page numbers in the text, using the following editions:

Amrita/To Whom She Will (New York: W. W. Norton, 1956).
The Nature of Passion (London: George Allen & Unwin, 1956).
Esmond in India (London: George Allen & Unwin, 1958).
The Householder (London: John Murray, 1960).
Get Ready for Battle (London: John Murray, 1962).
A Backward Place (London: John Murray, 1965).
A New Dominion (London: John Murray, 1972).
Heat and Dust (London: John Murray, 1975).
In Search of Love and Beauty (London: John Murray, 1983).
Three Continents (New York: William Morrow, 1987).

Notes to Chapter 1: Introduction

1. Dorothy Rabinowitz, review of *Travelers*, World 2, no. 12 (1973) p. 66; reprinted in *Contemporary Literary Criticism: Excerpts from the Criticism of the Works of Today's Novelists*, ed. Carolyn Riley (Detroit: Gale Research, 1975) vol. 4, p. 256.
2. Barbara Grizzuti Harrison, 'We're Off to See the Guru', *MS*, December 1973, p. 28; reprinted in *Contemporary Literary Criticism*, p. 257.
3. Unsigned review in the *Observer*, 7 June 1981, p. 33; as cited by R. J. Crane, 'Ruth Prawer Jhabvala: a Checklist of Primary and Secondary Sources', *Journal of Commonwealth Literature*, 20, no. 1 (1985) p. 203.
4. Reissued by Penguin Books in 1981.
5. Bernard Weinraub, 'The Artistry of Ruth Prawer Jhabvala', *New York Times Magazine*, 11 September 1983, p. 112.
6. From a letter to Yasmine Gooneratne, quoted in Yasmine Gooneratne, *Silence, Exile and Cunning: The Fiction of Ruth Prawer Jhabvala* (New Delhi: Orient Longman, 1983) p. 2.
7. Siegbart Soloman Prawer (1925–) is the author of a number of literary critical studies suggesting interesting commonalities with his sister's work: for example, *Caligari's Children: The Film as Tale of Terror* (Oxford: Clarendon Press, 1980; New York: Oxford University Press, 1980), or *Heine's Jewish Comedy: A Study of His Portraits of Jews and Judaism* (Oxford: Clarendon Press, 1983; New York: Oxford University Press, 1983).
8. From Ramlal Agarwal, 'An Interview with Ruth Prawer Jhabvala', *Quest*, 91 (1974) p. 36.

9. Gooneratne, *Silence, Exile and Cunning*, p. 2.
10. Ruth Prawer Jhabvala, 'Moonlight, Jasmine and Rickets', *New York Times*, 23 April 1973, p. 35: 'When one writes about India as a European and in English (as I do), inevitably, one writes not for Indian but for Western readers.'
11. John Updike, 'Raman and Daisy and Olivia and the Nawab', review of *Heat and Dust* in the *New Yorker*, 5 July 1978, p. 83.
12. Ramlal Agarwal, in *Times of India* (Bombay), 25 March 1973.
13. Ibid., pp. 33–4.
14. Ibid., p. 34.
15. Gooneratne, *Silence, Exile and Cunning*, p. 18.
16. Ibid., p. 17.
17. Hayden Moore Williams, *The Fiction of Ruth Prawer Jhabvala* (Calcutta Writer's Workshop, 1973) p. 65.
18. Vasant Shahane, 'Jhabvala's *Heat and Dust*: a Cross-Cultural Encounter', in *Aspects of Indian Writing in English*, ed. M. K. Naik (Madras: Macmillan, 1979) p. 230.
19. Ibid., p. 223.
20. And probably in the view of most who would call themselves feminists. See, for example, Margo Jefferson, 'The Bostonians Misses the Boat', *MS*, October 1984, p. 33. However, it seems only fair to add that one 'neo-Conservative' found the film irritatingly *feminist*, and denounced Jhabvala for having spinelessly capitulated to the forces of trendy feminism! (See Richard Grenier, 'The Bostonians Inside Out', *Commentary*, October 1984, p. 60.)
21. As quoted in Weinraub, 'The Artistry of Ruth Prawer Jhabvala', p. 64 (no source given).
22. Ruth Prawer Jhabvala, 'Myself in India', *An Experience of India* (New York: W. W. Norton, 1971) p. 19.
23. Charlotte Brontë, *Shirley* (1849), as quoted in Ellen Moers, *Literary Women: The Great Women Writers* (New York: Anchor Books, 1977) p. 192.
24. Jhabvala, 'Myself in India', p. 7.
25. *To Whom She Will* (London: George Allen & Unwin, 1955) p. 1.
26. Richard Nyrop et al., *Area Handbook for India* (Washington, D.C., 1975) p. 205.
27. Jhabvala, 'Myself in India', p. 8.
28. Hayden Moore Williams, 'The Yogi and the Babbitt: Themes and Characters of the New India in the Novels of R. Prawer Jhabvala', *Twentieth-Century Literature*, 15, no. 2 (1969) pp. 81–90.
29. Compare Carol P. Christ, *Diving Deep and Surfacing: Women Writers on Spiritual Quest* (Boston, Mass.: Beacon Press, 1980).

Notes to Chapter 2: Dangerous Quest

1. Charlotte Brontë wrote to her friend Ellen Nussey that passion is particularly dangerous for women. For ladies, 'une grande passion is une grande folie. . . . Mediocrity in all things is wisdom.' Since

reciprocal passion is rare, women are at risk: 'God help her, if she is left to love passionately and alone.' From Françoise Basche, *Relative Creatures: Victorian Women in Society and the Novel* (New York: Schocken Books, 1974) p. 166.

2. Kate Millett, *Sexual Politics* (New York: Doubleday, 1970) pp. 440–72.
3. Her friends caution her that he's no good. But 'I know that he's not bad, I know he's only sad.' Sung by the heroine as social worker in 'The Leader of the Pack', by Greenwich, Barry and Martin; The Shangri-Las, 1964. In Roger Lax and Frederick Smith, *The Great Song Thesaurus* (New York: Oxford University Press, 1984).
4. See H. Adlerfer, B. Jaker and B. Nelson, *Diary of a Conference on Sexuality: The Scholar and the Feminist. Towards a Politics of Sexuality* (Barnard College, New York, 1982).
5. Susan Griffin, *Pornography and Silence* (New York: Harper Colophon, 1981) *passim*.
6. See, for example, *The Female Gothic*, ed. Juliann E. Fleenor (Montreal: Eden Press, 1983), or Tania Modleski, *Loving with a Vengeance* (New York: Methuen Books, 1984). The term 'Female Gothic' is coined by Ellen Moers in *Literary Women: The Great Women Writers* (New York: Anchor Books, 1977) ch. 5.
7. Susan Sontag, 'The Pornographic Imagination', in *Styles of Radical Will* (New York: Farrar, Strauss & Giroux, 1969) p. 200.
8. Jessica Benjamin, 'Master and Slave: The Fantasy of Erotic Domination', in *Powers of Desire: The Politics of Sexuality*, ed. Ann Snitow, Christine Stansell and Sharon Thompson (New York: Monthly Review Press, 1983) p. 282.
9. René Girard, *Deceit, Desire and the Novel: Self and Other in Literary Structure*, trans. Yvonne Freccero (Baltimore, Md: Johns Hopkins Press, 1965) p. 176.
10. Ibid., pp. 182–3.
11. Sontag, 'Pornographic Imagination', p. 188.

Note to Chapter 3: Gurus: Short Stories

1. Ruth Jhabvala frequently uses the image of British cemetaries in India to conflate a number of themes: the vanished British presence, the cultural separateness of the British. In *Heat and Dust*, Olivia's wish to be cremated is one of the only clues that her retreat to the mountaintop is a willed embrace of Indianness.

Notes to Chapter 4: Gurus: *A New Dominion* or *Travelers*

1. *The Concise Oxford Dictionary*, 7th edn (Oxford: Clarendon Press, 1982).
2. James Ivory and Ruth Prawer Jhabvala, *Autobiography of a Princess, Being the Adventures of an American Film Director in the Land of the Maharajas*, compiled by James Ivory, screenplay by Ruth Prawer Jhabvala (New York: Harper & Row, 1975) p. 36.
3. In an interview with R. Agarwal, *Quest*, 91 (1974) pp. 33–6.

4. V. S. Pritchett, 'Ruth Prawer Jhabvala: Snares and Delusions', in *The Tale-Bearers: Literary Essays* (New York: Random House, 1980) p. 98.
5. Ellen Moers, *Literary Women: The Great Women Writers* (New York: Anchor Books, 1977) ch. 5.
6. Joanna Russ, 'Somebody is Trying to Kill Me and I Think It's My Husband', in *The Female Gothic*, ed. Juliann E. Fleenor (Montreal: Eden Press, 1983) pp. 31–57.
7. Susan Brownmiller, *Femininity* (New York: Simon & Schuster, 1984) p. 197.
8. S. Sondhi, 'Dowry Deaths in India', *MS*, January 1983, p. 22. Sondhi reports that two dowry deaths take place every day in Delhi alone.
9. Ann Bar Snitow, 'Mass Market Romance: Pornography for Women is Different', in *Powers of Desire: The Politics of Sexuality*, ed. Ann Snitow, Christine Stansell and Sharon Thompson (New York: Monthly Review Press, 1983) pp. 245–63. See also Tanya Modleski, 'The Disappearing Act: Harlequin Romances', in *Loving with a Vengeance: Mass-Produced Fantasies for Women* (New York: Methuen, 1984) ch. II.

Notes to Chapter 5: 'The Housewife'

1. P. Lal, *Great Sanskrit Plays in Modern Translation* (New York: New Directions, 1957) p. 74.
2. Ibid., pp. 3–74.

Notes to Chapter 6: 'Desecration'

1. Gita Mehta, *Karma Cola: Marketing the Mystic East* (New York: Simon & Schuster, 1979) pp. 68–9.
2. Susan Sontag, 'The Pornographic Imagination', in *Styles of Radical Will* (New York: Farrar, Strauss & Giroux, 1969) p. 50.
3. Ann Bar Snitow, 'Mass Market Romance: Pornography for Women is Different', in *Powers of Desire: The Politics of Sexuality*, ed. Ann Snitow, Christine Stansell and Sharon Thompson (New York: Monthly Review Press, 1983) p. 250.
4. Ibid., p. 255.
5. René Girard, *Violence and the Sacred* (Baltimore, Md and London: Johns Hopkins Press, 1977) p. 55. Originally published in Paris, 1972.
6. Jessica Benjamin, 'Master and Slave: the Fantasy of Erotic Domination', in *Powers of Desire*, ed. Snitow *et al.*, p. 290. See 'Pauline Réage', *The Story of O*, trans. S. d'Estrée (New York: Grove Press, 1965).
7. Girard discusses this idea in *Deceit, Desire and the Novel: Self and Other in Literary Structure*, trans. Yvonne Freccero (Baltimore, Md: Johns Hopkins Press, 1965) p. 112.
8. In this instance I refer readers to the American edition for the sake of convenience (it seems to be in wider circulation).
9. Ruth Prawer Jhabvala, 'Better than Dead', *New Yorker*, 24 May 1958.
10. Jean de la Fontaine, 'Le Loup et l'Agneau', *Fables Choisis* (Paris, 1668–9).

11. See, for example, William Ryan, *Blaming the Victim* (New York: Pantheon Books, 1971), or Andrea Dworkin, *Right-Wing Women* (New York: Perigree Books, 1983).
12. The perennial appeal of teenaged girls' serial detective stories may indicate the psychoanalytic importance of this somewhat 'gothic' idea, in which a young woman investigates a dangerous mystery. For an interesting discussion of the genre, see Bobbie Ann Mason, *The Girl Sleuth: A Feminist Guide* (Old Westbury, N.Y.: Feminist Press, 1975).

Notes to Chapter 7: Demon-Lovers and Holy Mothers: *Heat and Dust*

1. James Ivory, *Autobiography of a Princess: Also Being the Adventures of an American Film Director in the Land of the Maharajas* (New York: Harper & Row, 1975) p. 36.
2. Barbara Grizzuti Harrison, 'India, Inc.: Hullabaloo Over Merchant–Ivory Pictures', *Harpers*, March 1982, p. 67.
3. The evil spirit who was Adam's first wife, according to Hebrew legend. Raphael Patai, *The Hebrew Goddess* (New York: Avon Books, 1978) p. 183. Feminist historians see her as a negative recasting of the mother goddesses of the Near East. See Elizabeth Fisher, *Woman's Creation: Sexual Evolution and the Shaping of Society* (New York: McGraw Hill, 1979) p. 297.
4. J. S. Mill and Harriet Taylor, *The Subjection of Women* (London, 1869).
5. John Updike, review of *Heat and Dust* in the *New Yorker*, 5 July 1976.
6. My summary follows R. J. Furbank's in *Forster: A Life*, 2 vols (London: Secker & Warburg, 1978) vol. II, p. 68ff. 'Dyarchy' was recommended by the 'Montague–Chelmsford British Government Report' of 1918.
7. This point is made by R. J. Cronin, 'The Hill of Devi and Heat and Dust', *Essays in Criticism*, 36 (April 1986) pp. 142–59.
8. Furbank, *Forster: A Life*, p. 68.
9. Cronin, 'The Hill of Devi', p. 157.
10. Ibid., p. 144ff. However, Cronin also finds the modern narrator guilty of 'gauche, unimaginative prose' (p. 144), a view at odds with most reviewers. Gooneratne, for example, sees the modern narrator as 'a personality at once self-aware and generous', 'above all, an educated sensibility' with a style 'quiet, direct and thoughtful' (Yasmine Gooneratne, *Silence, Exile and Cunning: The Fiction of Ruth Prawer Jhabvala* (New Delhi: Orient Longman, 1983) pp. 222, 223, 224. Gooneratne's balanced view of the Nawab is given on pp. 210–34.
11. But Shahane unaccountably also calls the Nawab 'incredulous and perfidious . . . very erratic and sometimes childishly funny', in Vasant Shahane, *Ruth Prawer Jhabvala* (New Delhi: Heinemann, 1976) ch. 4, pp. 129–41. In my view he misreads the Nawab almost completely.
12. Dorothy K. Stein, 'Women to Burn: Suttee as a Normative Institution' (*Signs* 4, no. 2 [Winter 1978], p. 255).
13. Colonel Sleeman's *Rambles and Recollections of an Indian Official* (1844) is cited in Shirley Chew, 'Fictions of Princely States and Empire', *Ariel*, 17 (July 1986) pp. 103–16. Chew quotes his account of the widow's

self-immolation, as follows:

> As she rose up fire was set to the pile, and it was instantly in a blaze. . . . She walked once round the pit, paused a moment, and, while muttering a prayer, threw some flowers into the fire. She then walked up deliberately and steadily to the brink, stepped into the centre of the flame, sat down, and leaning back in the midst as if reposing on a couch, was consumed without uttering a shriek or betraying one sign of agony.

14. The anecdote, though delivered dead-pan by the narrator, is an example of the widespread habit of woman-blaming. Jhabvala also marks a sub-category thereof, mother-blaming, in *In Search of Love and Beauty*, where Shirley, a minor character, has a mother who 'like all mothers . . . had damaged Shirley and had been the first person she had to cut loose from' (p. 136).

    Indian woman-blaming appears to be widespread enough to escape notice; for example, in a sociologist's account:

    > The villagers as a whole strongly accuse women of causing the break-up of families, and they are justified in their condemnation. Many a man leaves his parents and settles down in a separate house as soon as he is married. . . . The men are instigated by the womenfolk to ask for a division of property. The women of the family always quarrel. These quarrels may not be of a serious nature, but the constant bickerings make life unpleasant. Quarrels are often due to very trivial causes such as a woman giving more food to her children than to other children in the family [this hardly seems trivial in a society of privation – L.S.]. The other women look upon such partiality with indignation and the result is a quarrel. Finally the quarrels get on the nerves of the menfolk and force a separation. (from D. N. Majumdar, *Caste and Communication in an Indian Village* (Bombay, 1961); quoted in Ronald Segal, *The Anguish of India* (New York: Stein & Day, 1965) p. 161)

15. The piano music of Robert Schumann accords well with the characters of Olivia and Harry, two dreamers.
16. Gita Mehta gives some horrible examples in *Karma Cola: Marketing the Mystic East* (New York: Simon & Schuster, 1979) p. 160. At the latest count, 1981, per capita income was $217 in India, as compared with $12,800 in the United States of America.
17. The thought is Gopi's in *A New Dominion*, p. 53. Inder Lal, too, fears the narrator: 'I could see . . . how everything he had heard about Western women rushed about in his head' (*Heat and Dust*, p. 127).
18. Kate Millett makes the point that they also serve to parody these roles. See her *Sexual Politics* (New York: Doubleday, 1970) p. 447.
19. On the jacket of the American edition of *In Search of Love and Beauty* (1983) and in subsequent books.
20. Simla was only the first and most populous of these hill-stations. The heat of the plains was thought to cause 'tropical neurasthenia' in

234 *Notes*

Europeans, that is, 'mental irritability, inability to work at full pressure and a mild depression . . . a preliminary stage of the more advanced condition of nervous breakdown'. The 1927 description by a British physician is quoted in Nora Mitchell, *The Indian Hill-Station*, University of Chicago: Department of Geography, Research Paper no. 141 (1972).
21. 'More than four-fifths of India's people are counted as villagers' (David G. Mandelbaum, *Society in India, I: Continuity and Change* (Berkeley, Cal.: University of California Press, 1970) p. 9.
22. Richard Nyrop *et al.*, *Area Handbook for India*, 3rd edn (Washington, D.C., 1975) p. 201.
23. Ibid., p. 200.
24. Sandra Gilbert and Susan Gubar, *The Madwoman in the Attic* (New Haven, Conn.: Yale University Press, 1979). In their view, literature by women characteristically contains a subtext of revolt beneath ostensible acquiescence to social norms. The madwoman represents a subversive female consciousness, only partially controlled.
25. V. S. Naipaul, *An Area of Darkness* (New York: Macmillan, 1964) p. 68.
26. E. M. Forster, *A Passage to India* (London: Edward Arnold, 1924; rpt. London: J. M. Dent, 1957) p. 219. All page citations are to this edition.
27. Ibid., p. 240.
28. Ibid., p. 253.
29. Furbank, *Forster: A Life*.
30. Quoted in ibid., vol. II, p. 126.
31. Ibid., vol. II, p. 126.
32. E. M. Forster, *The Hill of Devi* (1953); reprinted in *The Abinger Edition of E. M. Forster*, vol. 14, ed. Elizabeth Heine (London: Edward Arnold, 1983).
33. Ibid., p. 32.
34. Ibid., p. 98.
35. Ibid., p. 98.
36. Furbank, *Foster: A Life*, vol. I, p. 143.
37. Forster, *Hill of Devi*, p. 37.
38. Elizabeth Heine, Editor's Introduction to *The Abinger Edition of E. M. Forster*, vol. 14, p. ix. See also Furbank, *Forster: A Life*, vol. II, pp. 83–5.
39. E. M. Forster, 'Kanaya', in *The Abinger Edition of E. M. Forster*, vol. 14; Richard Cronin, 'The Hill of Devi and Heat and Dust', *Essays in Criticism*, 36 (April 1986) p. 154.
40. Ibid., p. 154.
41. Furbank, *Forster: A Life*, vol. I, p. 48.
42. Forster, *Hill of Devi*, p. 35.

Notes to Chapter 8: Difficult Adjustments: Three Stories

1. Adrienne Rich, 'Compulsory Heterosexuality and Lesbian Existence', in *Powers of Desire: The Politics of Sexuality*, ed. Ann Snitow, Christine Stansell and Sharon Thompson (New York: Monthly Review Press, 1983) pp. 177–205; see esp. p. 192.

2. Ibid., p. 182.
3. Ibid., p. 185.
4. Ibid., p. 178.
5. Ibid., p. 200.
6. Ruth Prawer Jhabvala, 'Myself in India', in *An Experience of India* (New York: W. W. Norton, 1971) pp. 12–13.
7. Stella Dong, '*Publishers' Weekly* Interviews Ruth Prawer Jhabvala', in *Publishers' Weekly*, 6 June 1986, pp. 54–5.
8. Ruth Prawer Jhabvala, 'Disinheritance', *Blackwood's Magazine*, April 1979.
9. See, for example, Helen Epstein, *Children of Survivors: Conversations with Sons and Daughters of Survivors* (New York: Putnam, 1979).
10. Bernard Weinraub, 'The Artistry of Ruth Prawer Jhabvala', *New York Times Magazine*, 11 September 1983, p. 112.
11. Jhabvala, 'Disinheritance'.
12. Ibid.
13. Weinraub, 'Artistry of Jhabvala', p. 112.
14. See, for example, Barbara McDonald and Cynthia Rich, *Look Me in the Eye* (San Francisco, Cal.: Spinsters Ink, 1983).
15. As, for example, in the scene in which Harry, Olivia and the Nawab discuss British racism (*Heat and Dust*, pp. 122–3).

Notes to Chapter 9: *In Search of Love and Beauty*

1. V. S. Pritchett, 'Ruth Prawer Jhabvala', in *The Tale-Bearers: Literary Essays* (New York: Random House, 1980).
2. Bruce Davidson (director), *Isaac Singer's Nightmare and Mrs Pupko's Beard*, with Isaac Bashevis Singer (New Yorker Films, 1974).
3. John Pym, *The Wandering Company: Twenty-one Years of Merchant–Ivory Films* (London: British Film Institute, 1983; New York: Museum of Modern Art, 1983) p. 50.
4. John Pym, 'Where Could I Meet Other Screenwriters?', interview in *Sight and Sound* (Winter, 1978–9) pp. 15–18.
5. Bernard Weinraub, 'The Artistry of Ruth Prawer Jhabvala', *New York Times Magazine*, 11 September 1983, p. 112.
6. Renée Winegarten, 'Ruth Prawer Jhabvala: A Jewish Passage to India', *Midstream: A Monthly Jewish Review*, March 1974, pp. 72–9; p. 79.
7. Weinraub, 'Artistry of Jhabvala', p. 112.
8. Ibid., p. 114.
9. The publicity brochure distributed by the MacArthur Foundation after its award to Jhabvala early in 1983 states that she is 'working on an original piece of fiction to be published both as a novel and adapted as a screenplay'. This was just prior to the publication of *In Search of Love and Beauty*, in June 1983.
10. Weinraub, 'Artistry of Jhabvala', p. 114.
11. Michiko Kakutani, review of *In Search of Love and Beauty*, in the *New York Times*, 19 July 1983, sect. 3, p. 14.
12. As noted by John Updike in his review in the *New Yorker*, 1 August

1983. Of course, Ruth Jhabvala's native city, Cologne, was also destroyed by bombing.

13. *Querschnitt* ['cross-section'] was an avant-garde literary and artistic periodical published in Berlin, 1921–36. Max Reinhardt (1873–1943), was an Austrian Jewish theatrical director. He is considered a master of spectacle. Like Leo, both he and Wilhelm Reich emigrated to the US.

14. Pietr Demianovitch Ouspensky, *In Search of the Miraculous: Elements of an Unknown Teaching* (New York: Harcourt Brace, 1949).

15. See Jeffrey Meyers, *Katherine Mansfield: A Biography* (New York: New Directions Books, 1980) pp. 238–52, for an excellent account of Katherine Mansfield's last days at Gurdjieff's 'Prieuré' at Fontainebleau. In fairness, it should be said that penicillin, which would have cured her tuberculosis, had not yet been discovered.

16. The name 'Marietta' connotes Victor Herbert's enormously popular operetta: 'Naughty Marietta', the story of a French princess who journeys to America and falls in love with an Indian scout. The witty allusion neatly conflates the themes in Marietta's life. It was naughty of her to have enjoyed the sexual encounter with her mother's lover. Her Protestant husband is as natively American as a white man can be, and she herself is a kind of disinherited princess.

17. John Updike, *New Yorker*, 5 July 1983; Robert Towers, *New York Times Book Review*, 12 June 1983.

18. George Henry Lewes thought the poem 'Goethe's most perfect creation'. Quoted in J. G. Robertson, *The Life and Work of Goethe* (London, 1932) p. 182.

19. Robertson, *Life and Work of Goethe*, p. 190.

20. Humphry Trevelyan, *Goethe and the Greeks* (Cambridge: Cambridge University Press, 1967) p. 205.

21. Pietro Citati, *Goethe*, trans. Raymond Rosenthal (New York: Dial Press, 1974) p. 32. Citati paraphrases: 'Men must not try to realize the hope, nor incarnate the radiance of myth within the confines of this earth. Mediocre and cautious bureaucrats, such as those in the small Duchy of Weimar and the German courts, were quite adequate to rule the destinies of our states.'

22. The title of this story alludes to a memoir by Jan and Rumer Godden, *Two Under the Indian Sun* (New York: Knopf, 1967). The latter is an account of a girlhood in Edwardian India. Perhaps Jhabvala's title is intended as an ironic comment on the contrast between the relationships that the two pieces portray. Jan and Rumer Godden are sisters so close that they tell one story between them, writing in the first person plural. They contrast to Elizabeth and Margaret, the two women 'friends' whose relationship is founded on a hidden jealousy and rivalry.

23. Fritz Perls, 'The Gestalt Prayer'. See F. S. Perls, *In and Out of the Garbage Pail* (Lafayette, Cal.: Real People, 1969).

24. Woody Allen, *Interiors* (United Artists, 1978).

Notes to Chapter 10: The International 'Trick': *Three Continents*

1. Harriet Shapiro, 'The Teeming Imagination of Novelist Ruth Prawer Jhabvala is Her Window on a World She Avoids', *People*, 28 September 1987, pp. 48–53; John Stark, 'Partners and Friends for 26 Years, James Ivory and Ismail Merchant Film Hotly Debated Gay Love Story', *People*, 26 October 1987, pp. 119–22.
2. Stark, 'Partners and Friends'.
3. Ibid.
4. Jane Perlez, 'High Ideals, Bad Ends', *New York Times Book Review*, 23 August 1987, p. 3.
5. Walter Goodman, book review in the *New York Times*, 20 August 1987, p. 28.
6. Robert Towers, 'Breaking the Spell', *New York Review of Books*, 8 October 1987.
7. Anne Duchene, 'Rawul Progress', *The Times Literary Supplement*, 13–19 November 1987.
8. Goodman, book review.
9. Shapiro, 'The Teeming Imagination'.
10. Ibid.
11. Ruth Prawer Jhabvala 'Myself in India', *An Experience of India*.
12. Shapiro, 'The Teeming Imagination'.
13. Towers, 'Breaking the Spell'.
14. Goodman, book review.
15. Quentin Crisp, 'Accepted Invitation: *Fatal Attraction* and *Maurice*', *Christopher Street*, issue 116, vol. 10, no. 8 (October 1987) pp. 8–10.
16. Ibid., p. 192. Forster's ellipses.
17. E. M. Forster, *Maurice* terminal note (New York: W. W. Norton, 1971) p. 250.
18. Ruth Prawer Jhabvala, 'Expiation', *New Yorker*, 11 October 1982, pp. 44–51.
19. Shapiro, 'The Teeming Imagination'.
20. Shapiro, ibid.

Selected Bibliography

I WORKS BY RUTH PRAWER JHABVALA

Novels

To Whom She Will (London: George Allen & Unwin, 1955); American edition retitled *Amrita* (New York: W. W. Norton, 1956).

The Nature of Passion (London: George Allen & Unwin, 1956; New York: W. W. Norton, 1957).

Esmond in India (London: George Allen & Unwin, 1958; New York: W. W. Norton, 1958; rpt. London: John Murray, 1978; Harmondsworth: Penguin, 1980).

The Householder (London: John Murray, 1960; New York: W. W. Norton, 1960; rpt. New York: W. W. Norton, 1977; Harmondsworth: Penguin, 1980).

Get Ready for Battle (London: John Murray, 1962; New York: W. W. Norton, 1963; rpt. Harmondsworth: Penguin, 1981).

A Backward Place (London: John Murray, 1965; New York: W. W. Norton, 1965; rpt. Harmondsworth: Penguin, 1980).

A New Dominion (London: John Murray, 1972); American edition retitled *Travelers* (New York: Harper & Row, 1973) (rpt. London: Quartet, 1976; London: Granada, 1983; New York: Harper & Row (Perennial Library), 1977).

Heat and Dust (London: John Murray, 1975; New York: Harper & Row, 1976; New Delhi: Hind Pocket Books, 1977; rpt. New York: Harper & Row (Perennial Library), 1976).

In Search of Love and Beauty (London: John Murray, 1983; New York: William Morrow, 1983).

Three Continents (London: John Murray, 1987; New York: William Morrow, 1987).

Collected Short Stories

Like Birds, Like Fishes, and Other Stories (London: John Murray, 1963; New York: W. W. Norton, 1964; New Delhi: Hind Pocket Books, 1969). Contents: 'The Old Lady'; 'A Loss of Faith'; 'The Award'; 'The Widow'; 'The Aliens'; 'The Interview'; 'A Birthday in London'; 'Like Birds, Like Fishes'; 'Lekha'; 'Sixth Child'; 'My First Marriage'.

A Stronger Climate: Nine Stories (London: John Murray, 1968; New York: W. W. Norton, 1968; rpt. London: Granada, 1983). Contents: 'The Seekers': 'In Love with a Beautiful Girl'; 'The Biography'; 'The Young Couple'; 'Passion'; 'A Spiritual Call'; 'A Young Man of Good Family'; The Sufferers: 'An Indian Citizen'; 'Miss Sahib'; 'The Man With the Dog'.

An Experience of India (London: John Murray, 1971; New York: W. W.

238

Norton, 1972). Contents: 'Introduction: Myself in India'; 'A Bad Woman';
'A Star and Two Girls'; 'Rose Petals'; 'A Course of English Studies';
'The Housewife'; 'Suffering Women'; 'An Experience of India'.

How I Became a Holy Mother, and Other Stories (London: John Murray, 1976;
New York: Harper & Row, 1976; rpt. New York: Harper & Row
(Perennial Library), 1979). Contents: 'Two More under the Indian Sun';
'The Englishwoman'; 'In the Mountains'; 'On Bail'; 'In a Great Man's
House'; 'Bombay'; 'Prostitutes'; 'Picnic with Moonlight and Mangoes';
'How I Became a Holy Mother'; 'Desecration'.

Out of India: Selected Stories (New York: William Morrow, 1986; London:
John Murray, 1986). Contents: 'Introduction: Myself in India'; 'My First
Marriage'; 'The Widow'; 'The Interview'; 'A Spiritual Call'; 'Passion';
'The Man with the Dog'; 'An Experience of India'; 'The Housewife';
'Rose Petals'; 'Two More under the Indian Sun'; 'Bombay'; 'On Bail';
'In the Mountains; 'How I Became a Holy Mother'; 'Desecration'.

Uncollected Short Stories

'Before the Wedding', *New Yorker*, 28 December 1957.
'Better than Dead', *New Yorker*, 24 May 1958.
'The Elected', *New Yorker*, 30 April 1960.
'Wedding Preparations', *Kenyon Review*, 23 (1961) pp. 408–22.
'Of Love and Sorrow', *Writers' Workshop Miscellany*, 10 (1962) pp. 31–5.
'Light and Reason', *New Statesman*, 19 July 1963.
'Foreign Wives', *London Magazine*, January 1968.
'A Very Special Fate', *New Yorker*, 29 March 1976.
'Parasites', *New Yorker*, 13 March 1978.
'A Summer by the Sea', *New Yorker*, 7 August 1978.
'Commensurate Happiness', *Encounter*, January 1980.
'Grandmother', *New Yorker*, 17 November 1980.
'Expiation', *New Yorker*, 11 October 1982.
'Farid and Farida', *New Yorker*, 15 October 1984.

Screenplays

The Householder, based on Jhabvala's own novel (Delhi: Ramlochan Books,
1963).
Shakespeare Wallah, with James Ivory (London: Merchant–Ivory Produc-
tions, 1965; New York: Grove Press, 1973).
The Guru, with James Ivory (London: Merchant–Ivory Productions, 1969).
Bombay Talkie, with James Ivory (London: Merchant–Ivory Productions,
1970).
'Autobiography of a Princess', in *Autobiography of a Princess, Being the
Adventures of an American Film Director in the Land of the Maharajas*,
compiled by James Ivory, photographs by John Swope and others,
screenplay by Ruth Prawer Jhabvala (New York: Harper and Row, 1975).
Roseland (London: Merchant–Ivory Productions, 1977).
Hullabaloo over George and Bonnie's Pictures (India: Merchant–Ivory Produc-
tions, 1978).

The Europeans, based on the Henry James novel (London: Merchant–Ivory Productions, 1979).

Jane Austen in Manhattan (London: Merchant–Ivory Productions, 1980).

Quartet, based on the Jean Rhys novel (London: Merchant–Ivory Productions, 1981).

The Bostonians, based on the Henry James novel (London: Merchant–Ivory Productions, 1984).

A Room with a View, based on E. M. Forster's novel (London: Merchant–Ivory Productions, 1986).

REFERENCES CITED

Note: This selected bibliography is a compilation of all works, other than Jhabvala's fiction, which I cite in my study, together with essays, reviews and interviews concerning Ruth Jhabvala and her work.

Adlerfer, H., Jaker, B. and Nelson, B., *Diary of a Conference on Sexuality: The Scholar and the Feminist: Towards a Politics of Sexuality* (Barnard College, New York, 1982).

Agarwal, Ramlal, 'An Interview with Ruth Prawer Jhabvala', *Quest*, 91 (1974) pp. 33–6.

——, 'Outsider with Unusual Insight', *Times of India*, 25 March 1973, p. 11.

——, 'Forster, Jhabvala and Readers', *Journal of Indian Writing in English*, 3, no. 2 (1976) pp. 25–7.

——, 'Two Approaches to Jhabvala', *Journal of Indian Writing in English*, 5, no. 1 (1978) pp. 24–7.

Asnan, Shyam K., 'Jhabvala's Novels – a Thematic Study', *Journal of Indian Writing in English*, 2, no. 2 (1975) pp. 38–47.

Bailett, Whitney, 'A Comedy and a Half', review of *The Nature of Passion*, in *New Yorker*, 22 June 1957, p. 101.

——, 'Post-Colonial', review of *Esmond in India*, in *New Yorker*, 29 November 1958, pp. 221–2.

——, 'The Weaning of Prem', review of *The Householder*, in *New Yorker*, 7 January 1961, pp. 83–4.

Basche, Françoise, *Relative Creatures: Victorian Women in Society and the Novel* (New York: Schocken Books, 1974).

Belliappa, N. Meena, 'East–West Encounter: Indian Women Writers of Fiction in English', in *Fiction and the Reading Public in India*, ed. C. D. Narasimhaiah (University of Mysore, 1967).

Benjamin, Jessica, 'Master and Slave: the Fantasy of Erotic Domination', in *Powers of Desire: The Politics of Sexuality*, ed. Ann Snitow, Christine Stansell and Sharon Thompson (New York: Monthly Review Press, 1983).

Blackwell, Fritz, 'Perception of the Guru in the Fiction of Ruth Prawer Jhabvala', *Journal of Indian Writing in English*, 5, no. 2 (1978) pp. 6–13.

Brownmiller, Susan, *Femininity* (New York: Simon & Schuster, 1984).

Campbell, Colin, 'Sapphires and Solitude', review of *Out of India*, in *New York Times Book Review*, 25 May 1986, p. 20.

Chew, Shirley, 'Fictions of Princely States and Empire', *Ariel*, 17 (July 1986) pp. 103–16.

Christ, Carol, *Diving Deep and Surfacing: Women Writers on Spiritual Quest* (Boston, Mass.: Beacon Press, 1980).

Citati, Pietro, *Goethe*, trans. Ramond Rosenthal (New York: Dial Press, 1974).

Crane, R. J., 'Ruth Prawer Jhabvala: a Checklist of Primary and Secondary Sources', *Journal of Commonwealth Literature*, 20, no. 1 (1985) pp. 171–203.

Crisp, Quentin, 'Accepted Invitation: *Fatal Attraction* and *Maurice*', *Christopher Street*, vol. 10, no. 8, issue 116 (October 1987) pp. 8–10.

Cronin, Richard, '*The Hill of Devi* and *Heat and Dust*', *Essays in Criticism*, 36 (April 1986) pp. 142–59.

Davidson, Bruce (director), *Isaac Singer's Nightmare and Mrs Pupko's Beard* (New York: New Yorker Films, 1974).

De Souza, Eunice, 'The Blinds Drawn and the Airconditioner on: the Novels of Ruth Prawer Jhabvala', *World Literature Written in English*, 17, no. 1 (April 1978) pp. 219–24.

Dong, Stella, '*Publishers' Weekly* Interviews: Ruth Prawer Jhabvala', *Publishers' Weekly*, 6 June 1986, pp. 54–5.

Duchêne, Anne, 'Rawul Progress', *The Times Literary Supplement*, 13–19 November 1987, p. 1248.

Epstein, Helen, *Children of Survivors* (New York: Putnam, 1979).

Fleenor, Juliann E. (ed.), *The Female Gothic* (Montreal: Eden Press, 1983).

Forster, E. M., *A Passage to India* (London: Edward Arnold, 1924; reprinted London: J. M. Dent, 1957).

——, *The Hill of Devi* (1953); reprinted in *The Abinger Edition of E. M. Forster*, ed. Elizabeth Heine (London: Edward Arnold, 1983) vol. 14.

——, 'Kanaya', posthumously published in *The Abinger Edition of E. M. Forster*, ed. Elizabeth Heine (London: Edward Arnold, 1983) vol. 14, pp. 237–40.

——, *Maurice* (written in 1913; posthumously published in New York: W. W. Norton, 1971).

Furbank, R. N., *Forster: A Life* (London: Secker & Warburg, 1978) 2 vols.

Gilbert, Sandra and Gubar, Susan, *The Madwoman in the Attic: The Woman Writer and the Nineteenth-Century Literary Imagination* (New Haven, Conn.: Yale University Press, 1979).

Girard, René, *Deceit, Desire and the Novel: Self and Other in Literary Structure*, trans. Yvonne Freccero (Baltimore, Md: Johns Hopkins Press, 1965).

——, *Violence and the Sacred* (Baltimore, Md and London: Johns Hopkins Press, 1977; originally published in Paris, 1972).

Godden, Rumer, *Two under the Indian Sun* (New York: A. A. Knopf, 1967).

——, 'A Cool Eye in a Parched Landscape' (review of *Out of India*), *New York Times Book Review*, 25 May 1986, p. 1.

Goodman, Walter, review of *Three Continents*, *New York Times*, 6 August 1987, p. C24.

Gooneratne, Yasmine, 'Traditional Elements in the Fiction of Kamala Markandaya, R. K. Narayan and Ruth Prawer Jhabvala', *World Literature Written in English*, 15, no. 1 (1976) pp. 121–34.

——, 'Film into Fiction: the Influence upon Ruth Prawer Jhabvala's Fiction of her Work in the Cinema, 1960–1976', *World Literature Written in English*, 18, no. 2 (1979) pp. 368–86.

——, 'Satirical Semi-Colon: Ruth Prawer Jhabvala's Screenplay for *Bombay Talkie*', *Journal of Indian Writing in English*, 8, nos 1–2 (1980) pp. 78–81.

——, *Silence, Exile and Cunning: The Fiction of Ruth Prawer Jhabvala* (New Delhi: Orient Longman, 1983).

——, 'Apollo, Krishna, Superman: the Image of India in Ruth Prawer Jhabvala's Ninth Novel', *Ariel* 15 (April 1984) pp. 109–17.

Gray, Paul, 'Tributes of Empathy and Grace' (review of *Out of India*), *Time*, 12 May 1986.

Grenier, Richard, '*The Bostonians* Inside Out', *Commentary*, October 1984, p. 60.

Griffin, Susan, *Pornography and Silence: Culture's Revenge against Nature* (New York: Harper and Row, 1981).

Grimes, Paul, 'A Passage to U.S. for Writer of India', *New York Times*, 15 May 1976, p. 14.

Hamilton, Alex, 'The Book of Ruth', *Guardian*, 20 November 1975, p. 12 (interview).

Harrison, Barbara Grizzuti, 'We're off to See the Guru', *MS*, December 1973, pp. 28, 31; reprinted in *Contemporary Literary Criticism: Excerpts from the Criticism of the Works of Today's Novelists*, ed. Carolyn Riley (Detroit: Gale Research, 1975) vol. 4, pp. 256–9.

——, 'India, Inc.: Hullaballoo over Merchant–Ivory Pictures', *Harper's*, March 1982, pp. 65–70.

Hartley, Lois, 'Ruth Prawer Jhabvala, Novelist of Urban India', *Literature East and West*, 9 (1965) pp. 265–73.

Ivory, James (compiler), *Autobiography of a Princess: Also Being the Adventures of an American Film Director in the Land of the Maharajas* (New York: Harper and Row, 1975; contains Jhabvala's screenplay *Autobiography of a Princess*).

Iyengar, K. R. Srinivasa, 'The Women Novelists', in *Indian Writing in English*, 2nd edn (New York: Asia Publishing House, 1973) pp. 450–61.

Jack, Ian, 'The Foreign Travails of Mrs Jhabvala', *Sunday Times Magazine*, 13 July 1980, pp. 32–6.

Jain, Daraki (ed.), *Indian Women* (Conn.: Thompson, 1975).

Jefferson, Margo, '*The Bostonians* Misses the Boat', *MS*, October 1984, pp. 33–4.

Jhabvala, Ruth Prawer, 'Moonlight, Jasmine and Rickets', *New York Times*, 22 April 1975, p. 35.

——, 'Disinheritance', text of Ruth Jhabvala's lecture in receipt of the Neil Gunn International Fellowship, *Blackwood's Magazine*, July 1979, pp. 4–14.

——, 'Writers and the Cinema', *Times Literary Supplement*, no. 4207 (18 November 1983) pp. 1287–8.

Kakutani, Michiko, review of *In Search of Love and Beauty*, *New York Times*, 19 July 1983, p. C14.

Kauffman, Stanley, 'A Civil War', review of *The Bostonians*, *New Republic*, 6 August 1984, p. 26.

Kemp, Peter, 'The Great Pursuit' (review of *In Search of Love and Beauty*), *Observer*, 10 April 1983, p. 33.

King, B. A., 'Three Novels and Some Conclusions: *Guerilla, The Adaptable Man, Heat and Dust'*, in *The New English Literatures* (London: Macmillan, 1980) pp. 214–31.

Lal, P., *Great Sanskrit Plays in Modern Translation* (New York: New Directions, 1957), contains Kalidasa's 'Skakuntala Won by the Sign of Recognition'.

Levy, Francis, 'A Passage to Nowhere', in *The New Leader*, 18 February 1974, p. 19; reprinted in *Contemporary Literary Criticism: Excerpts from the Criticism of the Works of Today's Novelists*, ed. Carolyn Riley (Detroit: Gale Research, 1975) vol. 4, pp. 256–9.

Mandelbaum, David, *Society in India* (Berkeley, Cal.: University of California Press, 1970) 2 vols.

Mason, Bobbie Ann, *The Girl Sleuth: A Feminist Guide* (Old Westbury, New York: Feminist Press, 1975).

May, Yolanta, 'Ruth Prawer Jhabvala in Conversation with Yolanta May', *New Review*, 2, no. 21 (1975) pp. 53–7.

McDonald, Barbara and Rich, Cynthia, *Look Me in the Eye* (San Francisco: Spinsters Ink, 1983).

Mehta, Gita, *Karma Cola: Marketing the Mystic East* (New York: Simon & Schuster, 1979).

Meyers, Jeffrey, *Katherine Mansfield: A Biography* (New York: New Directions Books, 1980).

Millett, Kate, *Sexual Politics* (New York: Doubleday, 1970).

Mitchell, Nora, *The Indian Hill-Station*, University of Chicago, Department of Geography Research Paper no. 141 (1972).

Modleski, Tania, *Loving with a Vengeance* (New York: Methuen Books, 1984).

Moers, Ellen, *Literary Women: The Great Women Writers* (New York: Anchor Books, 1977).

Mohanti, Prafulla, *My Village, My Life: Portrait of an Indian Village* (New York: Praeger, 1974).

Mukherjee, Meenakshi, 'Inside the Outsider', in *Awakened Conscience*, ed. C. D. Narasimhaiah (New Delhi: Sterling Publishers, 1978) pp. 86–91.

Naipaul, V. S., *An Area of Darkness* (New York: Macmillan, 1964).

Nossiter, Bernard D., 'Enjoying the Fruits of Detachment', interview, *Washington Post*, 9 December 1975, p. C2.

O'Brien, Timothy, review of *The Bostonians*, in *Commonweal*, 21 September 1984, p. 505.

Nyrop, Richard *et al.*, *Area Handbook for India*, 3rd edn (Washington, D.C., 1975).

Ouspensky, Peter Demianovitch, *In Search of the Miraculous: Fragments of an Unknown Teaching* (New York: Harcourt, Brace, 1949).

Owen, Lyn, 'A Passage from India to America', *Observer*, 9 April 1987, p. 30 (interview).

Patwardhan, Sunanda, *Change among India's Harijans* (Columbia, Mo.: University of Missouri Press, 1973).

Perlez, Jane, 'High Ideals, Bad Ends' (review of *Three Continents*), *New York Times*, 6 August 1987, p. C21.

Perls, Fritz S., *In and Out of the Garbage Pail* (Lafayette, Cal.: Real People, 1969).

Pritchett, V. S., 'Ruth Prawer Jhabvala: Snares and Delusions', in *The Tale Bearers* (London: Chatto & Windus, 1980) pp. 206–12.

Pym, John, 'Where Could I Meet Other Screenwriters?', *Sight and Sound*, 48, no. 1 (1978–9) pp. 15–18.

——, *The Wandering Company: Twenty-One Years of Merchant–Ivory Films* (London: British Film Institute, 1983) pp. 23–9; published in conjunction with the Museum of Modern Art, New York's retrospective screening of Merchant–Ivory–Jhabvala films, December 1983.

Rabinowitz, Dorothy, 'Making their Way through Small Troubles' (review of *Travelers*), *New York Times Book Review*, 8 July 1973, pp. 6–7; reprinted in *Contemporary Literary Criticism*, op. cit.

——, review of *Travelers*, *World*, 2, no. 12 (1973), p. 66; reprinted in *Contemporary Literary Criticism*, op. cit.

Radhakrishnan, Sarvepalli, and Moore, Charles A. (eds), *A Sourcebook in Indian Philosophy* (Princeton, N.J.: Princeton University Press, 1957).

Rau, Santha Rama, 'A Conflict of Loyalties' (review of *Amrita*), *New York Times Book Review*, 15 January 1956, p. 4.

——, 'Nimmi's Family Knew Best' (review of *The Nature of Passion*), *New York Times Book Review*, 23 June 1957, p. 6.

——, 'Like Pleasure, Like Pain' (review of *Get Ready for Battle*), *Saturday Review*, 16 March 1963, p. 88.

——, 'On the Surface of Sorrow' (review of *Like Birds, Like Fishes*), *New York Times Book Review*, 1 March 1964, p. 4.

'Pauline Réage', *The Story of O*, trans. S. d'Estrée (New York: Grove Press, 1965).

Rich, Adrienne, 'Compulsory Heterosexuality and Lesbian Existence', in *The Politics of Sexuality*, ed. Ann Snitow, Christine Stansell and Sharon Thompson (New York: Monthly Review Press, 1983).

Robertson, John George, *The Life and Work of Goethe* (London: George Routledge and Sons, 1932).

Rubin, D., 'Ruth Jhabvala in India', *Modern Fiction Studies*, 30 (Winter 1984) pp. 669–83.

Russ, Joanna, 'Somebody's Trying to Kill Me and I Think It's My Husband: the Modern Gothic', in *The Female Gothic*, ed. Juliann Fleenor (Montreal: Eden Press, 1983).

Rutherford, Anna, 'Ruth Prawer Jhabvala's Window on India', *ACLALS Bulletin*, 4th Series, no. 3 (1975) pp. 27–9.

Rutherford, Anna and Petersen, Kirsten Holst, '*Heat and Dust*: Ruth Prawer Jhabvala's Experience of India', *World Literature Written in English*, 15 (1976) pp. 272–7.

Sastry, L. S. R. Krishna, 'The Alien Consciousness in Jhabvala's Short Stories', in *The Two-Fold Voice*, ed. D. V. K. Raghavacharyulu (Vijaya-wada-Guntur: Navodaya Publishers, 1971) pp. 164–73.

Saxena, O. P. and Solanki, Rajni, *Geography of Jhabvala's Novels* (New Delhi: Jainson Publications, 1986).

Segal, Ronald, *The Anguish of India* (New York: Stein and Day, 1965).

Shahane, Vasant A., *Ruth Prawer Jhabvala* (New Delhi: Arnold–Heinemann, 1976).

——, 'Ruth Prawer Jhabvala and the Indian Scene', *Journal of Indian Writing in English*, 4, no. 2 (1977) pp. 21–4.

——, 'Jhabvala's *Heat and Dust*: a Cross-Cultural Encounter', in *Aspects of Indian Writing in English*, ed. M. K. Naik (Madras: Macmillan, 1979) pp. 222–31.

Shapiro, Harriet, 'The Teeming Imagination of Novelist Ruth Prawer Jhabvala is Her Window on a World She Avoids', *People*, 28 September 1987, pp. 48–53.

Singh, R. S., 'Ironic Vision of a Social Realist: Ruth Prawer Jhabvala', in *Indian Novel in English: A Critical Study* (New Delhi: Arnold–Heinemann, 1977) pp. 149–63.

Sleeman, Col., *Rambles and Recollections of an Indian Official* (1844); cited in Shirley Chew, op. cit., p. 115.

Snitow, Ann, 'Mass Market Romance: Pornography for Women is Different', in *Powers of Desire: The Politics of Sexuality*, ed. Ann Snitow, Christine Stansell and Sharon Thompson (New York: Monthly Review Press, 1983).

Sondhi, S., 'Dowry Deaths in India', *MS*, January 1983, p. 22.

Sontag, Susan, 'The Pornographic Imagination', in *Styles of Radical Will* (New York: Farrar, Strauss & Giroux, 1969).

Stark, John, 'Partners and Friends for 26 Years, James Ivory and Ismail Merchant Film Hotly Debated Gay Love Story', *People*, 26 October 1987, pp. 119–22.

Stein, Dorothy K., 'Women to Burn: Suttee as Normative Institution', *Signs*, 4, no. 2 (Winter 1978) pp. 253–68.

Summerfield, Henry, 'Holy Woman and Unholy Men: Ruth Prawer Jhabvala Confronts the Non-Rational', *Ariel*, 17 (July 1986) pp. 85–101.

Tinniswood, Peter, review of *Heat and Dust*, *The Times*, 6 November 1975, p. 10.

Towers, Robert, 'Leo and the Ladies of Temperament' (review of *In Search of Love and Beauty*), *New York Times Book Review*, 12 June 1983, p. 3.

——, 'Breaking the Spell' (review of *Three Continents*), *New York Review of Books*, 8 October 1987, p. 45.

Trevelyan, Humphrey, *Goethe and the Greeks* (Cambridge: Cambridge University Press, 1967).

Updike, John, 'Raman and Daisy and Olivia and the Nawab' (review of *Heat and Dust*), *New Yorker*, 5 July 1978, pp. 82–4; reprinted in Updike, *Hugging the Shore: Essays and Criticism* (New York: A. A. Knopf, 1983).

——, review of *In Search of Love and Beauty*, *New Yorker*, 1 August 1983.

Weintraub, Bernard, 'The Artistry of Ruth Prawer Jhabvala', *New York Times Magazine*, 11 September 1983, p. 64, pp. 106–14.

Williams, Haydn Moore, 'The Yogi and the Babbitt: Themes and Characters of the New India in the Novels of R. Prawer Jhabvala', *Twentieth-Century Literature*, 15, no. 2 (1969) pp. 81–90.

——, *The Fiction of Ruth Prawer Jhabvala* (Calcutta: Writers' Workshop, 1973).

——, *Indo-Anglian Literature 1800–1970: A Survey* (New Delhi: Orient–Longman, 1976).

Winegarten, Renée, 'Ruth Prawer Jhabvala: a Jewish Passage to India', *Midstream: A Monthly Jewish Review*, March 1974, pp. 72–9.

Unsigned, 'A Class Act Turns Twenty-Five: the Partnership of Ismail Merchant, Ruth Prawer Jhabvala and James Ivory', *Illustrated American Film*, September 1987, p. 75.

Index

architecture, as motif in fiction of
Jhabvala, 78–9, 168, 186
Austen, Jane, allusion to in fiction of
Jhabvala, 4, 5, 7

Backward Place, A, 17–18, 20, 26, 143
friendship in, 182
Basche, Françoise, 230
Benjamin, Jessica, 31, 61, 89
Bernini, *St Teresa* (sculpture), 198–9
'Better Than Dead', 92
'Birthday in London, A', 149–57
similarities to 'Commensurate
Happiness', 158
similarities to *In Search of Love and
Beauty*, 149
Bostonians, The (Henry James), 8, 9
British audience of R.J., 3, 229
British Raj
A New Dominion, 48, 54
Heat and Dust, 109–15, 134–40
Brontë, Charlotte, 26
Jane Eyre, 62, 100
Shirley, 13
Brontë, Emily, *Wuthering Heights*, 209
Brownmiller, Susan, 63

celebrity, as motif in fiction of
Jhabvala, 201–2
cinema, as motif in Jhabvala's fiction,
79
cinematic references in Jhabvala's
fiction, 9, 171, 220; *see also*
'narrative strategies'
'Commensurate Happiness', 144, 145,
150, 157–61, 204
Conrad, Joseph, *Heart of Darkness*, 102,
120–1, 124
Crisp, Quentin, 219–20
critics and R.J., 3–5, 110, 171, 176–7,
206, 213
Cronin, R.J., 110, 138–9, 232 n.10
Cults, 172–3, 190–2, 213–14; *see also*
Gurus, viewed satirically

'Desecration', 77–97
'compulsory heterosexuality', in, 147
'demon-lover' theme in, 7, 27, 75,
82, 110

isolation of heroine, 22–3
'knowledge' theme, 23–4, 81–97
marriage, 33–4, 87
and music, 117
plot, 80
similarities to *Heat and Dust*, 77–8,
110, 136
Desire, problem of, in Jhabvala's
fiction, 7–8, 11, 23–35, 196, 199
and Gothic motifs, 61–6 ('demon-
lover')
in 'On Bail', 202
in 'Desecration', 23–4, 68–97, *passim*
in 'An Experience of India', 41–3
in *Heat and Dust*, 98–9, 104, 107
in 'The Housewife', 69–73
A New Dominion, 49–50, 58–60, 64
in 'A Spiritual Call', 45–7
in *Three Continents*, 217, 219–20
and indifference of object, 91, 157
as ingredient of desire, 188–9, 196
and 'sado-masochism', 29–35, 39,
42–3, 46, 61, 82, 88, 91, 93, 105,
115
and social inferior as lover ('rough
trade'), 27–35, 40, 80, 82, 111,
202, 214–15, 216–17, 219–27, 230
(ch. 2, n.3)
spiritual essence of, 8, 10, 49–50, 61–
2, 81–2, 107, 162, 184–6, 192,
196, 199
Dewas, Maharajah of ('H. H.',
Forster's *Hill of Devi*) compared to
Newab of *Heat and Dust*, 136–40
Dickinson, Lowes (Forster's letters to),
136, 138
Dinesen, Isak, *Out of Africa*, 200
Disinheritance
as motif in Jhabvala's fiction, 150–1,
207
of India, 211
of Third World, 216–27 *passim*

'Englishwoman, The', 170
Esmond in India, 15, 24
'Experience of India, An', 15, 40–4, 60,
117, 148
'Expiation', 145, 206, 221–7

'Farid and Farida', 201–2
feminism, 8, 9, 25, 93–4, 227, 229 n.20;
    see also 'women: sender politics'
Forster, E. M.
    feelings about Indians, 135
    Hill of Devi, 9, 51, 136–40
    Kanaya, 138–9
    masculinist bias of, 136
    Maurice, 135–6, 200, 220–1
    Passage to India, 102, 121
    and *Heat and Dust*, 134–6, 139, 140
    and public schools, 139
    similarities to 'Harry' of *Heat and Dust*, 136
Furbank, R. N. (biographer of Forster), 135–8

Gandhi, 109
Genet, Jean, 119
Get Ready for Battle, 16, 25, 26, 130
Gilbert, Sandra, and Gubar, Susan, 131
Girard, Rene
    Deceit, Desire and the Novel, 31–2
    Violence and the Sacred, 85
Godden, Jan and Rymer, 236 n.22
Goethe, Johann
    Herman und Dorothea (alluded to in *In Search of Love and Beauty*), 181, 236 n.21
Gooneratne, Yasmine, 6, 50, 110
Gothic ('Female Gothic'), 6, 7, 8, 30, 44, 57, 61–6, 82, 106, 232 (ch.6, n.12)
    as architectural style, 186
'Grandmother', 32, 145, 161, 164–7, 204
Griffin, Susan, 29, 80
Gubar, Susan, and Gilbert, Sandra, 131, 234 n.24
Gurdjieff (Western mystic), 172, 236 n.15
gurus
    viewed without satire, 39, 56, 71, 74
    'The Old Lady', 161
    viewed satirically, 27, 38, 39–47, 49, 56–61, 172, 210

Heat and Dust, 6, 8, 9, 98–140, 211
    critics and, 5
    'demon-lover' theme in, 27, 33–4, 114–15
    double layers of, 8, 98–102, 107–9, 115
    ending of, 15, 34, 75, 193
    female friendship in, 183

Forster, E. M. and, 134–40
gay men in, 139, 145, 166
imagery of, 99, 121–7
Maji, 124–8, 19, 25, 39, 131
modern narrator ('Ms Rivers'), 103–7, 120, 124, 131–4
motifs in, 115–19
Olivia, 109–15
omission in, 51
pregnancy in, 101, 115–17, 123, 126, 134
problem of sexuality in, 114–15, 120, 225
Raj in, 100–3, 108–15, 134–9
similarities to 'Desecration', 77–8, 80–1, 86, 88, 90, 98–140, 225
widows, 161–4
hijra (eunuchs)
    Heat and Dust, 114, 118, 118–20
    Three Continents, 212
Hill of Devi (Forster, E. M.), 9, 51, 136–40
Holocaust, 3, 150, 151–5, 170, 226
Homosexuality, female: *see* 'women, lesbianism'
Homosexuality, male
    in fiction of Jhabvala, 9, 143–9
    in 'Commensurate Happiness', 158–61
    in 'Desecration', 82
    in 'Grandmother', 166–7
    in *Heat and Dust*, 110, 113
    in *In Search of Love and Beauty*, 135, 183–4, 187–90
    in *A New Dominion*, 50–1, 65
    in 'A Summer by the Sea', 203–5
    in *Three Continents*, 205, 207, 219–20
'Housewife, The', 33, 34, 39, 69–76, 110, 117, 216
Householder, The, 15, 25, 39, 54
'How I Became a Holy Mother', 39–40, 77, 151
How I Became a Holy Mother (collection), 77

Illusion, shedding of, as motif in Jhabvala's fiction, 8, 10, 21, 79, 125, 214
'In Love with a Beautiful Girl', 33, 54
'In the Mountains', 193
India, Jhabvala's ambivalent view of, 3–5, 10–11, 13–15, 16–18, 20, 28, 41–4, 48–54
    Heat and Dust, 98–140

India, Jhabvala's ambivalent view
of – *continued*
Three Continents, 200–27 *passim*
poverty in, 14–15, 41, 53, 105, 118,
129–30, 211, 216, 221–7
Western fear of, 104, 106–7, 123
Western misconceptions about, 77,
101, 106
'Indian Citizen, An', 153
Indian view of Western women, in
fiction of Jhabvala, 41, 53–4, 108,
118–19, 133
In Search of Love and Beauty, 9, 168–99
architecture in, 168–9, 187–92
autobiography in, 16, 154, 169–71
critics and, 171, 176–7
cults in, 59, 172–3, 190–3
desire, problem of in, 7, 23–4, 26, 29,
40, 61, 70, 174–5, 192–9
ending of, 15
gay men in, 16–17, 145–6, 166, 169,
183, 187–90, 194–6
Holocaust and, 151, 153, 169–71
mythological allusion in, 169, 177–82
Natasha, 16, 25, 192–9, 206, 209
plot, 171–6
preparatory stories, 143–67 *passim*
women, alienation from each other
in, 146–7, 182–4
Ivory, James, 3, 49
Autobiography of a Princess, 98

James, Henry
The Bostonians, 9
Turn of the Screw, 102, 121
Jewishness, 3, 4, 121
anti-Semitism, 90, 226
Jewish characters, 149–57 *passim* ('A
Birthday in London'), 172, 174
Jewish themes and values in fiction
of Jhabvala, 4, 201, 214, 226–7
Jhabvala, Cyrus, 168
Jhabvala, Ruth Prawer
birth, 3
celebrity of, 200–1
childhood of, 3, 4, 152, 226
education of, 4
Holocaust and, 3, 151–4, 170, 226
in India, 4, 5, 6, 10–11, 147–8, 229
marriage of, to C. S. H. Jhabvala, 4,
109
move to New York, 6, 170
North American audience of, 3, 200;
in *People* magazine, 201

outsiderhood and, 6, 90, 170
parents, 3, 4 (*see also* Prawer,
Eleonora Cohn and Prawer,
Marcus), 152, 154, 170, 177
as refugee, 4, 170

Kakutani, Michiko, review of *In Search
of Love and Beauty*, 171
Kalidasa, 'Shakuntala', 69, 73–4
'Knowing', as theme in Jhabvala's
fiction, 23–5, 81–97, 108, 140
Krishna, 55, 217

'Light and Reason', 149
'Like Birds, Like Fishes', 79, 151
Like Birds, Like Fishes (collection of
stories), 77
Lilith, 100, 232 n.3

MacArthur Foundation Grant, 3
'Man with the Dog, The', 7, 162
Mansfield, Katherine, 171, 236 n.15
Marhabharata, 73
Masood, Syed Ross (friend of Forster,
Passage to India dedicated to), 135
Mehta, Gita, 77–8
Merchant–Ivory Productions, 200
Maurice, 200, 219
Room with a View, 200
celebrity of, 200
Jhabvala's collaboration with, 3, 8–9;
as of 1986, 200–1, 219; decision
not to write screenplay for
Maurice, 201; flashback narrative
technique influenced by, 171
Mill, John Stuart, 102
Millett, Kate, 233 n.18
'Miss Sahib', 25, 26, 164
theme of disinheritance, 151
Moers, Ellen, *Literary Women*, 12, 13, 30
music, as motif in Jhabvala's fiction,
69–76, 117
'Myself in India', 5, 10, 13–15, 39, 53,
147–8
devotional poetry discussed in, 185

Naipaul, V. S., 132
Names in fiction of Jhabvala, 54–6, 78,
100, 133, 222
'Expiation', 236 n.16
Get Ready for Battle, 16, 17
The Householder, 15
In Search of Love and Beauty, 179, 188,
208

Narrative techniques
  flashback, 170–1
  omission, 51, 62–3, 183, 216, 224–5
  open-ended but pessimistic endings,
    15
  unreliable narrator, 203, 206, 214–15,
    217–19
Nature of Passion, The, 14, 130, 221
New Dominion, A (also called *Travelers*),
    5, 9, 15, 23, 25, 30, 32, 39, 40, 48–
    66, 75, 110, 129, 145, 206
  female friendship in, 148, 183
  Margaret compared to K. Mansfield,
    172–3
  old women in, 162
New Yorker Magazine, 3, 92, 202

'Old Lady, The', 25, 39, 184, 197
'On Bail', 27, 33, 202, 216
Ouspensky, P. D. (*In Search of the
    Miraculous*), 172
Out of India: Selected Stories, 200
outsiderhood and R.J., 6, 90, 170

Panchatantra, 14
'Parasites', 202
'Passion', 24, 27, 28–9, 34, 75, 110, 216,
    223
Passivity, 'active', 25, 26
  of Natasha (*In Search of Love and
    Beauty*), 193, 197–8
Perls, Fritz, 172
  'Gestalt prayer' satirised, 191–2
Persephone, 83
'Picnic with Moonlight and Mangoes',
    79
pollution taboos as motif, 131–3
pornography, related to romance, 18
Prawer, Eleanora Cohn (mother), 3, 4,
    152, 154, 170, 177
Prawer, Marcus (father), 3, 152, 154
    (suicide of), 170, 177
Prawer, Siegbart Solomon (brother), 3,
    152, 228
Pritchett, V. S., 51

Quartet (Jean Rhys), 113, 202
Quest theme in Jhabvala's fiction, 10,
    11, 22–7, 32, 40, 98, 124, 168

'Réage, Pauline', *Story of O*, 89, 91
Refugees
  'A Birthday in London', 149–57
  In Search of Love and Beauty, 168–70

Rhys, Jean, *Quartet*, 113, 202
Rich, Adrienne, 146–7
Romance, popular genre, 62–4, 82–3, 219
Room with a View, A (E. M. Forster), 9
'Rose Petals', 146, 162
Roseland, 161
Rossetti, Christina, 'Goblin Market', 86

self-delusion, as motif in Jhabvala's
    fiction, 10, 94–5, 112
Shahane, Vasant, 5, 110, 232 (ch.7 n.11)
Shakespeare Wallah, 5
Simla, 233 n.20
Singer, Isaac Bashevis, 169
'Sixth Child', 130
Sleeman, Colonel, 110, 232–3 n.13
Snow, C. P., 9–10, 147
Sontag, Susan, 'The Pornographic
    Imagination', 30, 34–5, 82
'Spiritual Call, A', 7, 40, 44–7, 54
Stein, Dorothy, 110
story-within-a-story technique, 102,
    107–9
Stronger Climate, A, 54
'Summer by the Sea, A', 202–5, 206
suttee, 74, 100, 110–11, 114, 127–8

Taylor, Harriet, 102
Towers, Robert, reviewer of *In Search
    of Love and Beauty*, 176
Three Continents, 5, 15, 27, 80, 143, 144,
    145, 146, 200–2, 204–20, 225, 226
  problem of desire in, 212–21
  'Sonya', 177
'Two More Under the Indian Sun',
    182, 216
To Whom She Will (also called *Armita*),
    14, 92, 130, 221

Updike, John, 4, 108
  review of *In Search of Love and Beauty*,
    176

'Very Special Fate, A', 202

Weinraub, Bernard, 38
'Widow, The', 127
withdrawal from society as theme in
    Jhabvala's fiction, 10, 21, 43, 101,
    121–4
  contrasted to engagement, 162
  of Jhabvala herself, 170
  of Natasha in *In Search of Love and
    Beauty*, 192–3

women in Jhabvala's fiction
alienation from each other, 11–12,
65–6, 88, 92–4, 116, 126, 130,
144–9; in 'Commensurate
Happiness', 160, 181–3; in *In
Search of Love and Beauty*, 146–7,
182–4; in 'A Summer by the
Sea', 203–5; in 'Two under the
Indian Sun', 236 n.22
as artists, 69–76 ('The Housewife'),
117, 134, 193, 197–8
autonomous, 124–5, 127–31
dowry death and, 63–4, 129, 231
(ch.4, n.8)
female sexuality (*see also* 'Desire,
problem of'), 87–8, 148, 225; in
Heat and Dust, 126–7, 168; in *In
Search of Love and Beauty*, 174,
190; nature of, 195
gender politics (*see also* 'feminism'),
9, 11, 51, 65–6, 75–6, 83–97
('Desecration'); 102, 111–18,
124–31 (*Heat and Dust*); in *In
Search of Love and Beauty*, 168; in
'A Summer by the Sea', 203–5;
woman-blaming, 233 n.14
lesbianism, 17–18, 146–9, 208–9

marriage, 33–4, 69, 96, 99, 109; in
'Commensurate Happiness',
157–61; in *Heat and Dust*, 114–16,
129–31
mother–daughter relationship, 144,
164, 174, 191
mother–son relationship, 189
old women in Jhabvala's fiction:
'Grandmother', 161, 164–7; *Heat
and Dust*, 161–2, 164; 'Old Lady',
161
quest and, 23, 24, 26, 98, 174, 184,
190–2
and rival 'other woman', 80, 93, 202
spirituality and, 19, 25, 77, 99; in
Heat and Dust, 123–6
as wanderers, 12–13, 118–20, 133,
183
widows (*see also* 'suttee'), 74, 100,
110–11, 114, 127–31
World War II, 3; *see also* 'Holocaust',
'refugees'

Yeats, William Butler, 214
Yogal
Heat and Dust, 126–7, 133
In Search of Love and Beauty, 174
'Young Couple, The', 112